The Subject Is reading

Essays by Teachers and Students

Edited by

Wendy Bishop

Boynton/Cook Publishers
HEINEMANN
Portsmouth, NH

Boynton/Cook Publishers, Inc.
A subsidiary of Reed Elsevier Inc.
361 Hanover Street
Portsmouth, NH 03801–3912
www.boyntoncook.com

Offices and agents throughout the world

Library of Congress Cataloging-in-Publication Data
The subject is reading : essays by teachers and students / edited by Wendy Bishop.
    p.   cm.
    Includes bibliographical references.
    ISBN 0-86709-472-9
    1. Reading (Higher education)   I. Bishop, Wendy.

LB2395.3 .S82 2000
428.4'071'1—dc21   99-058141

Editor: Lisa Luedeke
Production coordinator: Sonja Chapman
Production service: Denise Botelho, Colophon
Cover design: Darci Mehall/Aureo Design
Manufacturing: Louise Richardson

Printed in the United States of America on acid-free paper
04 03 02 01 00 DA 1 2 3 4 5

Contents

Preface and Introduction

With students in mind—

For some reason I wasn't running up and down the streets with the fellas much anymore. Harvey would get bent out of shape every time I'd tell him I had something else to do . . . This also bothered my mother because she kept telling me I was going to ruin my eyes if I didn't stop reading so much; and what was [it] that I spent all my spare time writing in a manila notebook? Was I keeping a diary or something? . . . But I kept right on reading and writing, looking forward to Miss Nettlebeck's class twice a week. I stopped fighting, too. But I was still rougish as ever. Instead of raiding Robert's Men's Shop, Smith's and Flagg Brothers' Shoes, I was stealing books by just about every poet and writer Miss Nettlebeck read to the class. That's how I started writing poems. (Lockett 1997, 77)

Reginald Lockett's literacy narrative points you toward many of the issues you'll find in this collection: how reading and writing are deeply interconnected, how both affect our relationships with our families and with the world, and how acquiring greater fluency as a literate citizen can represent a way of being that those around us may not accept or understand or may encourage without knowing quite why they encourage it. For Lockett, the answer to "Why do you write poems?" was not a simple one, but it was an answer he could arrive at by considering how his literacy past made him the literate individual of the present.

In many ways, *The Subject Is Reading: Essays by Teachers and Students* asks you to undertake a similar journey. As editor, I have tried to place teachers and students in dialog with each other about reading *as a subject*. While there are many books available to talk to you about improving as a writer—including a companion volume to this one, *The Subject Is Writing*, second edition—there are few that do the same with reading; perhaps that's because by the time our college years come around it's all too easy to assume we know how to read fluently enough. My experiences in writing classrooms, however, suggest that teachers and students are less fully aware of themselves as readers than they might usefully be and that many of us have forgotten what it meant to develop as readers.

Like Reginald Lockett, most of us can benefit from returning to our earliest memories of learning to read and write. Through attention to who we were then, we come to understand who we are now. We learn to improve our reading processes and in so doing we become better writers. I also believe that an improvement in reading abilities positively impacts the pleasure we take in reading print, media, and cultural texts. In fact, by becoming better at understanding what motivates us as readers, we often recapture an early interest in reading that many of us report became dulled or dissipated by negative encounters with assigned texts.

As you can see by reading their biographical notes, contributors to this collection in general are life-long readers, but their relationships to reading have not always been simple or easy. Because of that they encourage you—whether you consider yourself a reader or a nonreader—to further discuss and develop what are normally tacit skills; to explore the place of reading (and rereading) in your writing; to examine and question beliefs and myths you hold dear about reading in order to gain new insight into reading processes; and to understand the many ways reading abilities and practices influence the production of your written texts.

When you share responses to *The Subject Is Reading,* I expect you'll be looking at your own essays and perhaps at the stories, poems, plays, and essays of professional writers. That is, this book may be your main classroom text, helping you improve your work in a writing workshop. In other courses, it may be a secondary text, helping you understand yourself as a reader of the texts of others. In either case, the goal of the authors who share their ideas here has been to engage you—readers-who-write—in discussions of literacy issues, by offering arguments, insights, and best techniques for making more of reading.

With teachers in mind—

Although *The Subject Is Reading: Essays by Teachers and Students* text is envisioned for use in writing courses that are focused on literacy issues, you may also find it a useful ancillary for introductory reading courses in any genre. Because these essays have been composed by teachers and students for an audience of college-level writers, *The Subject Is Reading* will also support the introductory literature course designed to broaden students' approaches to reading through the use of interactive reading strategies and the development of their abilities to use theoretical perspectives as they read. I expect this collection will prove useful also for certain teachers of advanced composition and teacher education courses, for it offers a thought-provoking look at reading for general readers by providing insights into contemporary issues in the field.

With these goals in mind, Part I of the collection broadly addresses what it means to be a reader in college, with several of the essayists offering suggestions and techniques for becoming more efficient, more engaged, more intro-spective, and more flexible as readers. Essayists in Part II ask writers to remember how they first came to read and write in order to explore what that predicts for their literacy futures. Parts I and II also provide examples of student writers engaging in such literacy memory work within the genre of the literacy narrative. Part III offers discussions that will broaden readers' under-standing of texts to include examinations of TV, film, and culture in general. Part IV looks at reading processes by examining readers' beliefs, how teach-ers and students read texts, how revision is a form of active reading, and how we read as researchers. Part V looks to the future of reading, asking provoca-tive questions about collaboration and information technologies.

You and your students may wish to progress through *The Subject Is Reading: Essays by Teachers and Students* from start to finish or decide instead to read for specific class purposes, engaging first the chapters that suit your classroom design and the needs of those students who are learning to broaden their reading repertoires under your guidance. In support of those goals, Hint Sheets A through K offer flexible and field-tested classroom hand-outs and exercises, whereas Hint Sheets 1 through 5 provide advice for teach-ing with these essays for you, the teacher, using *The Subject Is Reading*.

Work Cited

Lockett, Reginald. 1997. "How I Started Writing Poetry." In: *Framework: Culture, Storytelling, and College Writing,* 76–81. Edited by Gary Colombo, Bonnie Lisle, and Sandra Mano. Boston: Bedford.

Acknowledgments

Lisa Luedeke was instrumental in bringing this book into being. My thanks for her friendship and for her expert editorial support on the project. Thanks too to the editorial and production staff at Boynton/Cook who always produce the most readable of texts and to Pavel Zemliansky who helped with last-minute preproduction editing and annotating. And of course, I'm tremendously grateful to the many students and teachers who contributed their work in the form of narratives, chapters, and quotable insights. Most authors shared drafts with readers in writing classes, and those readers helped us make the most of our works-in-progress. Final thanks to Morgan, Tait, and Dean, who this year have been helping me read a favorite new text, that small stretch of beach at Alligator Point.

Part I

Reading College,
Readers in College

Assigned reading?—honestly, it depends what it is—fiction, criticism, etc. Am I interested in it? When I am, reading is fairly easy—I usually sit on the couch w/my lapdesk and water nearby. I usually underline or highlight. Occasionally, I write notes in the margins. If I'm not interested I take more breaks, put it off until the last minute—skim enough to make one comment in class—or don't read it at all. Either way, I usually read all (or as much as possible) in one sitting.

—Amy

1

Making Meaning—
Your Own Meaning—
When You Read

Deborah Coxwell Teague

When I first began teaching high school English, I wondered if I had somehow completely missed out on an extremely important part of teacher training. I wondered if I had been absent—or perhaps I'd been doing some serious day dreaming—the day my college professor passed out the guide that revealed the secret to discovering the one true, correct meaning of a piece of literature. You see, when I was a high school student, my English teachers always had the answers, or at least I thought they did. Anytime we high school students were told to read a short story, a poem, or an essay for class, my teachers knew exactly what the selection meant. They knew precisely what the author was trying to communicate to the reader in the short story, poem, or essay. They had all the right answers. They had the knowledge and they gave it to us, their students. But when I became a teacher and assigned a short story, a poem, or an essay for my students to read, I was never sure I knew exactly what the author was trying to say to the reader. I knew what *I thought* the selection meant; I knew how *I interpreted* the text—but I didn't know if my interpretation was the correct one.

I clearly remember the dazed and confused looks on my high school students' faces when I first asked them what they thought about a selection I had asked them to read for class. "What do you think the author is saying in this poem?" I asked, and most of them looked at me as if I had lost my mind. I was the teacher. I was supposed to tell them what the author meant, not ask their opinions. I was supposed to know beyond the shadow of a doubt what the author had intended when she wrote the poem—but I didn't. I thought about discussing my problem—my shortcoming—with my colleagues, but I didn't want to let them know I wasn't the wonderful young teacher I fancied they thought I was. So I kept my thoughts to myself and continued to ask my students to read closely and share their interpretations with me and with the rest of the class. Together, we attempted to construct meanings for the texts we read.

That was more than just a few years ago, and since then I've made a discovery: My teachers were faking it—at least in some respects. They probably did not even realize they were faking it, but they were—at least some of the time. They had never sat down with William Shakespeare, Emily Dickinson, or Langston Hughes to discuss the one "true" meaning of *Romeo and Juliet, I'm Nobody! Who Are You?* or *Dream Deferred.* But when we discussed those literary selections in class, they *acted* as if they had all the answers. Looking back, I realize now that they did have many of the answers, and even when they didn't, their intentions were probably good: They were older and wiser than their students; they were more experienced readers and knew how to read a text closely; they had background information about the author that we, their students, did not have; they had knowledge of the historical and cultural contexts in which the selection had been written; and they were the literature teachers—the ones who were *supposed* to have the answers. Yes, they faked it when they led me to believe that they possessed the one, the true, the only correct way to interpret the text, but they weren't faking it when they shared information regarding plot, characters, point of view, or facts about the author's life and the historical and social contexts surrounding the literature.

In some of the writing classes you take at the college level, you will probably be assigned works of literature to read—short stories, poems, essays, perhaps plays and novels—but don't be surprised if your writing teacher doesn't ask you to focus on plot, character, and point of view. Don't be surprised if your writing teacher never asks you to write a formal literary analysis. And don't be surprised if your writing teacher refuses to fake it. In fact, she will probably tell you that there is no one correct way to interpret a text—that the interpretation depends on a number of factors such as the reader's experiences, knowledge, and feelings—and that her primary interest is in *your* interpretation and in how you reached it.

Okay, sounds easy, you might be thinking at this point. *After all, if there's no one right answer, how hard can it be?*

Sorry if I misled you. The reading you do for a writing class isn't as easy as it might sound. The easy classes, for me anyway, the ones that did not require much effort on my part, were the ones in which my teacher had all the answers and all I had to do was memorize the facts. That's not likely to be the scenario in a writing class. The reading you do for writing classes requires next to no memorization. The reading does, however, require lots of thinking about and writing about what you read, and lots of rereading, rethinking, and rewriting as you go about making meaning—your meaning—of the text.

We teachers sometimes forget that not all of our students know how to read.

What is she talking about? you might be thinking. *She's talking about college students, right? Come on, if you're in college, you know how to read.*

Not necessarily—not the way I'm talking about anyway,

A few years ago, toward the beginning of the semester, I asked the students in my second-semester first year writing class to read Alfred, Lord Tennyson's *Ulysses* for class. I love that poem; it's been one of my favorites for years, and I fully expected my students to be as excited about it as I was. I could hardly wait to hear their responses. We had read and discussed two or three pieces of literature at this point in the semester, and they had never failed to come to class full of ideas and ready for discussion. However, on the day we were to discuss *Ulysses,* my request for their responses, for their ideas, was met with silence and bowed heads as they stared at the texts before them on their desks.

"Well, what did you think of the poem?" I asked a second time. More silence. My first thought was that no one had read it, but then I realized that surely they had made time to read a two-page poem. They knew better than to think I would stand before them and deliver a lecture on the assigned reading. They knew I would ask for their ideas and opinions. More silence.

Finally one student spoke up. "I read it, but I couldn't figure it out. It was dumb."

Whoa—hold on there, young man. This is one of my favorite poems of all time and you are calling it dumb? Just who do you think you are? I somehow managed to keep my thoughts from coming out of my mouth, but doing so took a monumental effort.

"Yeah, I couldn't make any sense of it either," another student voiced.

"How many times did you read it," I asked, fully expecting my students to tell me that they had read it two, perhaps three times.

My students looked at each other and then looked at me as if I had asked the most stupid question they had ever heard. "Once, of course," came the reply.

At that point I realized that I had made several mistakes. To begin with, I had never talked with them about *how* to read. I had planned to—it was in my lesson plans—but I had gotten caught up in the maddening pace of the semester and hadn't made time for any talk of *how* to read. The other selections I had asked my students to read were easy to comprehend—one reading and they were able to share their thoughts and ideas with the rest of the class. The other texts we had read required no background knowledge of heroes from Greek mythology and contained no references to "the rainy Hyades" (10) or "the ringing plains of windy Troy" (17). The other texts were written in twentieth-century English and contained no sentences such as "Yet all experience is an arch wherethrough/Gleams that untraveled world, whose margin fades/For ever and for ever when I move" (19–21). I realized that I had not thought of

Ulysses as a difficult text because I had read it so many times over the years that I could repeat most of it from memory. I had read Homer's *Odyssey* and Dante's *Inferno,* and I understood the many references made in *Ulysses;* my first-year students, however, did not. At the least, I should have provided them with background information before assigning the poem, and I most certainly should have explained that this poem—like many of the selections assigned in a writing class—would require multiple readings.

Reading a selection more than once might at first sound like an unnecessary, unpleasant, redundant chore, but if you think about it, you've probably read many texts repeatedly. As children, most of us love to be read our favorite books over and over, until we know the words by heart. My little ones, now 3 and 4 years old, have had me read *Where the Wild Things Are* (Sendack 1963), *Runaway Bunny* (Brown 1942), and *Madeline* (Bemelmans 1939) so many times that they now "read" the books to me. And many of us can think of a favorite movie we've "read" over and over until we know every line, every look, every move before we see it on the screen.

To read *Where the Wild Things Are, Titanic,* or *Star Wars* over and over is one thing—to read an assigned text more than once is something else altogether—right? Not completely. Although our motives might be different, the result of the rereading is much the same. When we reread, at least the first several times, we almost always learn something new with each reading—we make connections and pick up on details we didn't notice the first or perhaps even the second time we read the text. Am I saying that we should read every assigned text over and over? No. I am saying that many texts, especially those assigned for reading in a writing class, need to be read closely—more closely than one reading allows.

Rereading is only one of many activities that can help us read a text closely. Several other strategies that can help include selective underlining, making marginal comments, keeping a reading response journal, and keeping a double-entry notebook.

Selective Underlining

Making marks in a text is often a difficult habit for college students to learn. In high school, most of the books you used probably belonged to the school system and were passed down from one student to another, and you were more than likely told to make no marks whatsoever in them. Now that you're in college and your books belong to you, you might be tempted to keep your books "clean" so that you can get a better price for them when you sell them back to the bookstore at the end of the semester. Don't give in to this temptation. Write in your books. Think of it as an investment in your education. Besides, the minuscule amount the bookstore will give you for your books is hardly worth what you'll lose if you refrain from making your books—and the information in them—your own.

As you read a text, underline or highlight words, phrases, and sentences that stand out to you. The words you decide to underline will depend to a large extent on your reasons for reading. For the reading you do in a writing class, you'll probably want to underline words, phrases, and sentences that are especially striking to you—for whatever reason. If you're reading an essay on a controversial topic, you might underline the main points the author makes in the argument. If you're reading a poem, you might underline phrases that, in your opinion, are beautifully written and/or especially meaningful to you. If you're reading a short story, you might underline parts of the story that remind you of similar experiences you've had. The parts of a text that you decide to underline are likely to be quite different from what someone else underlines— and that's fine. Underlining can help you pay closer attention as you read than you would without a marker in hand, and underlining also can help you later when you review the text.

Making Marginal Comments

In addition to underlining as you read, get in the habit of making notes to yourself in the margins. When I am reading a challenging text, one that is difficult for me to understand, or perhaps one that is not especially interesting to me, I've found that I'm less likely to let my mind wander as I read—less likely to be thinking about what I might eat for dinner that night or what I'm going to do over the weekend—if I make notes in the margin as I go along. I might write a phrase or a sentence in the margin beside each paragraph summing up the main point of the paragraph. If I finish reading a paragraph and have no idea what point the author was trying to make, I read it again. This strategy forces me to read more closely and keep my mind on what I'm reading.

Marginal comments serve lots of other useful purposes. When you're reading an essay on a controversial topic, you might respond to the author's argument in the margins of the text. If you disagree with the author's point, respond in the margin. If you don't think the author is providing sufficient evidence to prove her point, make a note of your reaction in the margin. When you're reading a short story and you make a connection between something that happens in the story and a personal experience, jot down a note in the margin. Marginal comments allow you to carry on a conversation with the text as you read.

Keeping a Reading Response Journal

This is a useful tool that provides a place for you to respond more fully than you might respond in marginal comments as you read a text. If you decide to keep a reading response journal, use it as a place to do more than simply summarize what you've read. Think of the journal as a place to carry on a more extended dialogue with the text. You might explore why you particularly disliked or liked a selection. If you disliked the selection, what caused your reaction? Did you disagree with the author's opinion? If so, how does your opinion differ from the author's? Did the author fail to make a strong argument? How could the argument have been made stronger? Do you feel the author was biased? If so, in what particular ways did the bias come across in the text? If you were not interested in the subject matter being discussed, what do you think caused your lack of interest? How is your opinion of the selection related to what's going on in your own life? Explore places in the text where you felt confused. What do you think caused the confusion? Explore places in the text where you had questions. If you especially enjoyed a particular selection, what was there about it that made you like it? Explore parts of the selection to which you could especially relate. Explore experiences in your own life that came to your mind as you read the selection.

Keeping a Double-Entry Notebook

The first time I was told to keep a double-entry notebook, I was less than excited about the assignment. We were told to draw a line down the middle of the page. On one side of the line we were to record phrases, lines, and/or passages from the text, and on the other side of the line we were to respond to what we had recorded. The whole assignment sounded to me like a lot of unnecessary busy work. I was wrong; it wasn't busy work. And today, years later, I still have that first double-entry notebook. There's something about recording others' ideas, and then responding to them that makes a text more meaningful for the reader. Keeping a double-entry notebook forces the reader to enter a dialectic—a discussion—with the author. No longer is the reader an outsider—a voyeur—looking on yet remaining invisible. Responding to the text requires involvement and helps the reader make his or her own meaning from the words on the page.

The reading you do for a writing class requires much more than reading for the main idea or reading so that you can write a plot summary or a character sketch. It requires more than reading to remember the characters' names and who did what to whom at what time and in what place. Reading for a writing class requires that you do much more than memorize what someone else tells you is the author's main intent or purpose.

Instead, the reading you do for a writing class requires involvement. It requires that you see reading as much more than simply mentally processing words on a page. It requires that you see reading as a process of investigation and reflection. It requires that you do some serious thinking about the way you read—about the way you go about making meaning of a text. It requires that you enter a dialectic—a conversation, your conversation—with the text. The reading you do for a writing class requires you to respond to the text, to make your own interpretation of the author's purpose for writing, and to make connections between the author's experiences, thoughts, and ideas, and your own. The reading you do for a writing class requires you to make your own meaning of the words on the page and to be ready to share that meaning with others. You may discover that your interpretation of a particular text is quite different from your classmates' or your teacher's—and that's okay. In a writing class, there's no need for anyone to fake it. Just read closely and make your own meaning.

Works Cited

Bemelmans, Ludwig. 1939. *Madeline.* New York: Viking.

Brown, Margaret Wise. 1942. *Runaway Bunny.* New York: HarperCollins.

Sendak, Maurice. 1963. *Where the Wild Things Are.* New York: Harper & Row.

Tennyson, Alfred. 1993. "Ulysses." *Windows.* Eds. Jeff Rackham and Olivia Bertagnolli. 483–84. New York: HarperCollins.

Student Narrative 1

Learning How Not to Read*

Kirk Parrott

Along with every other child in the world, I knew that I could read, so what was the point of constantly reading books when you could just watch television? The stories on TV were just as interesting and took about a fourth as much time. That's something you had to be a kid to understand and you lost as you became a grownup.

My earliest years could well be described by a lack of literary ability. I'm one of those Generation X'ers who grew up watching television because their parents were too involved in their own problems to have much time for them. Not to mention that they had me at an extremely young age and perhaps weren't ready to properly cultivate a young child's literary progress. Not to say that they weren't big on reading because both of them enjoyed reading in their spare time. Eventually, probably due to my low preliminary reading test scores, they decided that it was time they did something about my lack of interest in reading.

My interests lay in doing whatever pleased me at the time and avoiding as much work as possible. I remember trying to get out of mowing the yard by tying the lawnmower to my bike and riding around the yard. Although the lawnmower always fell over and never managed to cut the whole lawn, I still felt like I'd managed to avoid some work. That's just the kind of person I was.

Therefore, my true literary path began to develop the first time I was ever told to read a book that I didn't want to read. That's when I started doing anything that I possibly could to get out of actually having to do some work. Even if that meant that I would do twice as much work to get out of that original assignment, I'd definitely choose the latter. It's like going a long distance out of your way just to come back a short distance.

*The process narrative for Kirk's essay can be found in Hint Sheet A.

The first book I was ever forced to read was this mammoth work by the infamous Grimm Brothers. It was truly the definition of cruel and unusual punishment that I thought had been outlawed by the Constitution, but apparently parents somehow weren't bound by the forefathers. My parents always gave me some lame bullshit explanation about building character and learning responsibility. I never understood what they were talking about, but I'll probably tell my son the same thing.

Anyway, I was required to read one story a night and that was it. My first attempt to get out of the reading was the "I don't understand the words" bit. My father quickly ended that by handing me *Webster's Unabridged,* which is the one that gives you the definition in about four languages. Besides the fact that it was too complex, it took me half an hour just to find the word I was looking for. Like any kid was going to sit there and look up every unknown word? Hell no. I was just going to skip it whether I understood it or not.

My next solution was just not to read it at all and pretend like I was reading it. I allowed myself about 6 minutes a page, waited the allotted time, and then just put the book up. To kill my boredom while watching the clock go by, I'd smuggle in a GI Joe or two and use them to pass the time away. It wasn't but a day before that scheme was uncovered. My cover was blown by my mom, thank God, because she was much more lenient than my dad would have been. She decided that after each reading session she would give me a little pop quiz to see whether or not I had actually read the assigned material.

By this time it had become a game as to whether or not I would read the Grimm Brothers. I was determined not to read the stories come hell or high water. The only problem was how to get past the exams given after each story. This was something I had to think about long and hard. I wasn't going to be defeated no matter what the cost. If I read one of those stories, then I'd have lost and I just couldn't have that on my conscience. After staring at the book for a while, I decided that maybe I should just read the first story and see just how difficult these quizzes were going to be. To my surprise, the quizzes were incredibly easy. All she asked were questions like, "Who was the main character, and was he/she good or bad?" That's when I felt like a complete loser, after all, I'd read the entire story, and for what? There was no way that she was going to get the better of me the next night.

I was sly on the next quiz. All I did was skim the story to find out who the people were and read the first and last page to discover the point of the story and how it ended. I passed the quiz that night as well and figured I'd gotten the better of my mom. I'd taught her to try and outsmart me—I mean what was she thinking?

The third quiz I must have missed something. Maybe it was a name, maybe I just didn't catch something on that last page. Whatever it was, I'd been nailed and boy did I feel stupid, but I wasn't going out like that. Just because she'd figured out that I hadn't read this story didn't mean that I was going to start reading. She told me to read the story back over, but I decided that I could get around it by just finding the answer to that one question I missed. It took a while, but I pinpointed the careless mistake I'd made and prepared myself for the next barrage of questions. My confidence was shattered by a completely different set of questions. They had absolutely nothing to do with the first set and I was confounded. Besides being totally different, they were also much more in-depth. It wasn't a question like, "Where'd little Red Riding Hood go?" It was one like, "In the context of the time period, what were Little Red Riding Hood's intentions in going to grandma's house and contrast them with the Big Bad Wolf's." Boy, this lady was getting tough. Needless to say, after about the fifth quiz I was simply sent to bed with a spanking and told I'd better do better tomorrow.

They were winning at the moment, but I couldn't let them make me out to be the fool. That night, I didn't really read the story but I examined it and picked it apart. I knew it front and back and figured there was no way she could beat me on this one. It was no longer a matter of reading the text but more of a matter of whether or not I'd pass the quiz. I studied, and studied, and studied the story until I was sure I knew it. It was a good thing I'd spent so much time on it because that night I swear I had to diagram every sentence in the fable. I felt triumphant that night and didn't hold back from gloating to my mom that she couldn't make a quiz that I couldn't pass tomorrow.

Now when I look back at all of my attempts to get out of reading I realize that I learned a whole lot more than if I'd actually just sat down and read the book. Oh yeah, in case you're wondering, me and the Grimm boys didn't ever get along so well. That's why I celebrated finishing their book by toasting marshmallows over it in the backyard. I considered it a pretty good way to end such a traumatic event.

It also amazes me that this type of behavior didn't end with this one incident. I continued this type of juvenile behavior all the way up through high school; imagine that. I'd continue to attempt anything that appeared to be less work than the actual assignment. Of course, that strategy would fail miserably and I'd be forced to go and do the original torturous assignment.

One of the examples that really sticks out in my mind was my unsubstantiated confidence in *Cliff's Notes*. For some strange reason I thought that teachers had no idea that they existed and I was getting away with something. Once those myths were dispelled by my failure on a quiz, I was again stuck reading the book, just with a little more guidance from my parents. This is not to say that *Cliff's Notes* have no value; as a matter of fact, I found that they did help me with the symbolism that I could never seem to find in those novels.

These setbacks are only examples of the few times that my sneaky tricks didn't work. For the most part I did well in high school and managed to get away with avoiding the assigned work altogether. These are only the examples of when trying to get out of reading actually backfired and forced me to learn more than necessary. That's a horrible thought. I can't fathom what would have happened if I'd been busted every time. I'd probably be a member of the Mensa Society by now or at least have an extremely inflated ego.

Now that I've reached the college level I've discovered that skimming the pages and hoping that the lectures cover everything that will be on the tests doesn't quite cut it. The first test that I had in Psychology was one that I thought I could use common sense for. Boy was I wrong. I discovered that common sense does nothing to help me figure out what Skinner's main focus in his psychological experiments were. That was probably my awakening to the world beyond high school. Now I've come to realize that reading, as well as studying the text, is the only thing that can help me succeed on the tests. This is not to say that my avoidance of reading did nothing for me. On the contrary, I believed it has helped me to achieve the level of reading that I now enjoy. I just realize that now it is time for a completely different approach: doing it right the first time.

2

Reading . . . It's Not Just Books Anymore

Dan Melzer

In my classes in high school, I never "read" anything besides books, newspapers, and magazines. However, when I got to college, I was exposed to a different kind of "reading." In my anthropology class, we were required to view about four films per test. I thought that was a pretty neat way to gain knowledge in school, because it was something new. Another type of reading that was new to me was websites for my class.

—Haley, first-year writing student

In college you will probably "read" films, websites, advertisements, and even cultural events. You can expect to read much more in college than you did in high school, and the reading you do for most of your college classes will be more challenging than most of the reading you did in high school. Like many of my students, Haley was surprised by how much different college reading is from high school reading.

So what exactly can you expect from the reading you're required to do in college, and how should you approach this reading? To find some answers to this question, I interviewed two sections of my freshman composition class and a number of professors at the school where I teach, Florida State University. I also went on the Internet and collected syllabi and assignment sheets from teachers at 4-year colleges across America to discover their attitudes toward reading. I want to use this research to give you a glimpse of the kinds of reading required in a variety of college classes. I also want to suggest ways to approach this reading, based on tips from students and professors.

From Books and Articles to Websites and Newsgroups

At first glance the answer to the question, "What are students reading in their college classes?" seems obvious. Your gut reaction to this question might be, "Books, of course." But according to the teachers and students I talked to, college students are just as likely to "read" things like films and websites, as Haley mentioned in the opening quote.

Websites are quickly becoming primary reading material for college classes. A business professor explains that in his class, "the media most often read are company websites" (Dawley 1998). Often teachers who require their students to read websites are asking them to do a similar kind of reading of the website that they would do for a book. A number of the assignments I collected asked students to summarize websites, just as they would a book or article. One teacher even has students summarize what is said in a newsgroup (Zimmer 1998). Some students feel that reading websites is a nice complement to more "traditional" reading. One of my students, Liz, says, "my oceanography class requires a lot of website reading. I enjoy this because it is not boring—it's fun to search for the information and look through pictures and diagrams."

In college classes you also might be required to "read" films, advertisements, and works of art. For example, a meteorology professor at San Francisco State University requires his students to take notes and comment on television programs and radio shows, and a history professor at Radford University has his students compare and contrast the film *Gettysburg* to the chapter about the battle of Gettysburg in the textbook (Dempsey 1999, Hepburn 1998). A communications professor has his students analyze cartoons, and a psychology professor at the University of Michigan assigns magazine and television advertisements to be "read" and critiqued (Brooks 1999, Price 1999).

In humanities classes, it's not unusual to be assigned "reading" that includes artwork and plays. A classics professor at Trinity University requires students to visit the local art museum and compare and contrast artwork from the exhibits and the information in the textbook, and a modern languages professor says her students "are expected to describe and frequently interpret or 'read' cultural products such as paintings and architecture" (Dangler 1998, Garrison 1998).

The interpretation of architecture and art is similar to the interpretation of books. The same is true for the interpretation of live plays. Kent says of his theater class, "I had to watch plays and write a response about them. If I didn't watch the play and pay close attention, I wouldn't have been able to complete the writing assignments." Later in this essay I'll talk about the need to be an active and close reader, as Kent is when he "reads" plays.

Plays aren't the only "live event" you might be reading and analyzing in college. In classes like sociology and anthropology, you'll most likely have to read cultural events just as you read texts. For example, a human primatology professor at Indiana University has students observe human interaction at shopping malls, sporting events, and parties, and then summarize and evaluate their observations. And a behavioral science professor at Palomar College had his students observe and reflect on a religious ceremony at a local church (Balch 1998). In all of these examples, the traditional definition of reading as interpreting written text is expanded. But your approaches to reading these other kinds of "texts" are often the same approaches you take when reading written text.

Being an Active Reader

One thing to keep in mind, no matter what you're reading and what class it's for, is the importance of being an active reader. It's one of the keys to understanding a text. According to my students, an active reader is someone who highlights important points, makes notes in the margins, and even makes separate notes and outlines as she reads. This is especially true of the kind of reading you will be expected to do in most college classes. As a psychology professor at the University of Minnesota says, "For you to gain an adequate understanding of most research articles, more than a single 'passive' reading of them will be required" (West 1998).

Understanding that academic writing can be challenging, my students discussed a number of tips for approaching this kind of required reading. The number one piece of advice is to highlight or underline key points. Donald says, "I sit down with a highlighter in my hand. When I come across something that seems paramount, I highlight it." Brent says, "I find that highlighting the main points in the book and reading the highlighted portions over and over helps me to remember them." The key expression here is *main points*. If you find yourself highlighting almost everything, you're probably not understanding which points are most important.

Not all readers highlight. "It's very rare that I highlight as I read," says Laura. Even though Laura doesn't annotate a text as she reads it, most of my students read with a highlighter or pen in hand, and by underlining and making notes in the margins they read more actively. We can all remember times when we laid back on the couch with a book for class, only to doze off to dreamland a few minutes later. Not only will you understand texts better by highlighting and writing notes in the margins, you will be a more active, alert reader. And don't be afraid to write in your books! I can remember high school classes where I had to return the textbooks at the end of the year free of any marks, but in college you're encouraged to underline and make notes in your books.

Some readers also make separate notes in their notebook while they read. Liz says, "As I read I also take notes. I usually start with the headline and then write down the main points." Writing a summary like this is a useful technique, especially when you're reading something complicated. Karen says, "Usually I will stop and take notes on the important material. Then I go back and read the notes I took." Both Liz and Karen feel that writing your own summary of the main points of a text is worth the extra time and effort. As Elizabeth Flynn (1982) points out, "Through writing, students gain a fuller understanding of their reading" (149). Think of note taking as a way to better your understanding of a text. Note taking is especially important when you're "reading" films, artwork, plays, websites, and cultural events.

Some of you are probably thinking that all of this advice will only slow you down. It's true that rereading and note taking are time consuming. But don't be fooled by the latest advertisements for speed reading. Reading is not a race to the finish, and faster reading is not always better reading. Haley points this out when she says, "My reading usually takes a while, not because I am a slow reader, but because I read very carefully, paying attention to detail and trying not to miss a thing." Of course, your reading speed depends on your purpose. In a psychology class I took when I was an undergraduate, I read enough to get the gist of a theory or example, but I didn't get bogged down in every detail because I knew I would only need to understand the basic concept. On the other hand, in most of the essays I read for English classes, I read more slowly and did more note taking because I knew that I would have to write detailed essays in response to what I read. This need to slow down and read carefully is also true when you are "reading" films, advertisements, and websites. As one science teacher at the University of Arkansas suggests in his syllabus, "Slow down as you travel through cyberspace and become active observers—able to absorb the images and text, process it through your mind and come to a greater understanding" (Boss 1998). Good readers usually work at a happy medium between poring over every word at a snail's pace and speed reading through a text without rereading.

One reason that some students think faster reading is better reading is because of the amount of reading they have. Most of my students say that they have much more reading assigned in college than they did in high school. Regina says that she has over 300 pages a week to read for her classes, and Angie says that she reads for 1 or 2 hours a night. Because you'll probably have a lot to read in college, it's important not to wait until the last minute to read a novel, textbook, website, or film. Most of us do poorly when we write a paper the night before it's due, and the same is true of last minute reading. Devin admits that "any assignments that ask me to read something are usually done about 15 minutes before the class starts . . . Any 'recommended' reading for classes never happens until exam time, and then I skim through the reading." If you're not staying on top of your readings, you'll find yourself in Devin and Jen's position. Jen says, "I find myself putting other things first and not reading as much as I should, falling behind and having to cram later." Since you do some type of reading in most college classes, it's easy to fall behind.

Reading Is a Process

Good writers revise their writing and take it through many drafts. Few writers can sit down at the computer and write a polished essay in a single draft. The same is true for reading. Besides reading closely and annotating, my students also approach reading as a process. They don't expect to understand everything they read the first time they read it; especially the less familiar "academic" reading they are assigned. When you read your college newspaper or your favorite magazine, you can often just read it through once, from start to finish, and understand what you read. This is usually because you bring a lot of prior experience and context with you when you read. But many college texts require you to enter new territories in your reading, and rereading becomes an essential part of the reading process. For some of my students, the first step in this process is *prereading.*

Most writers brainstorm before they start writing. They might jot down ideas, make an outline, or just write the first thing that comes to their mind and then reshape it later. This is sometimes called *prewriting.* The same technique can be applied to reading: prereading. Haley says, "I begin by skimming the chapter to see what it is about and viewing some of the pictures. Then, I begin reading the chapter." Before you open a book for class, consider doing a little prereading. Look at the table of contents or skim the chapter you're assigned. Sometimes the books you're assigned to read will have summaries on the back or inside covers, and it's worth your time to read through these to get a sense of what the book will be about. The more prior knowledge you have, the more successful your reading will be.

Our best advice is to reread what you're having trouble understanding. As Anne Falk says in her chapter from the book *Language Connections,* "Good readers constantly ask themselves, 'Does this make sense?'" (124). If a sentence or paragraph doesn't make sense, committed readers will take the time to reread. Kent says, "If I don't understand the material, I will read it over a few times to try to get a better understanding." Kent not only takes the time to reread, but he reads something as many times as he needs to get an understanding of it. "Usually in geology, I will skim the material first and see if I can understand it," Karen says. "Usually I can't, so I will reread, and stop and take notes on the important material. Then I go back and read the notes I took. If I am still confused, I will reread the chapter one more time." Donald goes through a similar process. "When I don't understand something I read," Donald says, "I reread it until I finally comprehend it."

Donald also says he sits "with a dictionary nearby, because sometimes the vocabulary can be confusing." When you read the latest Stephen King novel there usually aren't that many words you can't understand, but when you're reading a philosophy or chemistry textbook, you will probably need to look up the meaning of words as you go along. The number of words you need to look up, and the amount of rereading you need to do, might depend on the class. Wanda says, "Most things in science and math I have to read more than once to understand." On the other hand, some students feel that the reading they do in math and science classes is much easier than reading a novel or a history book.

Of course, not all of my students take the time to reread. One student says, "My reading process involves reading the material once through, and if I didn't understand it then, chances are I never will." When I was an undergraduate there were textbooks in philosophy and science that I thought I'd never understand, no matter how many times I reread them. Looking back on those times, I realize that I could have used some of the tips my students gave me for this essay. If I knew then, what I know now, I might have had less trouble comprehending those texts.

Reading aloud can be another useful part of anyone's reading process. Carrie says, "I try to reread and read aloud. I think it helps me stick the information in my brain better." Reading a text aloud helps you comprehend it. If you're having trouble understanding something you're reading, try reading aloud. You can also talk to someone else about what you're reading. Theresa says, "If there's a concept that I'm having problems with, I'll go back and read the section until it makes more sense or until I'm so frustrated with it that I ask someone that understands the material." One of the best ways to improve your writing is to get feedback on it from an outside reader, and the same is true of reading. Some college classes are so large that it's difficult to communicate with the professor, but if your teacher is available, schedule an office appointment when you can't understand an assigned reading. Sometimes you ask the professor for feedback on your writing, so why not do the same with your reading? Many colleges having a reading/writing center, and you may have already taken essays there to get feedback. Why not do the same when you're having trouble understanding a passage in a book, or a scene in a play?

If you're fortunate, you'll get to discuss what you're reading in class. That's the perfect time to ask questions about passages you didn't understand. Of course, you need to keep up with the readings to do this! Linda says, "The classes that I have a lot of reading in are Multicultural Film and Marriages and Families. These two courses assign readings every class that are crucial in following discussions." Many teachers judge participation primarily by class discussion, which usually involves discussing what you've read or asking questions about passages you didn't understand. As Angie says, "In religion class you must show participation in the class discussions about what you have read." This usually means asking questions about and coming to an understanding of the concepts you've read about, and not just memorizing facts. In most college classes, if you don't do the readings, you will be lost during class discussion.

The Reading/Writing Connection

In *Understanding Reading,* Frank Smith (1994) says, "It's only through read-ing that anyone can learn to write" (175). Like Smith, I find there is a close connection between reading and writing. As one communications professor says, ". . . writing helps students to articulate the concepts they learn about through reading" (Brooks 1999). Much of the writing you will do in college requires you to respond to, synthesize, or evaluate what you've read. This kind of writing requires active reading, and when you respond to a text or synthe-size ideas, you come to a deeper understanding of what you've read. According to Anne Chapman (1993), the author of *Making Sense,* most high school tests ask for verbatim recall of facts from the reading, whereas most college tests require "integration and understanding of knowledge" (40).

Unfortunately, despite Chapman's claim, my students say that many of their classes test only on "fact finding." This kind of writing is just spitting out facts from the textbook, and it doesn't require you to think very hard about what you've read. Haley talks about the disadvantages of this kind of fact find-ing when she says that her classes have mostly multiple choice tests on the readings. "I was not required to think about the information," Haley says. "I just had to memorize it. Therefore, the information left my head after the test just as it entered it, not really benefiting me in the end." Another student says, "When they ask for facts about it [the reading material], you spit out answers like a calculator." This kind of reading and testing is much less helpful than when a teacher challenges you to think and write about concepts. As Linda says, "I feel like I learn more if I am forced to pick the reading apart, and make use of every piece of knowledge given." You're bound to have a number of classes that test you only on "facts" from the reading, but many of your college courses will require you to read more deeply than just skimming for facts. In these classes, reading is often seen as a way to improve writing.

A professor at Brigham Young University made this connection explicit in his syllabus: "Writing is intellectually challenging. The only ways I know to improve are to read things that are well-written, using them as models for your own work" (Deardon 1998). Clearly, reading improves writing. Kelley says, "The more mature writing I read, the more mature my writing becomes." Liz agrees: "I find that the more I read and research the better and also easier my paper becomes."

Students who don't read or aren't active readers find that their writing suffers because of this. "I think reading has a lot to do with writing," says Regina. "I can see a difference in my writing when I have done more reading throughout the year . . . It takes me a long time to write even the simplest assignments. Maybe that has to do with my lack of reading." Devin claims, "I don't really enjoy reading. Honestly, I avoid it whenever possible. So my writ-ing is pretty bad and sort of the same as it's been since high school." Even though these two students admitted that they didn't read often, they saw reading as the a key to writing better.

There's a moral here: When you're assigned reading in college, don't think of it as separate from writing, even if your teacher never makes a connection between the two. Karen says, "Besides English, I don't think the reading I do in class connects to anything I write. The only classes that I read anything in, there is no writing required." But it's possible that the reading Karen does this semester will help her with writing required in another semester. *You never know when the reading you do for one class might help you with your writing in another.* Donald provides a good example of this kind of connection:

> I took speech class last semester and witnessed a person talk about Nike sweatshops. This made me very inquisitive about this particular topic. So I decided to search on the web and read articles regarding it. Then a paper in my English class came up when we had to write a business letter to a company. So I pooled together the knowledge I learned from the speech and the websites and I was able to put together a pretty nasty letter to Nike.

Think about using Donald's technique of connecting classes with the reading and writing you do in college. Any reading you do for any class has the potential to help with your reading or writing in another class, and even Karen acknowledges this: "When I read, sometimes I pick up new ideas or language that I can transfer over and use in some of my other classes."

Karen talks about picking up new language, and an increased vocabulary was something valuable my students gained from the reading they did in each of their college classes. "My reading in my other classes connects to my writing in my other classes by the building of my vocabulary," Matt says. "It also gives me exposure to other styles of writing." Brent says, "By reading the textbooks, I have found that I have increased my vocabulary and ability to comprehend difficult concepts."

Whether it was through improving writing style, increasing vocabulary, or gaining a better ability to comprehend difficult concepts, most of the teachers and students I interviewed saw a close connection between reading and writing across the curriculum. To help you reread and write about *this* essay, I'll end with a summary of the advice I collected:

1. "Reading" can mean more than just reading printed texts.
2. The key to understanding a text is being an active reader.
3. Writing about what you're reading can aid comprehension.
4. Faster reading is not necessarily better reading.
5. Good readers preread and reread.
6. Good readers ask questions and get feedback about what they're reading.
7. Reading improves writing.

I invite you to think about your reading process and the reading you do in your classes and add to my list. Good luck with your many types of college reading!

Works Cited

Balch, Grace. 1998. "Writing Assignments." Online. Netscape. August 4, 1998. Available at WWW: http://www.palomar.edu/more/beh_sci/balch/writing.html.

Boss, Stephen K. 1998. "Earth Systems Science." Online. Netscape. July 19, 1998. Available at WWW: http://comp.uark.edu/~sboss/esswritnotes.htm.

Brooks, Robert. 1999. Personal E-mail, March 18, 1999.

Chapman, Anne, ed. 1993. *Making Sense: Teaching Critical Reading Across the Curriculum.* New York: College Entrance Board.

Dangler, Jean. 1998. Personal E-mail, March 1, 1998.

Dawley, David. 1998. Personal E-mail, February 28, 1998.

Dearden, David. 1998. "Class Policies." Online. Netscape. August 3, 1998. Available WWW: http://chemwww.byu.edu/faculty/dvd/classes/CHEM391/policy.html.

Dempsey, Dave. 1999. "A Guide to Keeping Your Meteorology Journal." Online. Netscape. April 28, 1999. Available at WWW: http://twister.sfsu.edu/courses/metr302.2/syllabus/journal_guide.html.

Falke, Anne. 1982. "What Every Educator Should Know about Reading Research." In: *Language Connections,* 123–37. Edited by Toby Fulwiler and Art Young. Urbana, IL: National Council of Teachers of English.

Flynn, Elizabeth. 1982. "Reconciling Readers and Texts." In: *Language Connections,* 139–52. Edited by Toby Fulwiler and Art Young. Urbana, IL: National Council of Teachers of English.

Garrison, Mark B. 1998. "Classics 1305: Classical Mythology." Online. Netscape. July 24, 1998. Available at WWW: http://www.trinity.edu/~mgarriso/Myth/MythProject1.html.

Hepburn, Sharon Roger. 1998. "History 365: Civil War and Reconstruction." Online. Netscape. July 16, 1998. Available at WWW: http://www.runet.edu/~shepburn/cwwrite.htm.

Price, Paul. 1999. "Writing Assignments." Online. Netscape. April 28,1999. Available at WWW: http://www.umich.edu/psych112/wri.112.html.

Smith, Frank. 1994. *Understanding Reading: A Psycholinguistic Analysis of Reading and Learning to Read.* Hillsdale, NJ: Lawrence Erlbaum.

West, Tiffany. 1998. "Journal Article Assignment." Online. Netscape. July 15, 1998. Available at WWW: http://icd.coled.umn.edu/Fall97/CPsy3343/journal.htm

Zimmer, JoAnn. 1998. "International Protocol: Cultural Awareness." Online. Netscape. July 22, 1998. Available at WWW: http://www.sheridan.om.ca/academic/crosscollege/international/bib.html.

Student Narrative 2

Why It Took So Long*

Lysa Moorefield

Reading and writing are two words that could send a chill up my spine. In high school, I would have rather jumped off a cliff than read a book or write a paper. History and English were my worst subjects, and they were also subjects that I had to take my freshman year in college. In high school, I made a "D" in History my junior year, and then busted my butt my senior year to make an "A." I think English class remained at a steady "C" all the time. There was little chance that I was going to succeed in college if I had to take History and English.

American Civilization was my first class of the fall semester. I received my syllabus and saw the words *book report* before anything else. Not just one but two book reports. I hate reading, but I hate reading more if it's a book that I have no interest in at all. Even though the books may be useful for the class, I hate to even think about reading a book, knowing beforehand that I am not going to like it. I was doing fine in the class, as far as taking notes and paying attention to the lectures, but when the teacher would ask us how our reading was coming along, I felt like sliding down in my seat because I did not want him to know that I was not reading the book.

For our first book report, I probably did what a lot of the other students attempted. We were supposed to read *The Autobiography of Benjamin Franklin,* but I think that a majority of the class, including me, just skimmed through the book about 3 weeks before it was due. I tried to come up with some amazing paper, giving a summary of the book. For this reason my paper was not an "A" or a "B," but good enough to pass the Gordon Rule. This was a [state of Florida] rule that in specific classes students have to accumulate so many points by writing essays or reports before the end of the semester. It also

*The process narrative for Lysa's essay can be found in Hint Sheet A.

requires that you make a "C" or above on the paper for it to count toward your points. If the Gordon Rule is not achieved, then your class isn't either.

Toward the end of the semester, our next report was due. We were reading *The Jungle* by Upton Sinclair. I actually read some of this book. I also got the *Cliff's Notes* to help out a little. This book was truly interesting to me; it told a story that was exciting. It was not some book that explains facts about a person and what they accomplished in life. This book actually had a plot and was very interesting.

The only books that I really like are suspense, mystery, and horror novels. Those are the only books that can keep my attention long enough to read the whole thing. Since I actually read *The Jungle* and did my book report, I received an "A." I was really shocked at the fact that I, someone who hates reading so much and can not even pick up the newspaper, could make an "A" on a book report in an American Civilization class in college. To this day I still suspect there might of been some sort of mistake.

However, my English 101 class may have had an impact on my reading and writing skills also. This was my second class of fall semester. Throughout the semester we took the word *authority* and analyzed it in many different perspectives. We learned about authority and how much it is in our lives. Authority in school, home, and media were just a few examples that were discussed in the class.

As I mentioned earlier, being told to write something gives me a feeling of discomfort. I get this look of fear and disappointment on my face. I hate the pressure of brainstorming, knowing that you have to write a paper on something that you could probably care less about. For my first paper in English 101, I decided to write on authority in my life. I told some stories from middle and high school, and explained some experiences from the fall semester that I was adjusting to. I contrasted teachers and coaches from grade school to professors and coaches in college. With that I explained how I was an authority figure, just like my parents were. It was interesting to find that there were many authority figures in my life, and to learn that there would be more in the future and that it was something that I looked forward to.

After writing that first paper, I started feeling very positive about the class and found myself being interested in the next assignment. I felt good until I heard the words *reading workshop*. The teacher said that we would have to be in groups and read each others' papers and give comments on them. If I cannot even read the paper I just finished writing myself; how was I supposed to read someone else's?

Everyone broke into their little groups, and we started reading. I read the first paper, and found it very interesting because my experiences dealing with authority were totally different from Laura's, the person's paper that I was reading. I knew they were going to be different in some way, but not to the point where nothing was the same. As I read Laura's paper, I learned a lot about Laura the person. I could tell that she was introverted, with a nice personality, and very delicate because of the soft tone that she wrote in. It was nice finding out about someone from their writing, also thinking that they may be learning about me from my writing. Reading was actually becoming not such a bad thing after all.

In my second semester now, I really do not mind reading as much, and sometimes I actually enjoy reading. I never thought that I would change into a person who takes books with them on trips or vacations. Being on the basketball team and traveling a lot, a book can sometimes become my best friend. On our trip to Puerto Rico, I read a horror novel by Stephen King—the whole book! Since I have started reading more, I have found that reading makes me a more intelligent person and has helped improve my writing skills. I feel that reading, depending on what type of reading it is, makes me think and be more creative with my mind. Reading is a great stress reliever because I can get carried away and very involved with my book. This way it takes my mind off things that are bothering me for a while, or at least gives me some time to relax. I actually find myself reading a lot in those situations. I have now learned that reading is not something to be afraid of because I can be taken into a whole different world with reading.

3

Reading Radically or Radically Reading . . . How I Try to Get to the Root of Things

Lisa Albrecht

What do all these newspapers, magazines, and periodicals have in common?

- *Minneapolis Star Tribune*
- *Gay Community News: The National Queer Progressive Quarterly*
- *Radical Teacher: A Socialist and Feminist Journal on the Theory and Practice of Teaching*
- *Ms. Magazine*
- *Dollars and Sense: What's Left in Economics*
- *Utne Reader*
- *The Nation*
- *Teaching Tolerance*
- *Radiance: The Magazine for Large Women*
- *Democracy and Education: the Magazine for Classroom Teachers*
- *Lilith: The Independent Jewish Women's Magazine*
- *Bridges: A Journal for Jewish Feminists and Our Friends*
- *Race Traitor: Journal of the New Abolitionism*
- *George*
- *Re-thinking Schools: An Urban Educational Journal*

- *College English*
- *College Composition and Communication*
- *Extra!: The Magazine of F.A.I.R. (Fairness and Accuracy in Reporting)*
- *Color Lines: Race, Color, Action*
- *Journal of Education*
- *Evergreen Chronicles: A Journal of Gay, Lesbian, Bisexual and Transgender Arts and Cultures*

I know you might find this hard to believe, but I subscribe to all of these rags (that's what I call magazines, newspapers, and periodicals). You probably think I'm crazy, and that I spend my whole life reading! I really don't. I do way too many things at once most of the time; my mind flits like a butterfly among all the projects I juggle. Reading for me is like gardening—I do it in fits and spurts. Sometimes the weeds get incredibly out of control because I don't find the time to get outside to crawl around and hang out with my vegetables and flowers. I make excuses to myself that it's too much work to pull up the crabgrass that surrounds my tomatoes. I let myself forget how wonderful I feel after I've gotten down on my knees and rolled around in the dirt for a few hours. I know for sure that my tomatoes do better if I give them some attention.

Reading, like gardening, sometimes feels like too much work. I'd rather watch TV or a video, listen to a new CD, talk on the phone, go out to eat with friends, or play with my dog and cat. But my mind is always questioning why the world is the way it is; when I stop long enough to catch my breath, picking up a newspaper, magazine, or journal helps me sort out what I already know, what I need to find out, and how to think analytically about working for social justice in the world. I don't always have time for a "big" book, but I can always find time to read an article. I carry around rags in my backpack when I go to the dentist, when I travel by air, car, train, or bus, when I'm waiting for a friend in a restaurant . . . everywhere. There are magazines in my bathroom reading rack, on the living room coffee table, on the floor next to my bed, on the dining room table, and in stacks on the floor of my office. There's even old feminist newspapers from the 1970s that I've catalogued in boxes in my basement. I tell myself that you never know when you might need them for a project. Yes, I admit it; I am a terrible pack rat. My partner worries that in a few years, there will only be narrow, winding paths in our home, with newspapers stacked to the ceiling.

There is, however, another really important key to my reading life. I'm an activist and educator and have spent most of my adult life working for a more just world. Call me a feminist. An antiracist. A queer. A radical Jew. A middle-class professional working for economic justice. All of the above. For me, one way that I work for social justice in this world is by learning as much as possible about how power and privilege operates in the world. To do that, I need to be able to find information that challenges what mainstream media circulates as "fact."

What do I mean exactly? Simply put, the information that most of us take in from the media often contradicts other, less available information. For example, throughout 1999, newspapers all over the United States have been headlining how great our economy is going, how low unemployment is, and how well the stock market is doing. Yet, at the same time, the gap between the rich and the poor in this country is at its greatest in over 20 years and unemployment remains staggeringly high in communities of color (Collins et al. 1999).

Something doesn't jive here. That's why I go out of my way to find information from progressive publications. I need to "see" the big picture, come to my own conclusions, and, as an educator and activist, help people learn how to find alternative information sources and how to "read" the media more carefully.

I also read alternative rags because I want to learn more about the lives of historically marginalized peoples, especially when they are characterized more thoughtfully. As a lesbian, when I read *Evergreen Chronicles* and *Gay Community News,* I see positive and interesting characterizations of gay, lesbian, bisexual, and transgender people (not just limp-wristed drag queens or very masculine dykes). When I read *Bridges* and *Lilith,* I learn more about my heritage as a Jew, and what Jewish women think and care about today. In reading *Race Traitor,* I find the work of other white people who want to eradicate racism. If I were to stick with the *Minneapolis Star Tribune, Time, Newsweek,* and the *New York Times,* I'd get a fairly one-sided view of many of these issues and people. How come?

If you read Ben Bagdikian's *The Media Monopoly* (1997), you can learn about who "owns" most of the media in this country. For example, in 1996, in a $19-billion dollar deal, Disney merged with ABC. The conglomerate that exists now owns newspapers, magazines, books, radio, broadcast TV, cable systems, movies, recordings, and videocassettes (xiii). This affects what gets advertised, what information is considered important to print, and what information isn't considered important to release to the public. As of 1996, approximately ten media companies (among them Viacom, Time Warner, Sony, Seagram, Westinghouse, Gannett, General Electric, Murdoch, and Disney) controlled over 90 percent of the media in this country. As Bagdikian says, "media power is political power" (xiii).

So where do we go to find other sources of information? I often wander into independent bookstores and cruise the magazine racks. Independent bookstores are different than huge chains. The chain bookstores have deep financial ties to the mainstream media, so their magazine and book selections are usually not as diverse as the smaller bookstores. I know that sounds weird—big bookstores should have a greater variety of sources of information, but given who controls the media, that's not the case (see *The Nation*, March 17, 1997, for an entire issue devoted to mainstream publishing).

I also depend on searching the World Wide Web for alternative sources of information. That sometimes feels like looking for a needle in a haystack, but there are some great places to start. Try the *Alternative Press Directory* (www.altpress.org/index.html) and *F.A.I.R.—Fairness and Accuracy in Reporting* (www.fair.org). Both organizations are devoted to broadening people's viewpoints. Their websites have links to lots of other great resources.

Because I love pop culture, I watch TV and also pick up *Time, Newsweek,* and *People Magazine.* Yes, there's lots of information transmitted in these sources, but what I've taught myself to do is not simply accept it all, but critique it as well. I ask questions like, How come good looking, skinny white women in expensive gowns often are shown on TV commercials and in magazine ads selling us fancy sports cars? Is the message that you—the man—get the woman if you buy the car? How come there are so few positive stories about African Americans or Mexican Americans in the news? We usually hear about poverty and violence in these communities, not about folks who are creative and brilliant. *Making Sense of the Media: A Handbook of Popular Education Techniques* by Eleonora Castano Ferreira and Joao Castano Ferreira (1997) is a great tool to help teach us how to critique mainstream media. I've used it in the classroom and with friends to help people have fun while learning how to perform a critical analysis of the media.

I must admit that sometimes, it feels very difficult for me to read with a critical eye. It *does* take more work! Why not just watch the nightly news, read the daily newspaper, and pick up *Time* and *Newsweek*? They are easy to read, and the pictures are great. I really do believe that as citizens in this democracy, it is our responsibility to "read" the world critically. How else will democracy work if we don't take responsibility? When I get lazy, I often give myself a reading assignment to challenge myself. I'll read the morning local newspaper, and some story will catch my eye.

In July 1999, President Clinton visited an American Indian reservation in North Dakota as part of a tour he did of poor regions in the United States. The story made national news—both TV and newspapers. The news emphasized how Clinton was the first sitting president to visit a reservation in sixty years. The articles I read also discussed the poverty on the reservation and interviewed Native people who were glad Clinton came to see them. The articles were fairly short, and did not go into great detail, beyond mentioning the high unemployment on the reservation and the high rates of alcoholism. For an uncritical reader, this kind of a story can reinforce negative racial stereotypes that all Indians drink and don't want to work. The question I've been asking myself is, What do Native-owned newspapers and magazines have to say about this story? There are no Native-owned daily newspapers, but there are quite a few monthly newspapers, as well as monthly and quarterly periodicals produced by Native people and other communities of color that do a more in-depth analysis of Native life (see *The Circle,* a Minneapolis-based monthly newspaper). What is the history of the federal government's commitment to Native peoples? Why is there a high rate of alcoholism on the reservation? I will go to these sources to give me a better perspective on what I read in my local newspaper.

You can also do this in classrooms or community reading groups. Pick a topic that's been in the news for the past year. Go to your library and get several articles about it from mainstream sources, and then several articles from alternative sources. Read both sets of articles, and see for yourself. Do you get the same "facts?" Probably not. It seems to me to be worth the effort and part of my responsibility as a citizen to be informed about the world around me.

This is what I call reading radically or radically reading . . . getting to the root of things. I urge you to give it a try. You don't have to give up much to do it, and you gain a whole lot more as an informed citizen-participant.

Here are the addresses of some of the journals and magazines I mentioned. You might want to start with some of these, but even better, make a list of your own and share that list—and the results of your radical but informed reading—with others as I've done here.

Radical Teacher: A Socialist and Feminist Journal on the Theory and Practice of Teaching
P.O. Box 383316
Cambridge, MA 02238

Ms. Magazine
www.msmagazine.com

Dollars and Sense: What's Left in Economics
One Summer Street
Somerville, MA 02143
www.dollarsandsense.org

Utne Reader
1624 Harmon Place
Minneapolis, MN 55403
www.utne.com
The Nation
33 Irving Place
New York, NY 10003
www.TheNation.com

Teaching Tolerance
Southern Poverty Law Center
400 Washington Ave.
Montgomery, AL 36104
www.splcenter.org

Radiance: The Magazine for Large Women
P.O. Box 30246
Oakland, CA 94604
www.radiancemagazine.com

Democracy and Education: The Magazine for Classroom Teachers
College of Education
Ohio University
321 McCracken Hall
Athens, OH 45701
www.ohiou.edu/ide/home.html

Lilith: The Independent Jewish Women's Magazine
250 W. 57 Street
New York, NY 10107
www.lilithmag.com

Bridges: A Journal for Jewish Feminists and Our Friends
P.O. Box 24839
Eugene, OR 94702
www.pond.net/~ckineberg/bridges

Race Traitor: Journal of the New Abolitionism
P.O. Box 603
Cambridge, MA 02140
www.postfun.com/racetraitor

Re-thinking Schools: An Urban Educational Journal
1001 E. Keefe Avenue
Milwaukee, WI 53212
www.rethinkingschools.org

Extra!: the Magazine of F.A.I.R. (Fairness and Accuracy in Reporting)
www.fair.org

Color Lines: Race, Color, Action
4096 Piedmont Avenue, #319
Oakland, CA 94611
www.arc.org/Pages/ArcColorLines.html

Journal of Education
Boston University School of Education
605 Commonwealth Avenue
Boston, MA 02215

Evergreen Chronicles: A Journal of Gay, Lesbian, Bisexual and Transgender Arts and Cultures,
P.O. Box 8939
Minneapolis, MN 55408
evergchron@aol.com

Works Cited

Bagdikian, Ben. 1997. *The Media Monopoly,* 5th edition. Boston: Beacon Press.

Castano Ferreira, Eleonora, and Joao Castano Ferreira. 1997. *Making Sense of the Media: A Handbook of Popular Education Techniques.* New York: Monthly Review Press.

Collins, Chuck, Betsy Leondar-Wright, and Holly Sklar. 1999. *Shifting Fortunes.* Boston: United for a Fair Economy. www.stw.org.

Student Narrative 3

Learning to Read
For Me It's Been the
Struggle of a Lifetime*

Chris Olson

Imagine having to double your study time because you just learned to read 3 years ago. Ever since I can remember, I have been a horrible student. I never understood much when I was little and was the troublemaker of the class, and always the one to be sent to the office. I made one trip to the office just about every day. On some days, when the teacher thought I had too much sugar in me, a second trip that would land me there the rest of the day. My parents did not have much to say about it at first, but when they had to leave work early and come pick me up because the school did not want me in their classrooms, things began to change.

I had made it up to the fifth grade, surprisingly only repeating third grade on the way. You can imagine the grades I was getting only being in class half the time. With the end of the fifth grade approaching, I received a letter in the mail explaining that I would have to repeat it. I was emotionally destroyed at that point. Twelve years old, a year older than most kids in the class, and I had to find out that I would be thirteen and still in the fifth grade. I began to think that teachers would not give me a break. They heard I was a bad kid, and the smallest little slip up and I was on my way. Sometimes I would be sent out not knowing what it was that I did. If I did not know what I did, how could I fix it, and then, did I want to? Their practices turned me against them, and I never won.

Upon receiving the letter, my folks had had enough. I was tested by the public school system a dozen times and they had no answers, which my parents desperately needed. I began to find myself not attending school very

*The process narrative for Chris' essay can be found in Hint Sheet A.

much. Instead I spent most of my remaining days of fifth grade undergoing tests. Still there were no answers.

Frustrated as hell at the no-answer scenario, my parents began to do some research of their own. They found Dr. Grosglen, who was world renowned for working and diagnosing learning disabilities. She worked out of the Mailmen Center for Child Development in Miami, and my parents squeezed me in to see her, which wasn't very easy. This was an intense time because it was just about my last hope. I underwent several days of testing—much of it I never understood, blocks with shapes and colors that had to match and pictures with odd shapes that didn't make sense. Just about the only thing that did make sense was the reading comprehension, and at this point I could hardly read. It was horrible not being able to read. I would sit in class and have stomach cramps from fear that the teacher would call on me to read a paragraph to the class, as they do in grade school.

When the testing ended there was a week wait before they brought me in to explain the results. I sat at a big oval office table that extended from one end of the room to the other, and had gentlemen in suits scattered about it as a Christmas tree would have ornaments. The angel at the top of the tree was Dr. Grosglen. It was from her that I would learn the fate of my struggle which was not over but just beginning. They explained to me that I suffered from what they called dyslexia, disturbance of the ability to read. She also explained that I had a slight attention deficit disorder. Despite all of this, she explained to me that my I.Q. was high, "above average" she said. "There is a lot of hope for you," she explained, "but you are going to have to work hard your entire life." I could not figure out what hard meant, but I knew I couldn't read. This scenario amazed me—the entire time I thought I was stupid, I wasn't. She went on to tell me that a lot of people suffered from this, and many are prominent. A few she named were Albert Einstein, Ben Franklin, Tom Cruise, and Cher.

Upon hearing the news, a few recommendations were made on where I should attend school. The chosen school was Vanguard, which specialized in cases such as mine. The school had no grades, so you worked at your own pace. My pace was 3 years, and much of those 3 years I learned to read and to function in the classroom. It all started with lousy reading comprehension books. Read the passage and answer the questions. It sucked and I quickly developed a distaste for it, but with persistence I finally came to the point where I could understand what I was reading. You see, at Vanguard it was a no-slacking environment, and they stressed control. Outside the small classrooms, I worked to be rewarded. Each night I would be given a certain amount of work that had to be done by the next day, and it had to be correct, absolutely correct. If it was incorrect, I would find myself doing the work at lunch instead of eating. And if it was not done correctly at lunch, I would find the work 3 hours later on my lap as my peers had fun in PE class. There was incentive for me to do the work then.

This is where I learned to read. For many days of the year, I sat lonely in the classroom learning and sounding out words. It was horrible. Sitting inside while my friends played outside in the warm south Florida sun drove me nuts, but I knew the only way out was to get the work done. It was a grueling process of learning to understand everything I read.

There seemed no doubt in my mind that after learning the concepts, I would conquer my disability and find a way. I just decided I was going to do it no matter what, so I dug in and improved. This is what gave me the confidence I have today—the struggle of learning to read. There was so much frustration and hardship, I had to get through it. It had to be over, and I was the only one who could end it.

I learned the basics, enough that I was admitted into a college prep school in Miami. I, for the first time in my life, amazed myself by breezing through a year there with a 2.9 grade point average, which I thought I would never do. It almost seemed too easy.

The real challenge came when I entered college. As a freshman, I quickly became overwhelmed with work. No matter how many hours I put into it, I got the same result. I began to notice students around me studying half the time I was and they ended up with better grades. What was going on? This seemed to be the case with every class. It was getting to the point that all I would do was study. It would extend from the time I woke up to late into the evening. I began to close the library. Still, I was not able to get above a "C" average. I began to pull my hair out. In high school I was an "A" student in algebra, and I was still not very good at reading, but as a college student, I was excellent in reading and failed math three times.

This has caused some very frustrating times in college. Most of the time I walked away from a test thinking that I definitely got an "A," only the next week to find it came back a "C." I often looked over a test after the fact and I would find the most basic mistakes. The markings of "B" and "D" on the answer sheet would often be backwards, among other fundamental mistakes. It wasn't that I did not know the material. This was caused by the dyslexia and it was the first time I began noticing what the doctor and I had spoke about. I would find, by going over the test with the teacher, that I knew all the material and even more. It was just the transition of it onto the test that became a problem—the same problem I had with comprehending what I was reading.

As a senior in college I seem to be more relaxed about my disability because I often can find my biggest mistakes. The small ones are what get away from me. Looking back on the days I had to learn to read, I realized that I learned a lot more than just reading. I learned to struggle and survive. It seems corny but reading has been the greatest struggle in life for me so far, and today I think I can read better than most people my age. My new goal is learning to spell and write. Things still come slowly to me, and I still find that I study twice as long as my peers. "But this too shall pass."

4

An Open Letter to Jason Smith*

Ormond Loomis

Dear Jason,

Before you dropped out of ENC-1102, you wrote in your last journal entry something like, "What's the point of all this reading and writing anyway, I just want to get a degree and get on with my life." And I thought, "Yes! I know what you mean. I'm there." I wish we'd had a chance to discuss your question. Others in class were probably wondering the same thing, but didn't ask. I've meditated on the question—occasionally before you expressed it and more since then. Maybe it would've helped if we'd talked about the point and I'd offered some advice about relating the second semester of First-Year Writing (FYW) to your life.

From what you told me about your reasons for arriving late to classes, missing others, and getting behind with assignments, I gather you had trouble balancing your social life with classes. Maybe that contributed to your leaving ENC-1102. High school teaches people to juggle assignments due on the same date—say, math problems and an English paper, sometimes a big exam as well—right? Life at college and the university brings conflicts between class work and washing clothes, fraternity projects, parents' visits, increased freedom in dating and partying, eating properly and regularly, and other new uses for time. Sometimes social life needs to come first; other times class work does.

"Reading and writing" can help you sort out priorities. That's one reason for studying these processes, one answer to your question. Perhaps it's the most important one. But I expect you know, like most first-year students, how to use writing to evaluate the pros and cons of a Business, Music, or Pre-med major; rank and schedule activities on a plan of work; and sort out your feelings for someone you're attracted to. With that kind of writing, you are your own audience; you read and interpret sources on your own; you're responsible to yourself for the clarity and honesty of the ideas your work contains. It's not usually for a class.

Another reason to study "all this reading and writing"—the one that fits your question as I suspect you meant it—is to improve your ability to share ideas with other people. Composition courses at FSU, and at most universities these days, are designed to give students practice expressing their own ideas in writing. In high school, you get the basics of vocabulary, spelling, grammar, and structure—especially the five-paragraph essay. You also learn to interpret a teacher's point of view and how to reflect it back in your work. Your last journal suggests to me that you're ready to move on. College composition requires more of your own perspective in your writing.

There's debate among composition teachers over whether their courses should equip you to write primarily for your personal purposes or as a member of the university and one of its many professional subcommunities. Although the skills you develop in FYW improve your ability to put words on paper whenever you need to, the courses are usually less for work on writing that's strictly for yourself and more for writing in school and beyond. Teachers sometimes refer to a group of people who share a particular vocabulary and way of using language—such as you and your fraternity brothers, the people from your hometown, lawyers, or people who were hippies in the 1960s—as a *discourse community*. The goal in FYW is to help you learn to recognize and use the language of different discourse communities appropriately, especially the ones that you'll belong to as you "get on with . . . [your] life."

Since you'll probably retake ENC-1102, perhaps some advice on how to approach it would be useful. I assume you passed ENC-1101 and learned the importance of incorporating your personal experience and perspective in your work, using revision to deepen the expression of your initial ideas and perhaps to find unanticipated meaning in them, and getting responses from small groups of peers to gauge the effect your writing has on readers. Build on those activities. The second part of FYW emphasizes the relationship of reading to writing and the skills for appropriately representing other people's ideas in your writing. Here are some pointers.

Continue to Draw from Your Own Background

This is old, often repeated advice. Authorities on writing have emphasized working from what you know—what you read and experience—for more than a century. George Lewes (1865)—husband of Mary Ann Evans, usually known by her pen name, George Eliot—addressed the issue in *The Principles of Success in Literature*:

> We cannot demand from every man that he have unusual depth of insight or exceptional experience; but we demand of him that he give us of his best, and

his best cannot be another's . . . Let the original observer speak for himself
. . . Personal experience is the basis of all real Literature . . . Importance does
not depend on rarity so much as on authenticity.(12–13)

More recently, William Zinsser (1976), a former editor of the *New York Herald Tribune* and writing teacher at Yale, echoed the idea:

Ultimately the product that any writer has to sell is not his subject, but who
he is. I often find myself reading with interest about a topic that I never
thought would interest me—some unusual scientific quest, for instance.
What holds me is the enthusiasm of the writer for his field. How was he
drawn into it? What emotional baggage did he bring along? How did it
change his life? . . . This is the personal transaction that is at the heart of good
nonfiction writing.(5)

Composition teachers these days are increasingly concerned with acknowl-
edging the authority that grows out of students' diverse backgrounds and
knowledge. More than a generation ago, the conference on College and
Communication (CCCC) adopted a report that asserted "Students' Right to
Their Own Language." Most would agree with a speaker at a recent meeting
of the CCCC, the foremost organization of university writing teachers.
Describing the difficulties that first-year students face, she observed that her
students' work improved in assignments that "gave them a chance to make
their special knowledge and skills visible":

When they were asked to write on subjects about which they have unusual
knowledge or uncommon understanding, they were excited by and grateful
for the chance to reveal their personalities and "show off" their authority.
Their work . . . was infused with a kind of confidence that student writing
frequently lacks, and so their papers were expressive and compelling in ways
that their responses to other assignments often were not.(Cox 1999)

Connect Your Experience to Topics You've Been Asked to Write About

If you relate an assigned topic to your interests by asking questions about it
based on your experience, you make the topic your own. As you do, your
perspective becomes essential to your paper. Pieces you're asked to read,
prompts that follow them, and discussions on them during class are often
designed to encourage you to make connections between ideas in them and
activities or experiences in your life. If you've read Jonathan Swift's "Modest
Proposal" and find his proposal outrageous, can you think of anything outrageous you've done to provoke a reaction? Your behavior can be a point of
connection for you to develop in an essay. If you've read Langston Hughes'
"Theme for English B," do the instructions your teacher has given raise any

concerns that make you wonder, as Hughes did, whether what you write will be acceptable? The way Hughes, your teacher, and you use language can be a point of connection.

The principle of connecting personal experience to topics for writing applies to research papers—which are standard exercises in most FYW courses, especially during the second semester—as much as it does to open essay topics. Some students think of research assignments as the antithesis of the personal experience papers. They claim they have no problem writing about their own experiences, but research throws them. Maybe you're one of them. Yet they, and I expect you, do research of a sort to select the best elective courses to take, the best party to attend on Saturday, or the right NBA team to support. It seems to me that a research paper amounts to putting in writing what you might say orally: an explanation of what you read, who you talked to, and what you base the selection of your sources on. If you relate the topic of the paper to your interests, gathering information and working out the explanation in writing is a way of making sense of your impressions.

From the point of connection you establish, you've given yourself leverage to draw in anything else from your experience that relates to your topic. As you do this, however, explain the relationships—the connections—you find. Make them apparent to your readers. Whether your teacher asks you to write about a well-known piece of literature, an article that strikes you as esoteric, or a topic of your choice, include books and articles you've found on your own; movies, songs, and TV shows you know; personal experiences that connect. The associations you see reflect your thinking. The individuality, the authenticity, of your writing comes from your experience.

Use a Broad Definition of "Reading," and Whenever an Assignment Allows, Refer to Sources that You Know Well

Your perspective grows out of what you've experienced, right? Whatever you've experienced—books, movies, songs, personal events, or anything else—can be read if "read" is understood as "to interpret the nature or meaning through close examination or observation" (*American Heritage Dictionary*, 1985). Although this isn't the first meaning of the word, it's a valid one, and it can expand your thinking to include sources that empower your writing.

How much and what do you read? The amount is greater if you include material that's not assigned for classes than if you limit it to course materials, right? It's probably much greater, especially if you consider nonprint and nonverbal materials as well—items like films, music, E-mail, clothes. They're things you "interpret . . . through close examination or observation." I sometimes ask students to use a broad definition of *reading* and list everything they've read in the last 6 months that's not directly related to a school class. I'm always impressed with the results, and I think you'd be if you tried it yourself.

The last time I asked a class to perform this activity, 21 students were present. They named 585 distinct items in 15 minutes. I'm sure each of them could have named more if I'd allowed more time for the activity. Most mentioned from 30 to 45; the person with the fewest had 16; one young woman included 71. There was considerable overlap among some of their answers. For example, 10 people listed *FSView,* the campus paper; seven listed *Shakespeare in Love*; six listed *The Simpsons*; three listed shoes. At the end of the course, one of the students wrote, "One activity that this class did made me realize that we read things every day without knowing it. I really enjoyed listing things we've read this semester besides books. I never even thought about watching movies and looking at people to be reading. After that exercise, I noticed myself reading a lot more" (Stultz 1999).

Marketing specialists who study young adults' habits might be able to predict much of what these surveys reveal. For example, among my 21 students, more list films (93) than anything else. They mention TV shows of one kind or another (89)—especially serial dramas and comedies (37)—about as often as they do music CDs and radio (88). They recall reading popular books (45) and scripts of plays (13) more than, but perhaps not as frequently as, magazines (37) and newspapers (11), and not as much as miscellaneous texts (88) such as signs (23), packaging (19), financial statements (10), flyers (6), and menus (6). Such a survey isn't reliable because it's not standardized. I don't use a questionnaire suggesting equivalent categories, and people may have different understandings of terms like *nonprint* and *nonverbal.* As a result, the level of detail in the responses varies from "church bulletins" to "top 40 radio shows."

Still, I like the detailed information my students generate because it's uniquely theirs. It implies some of them know enough about characters on "Dawson's Creek" to write about the ethical choices the characters face. Others among them appear to know enough about the dancing in *Chicago* to analyze Bob Fosse's style; others enough about the vocabulary, grammar, and rhetoric of a credit card flyer to analyze the promotion. When students deal with such topics—and many of mine have—the writing is more engaging because they know the sources well.

Pay Attention to the Authority of the Sources You Find, Use Sources that Matter the Most to Your Subject, and Explain Their Significance to Your Readers

If you wanted to write about athletes' knee injuries, would you read the sports section of the campus newspaper or a study written by a specialist in sports medicine? The paper might have more immediacy, but wouldn't you expect the specialist to offer more breadth and depth? Unless you wanted to make the point that sports injuries are a current problem at FSU, the specialist would be the better authority and would matter more to your subject. If you wanted to know about weaving, would you ask a tourist who'd bought a rag rug on her vacation, a dormmate who had one her grandmother made her, or your dorm-mate's grandmother who'd been making them for 50 years and learned the tradition from her Finnish father? Each source gives a different perspective; each could be useful in a way; but the grandmother would have the most authority—as a historian, maker, and tradition bearer.

Evaluating sources contributes to critical thinking; including the source's ideas when you develop your own ideas strengthens your work; and explain-ing the authority of the sources you cite lets your readers know why they matter. Don't expect readers to understand your reasons for picking a source even if you're sure they share your acquaintance with it. Your teacher and classmates may have read "Theme for English B" because it was assigned. "Everyone" may have seen *Shakespeare in Love* because it was a hit, but they won't know your perspective unless you discuss it. And learning about your perspective is the reason people read the papers you write.

The explanations frequently involve giving your readers an introduction to the speaker or writer you cite. Many times writers use a phrase such as "According to" before naming the authority—for example, "Terry Gilliam"—and some identification, like "coauthor and a leading authority on the history of 'Monty Python's Flying Circus'." But beware of overusing the formula. You may need to expand on a point to clarify the connection you see between the authority's ideas and the topic you're writing about. If you claim that "My roommate notices brand names on clothes," you may need to explain with a comment like "Students at FSU pay more attention to sports logos on shoes, shorts, shirts, and hats ever since the athletic department agreed to promote Nike products." You're basically telling your readers why they should accept the words of your source. By extension, your explanation helps persuade read-ers to accept your words as well, since you've selected and interpreted the authority you cite.

Rely More on Printed Sources than on Other Types of Sources

When you choose sources, it's tempting, I think, to favor films, TV, CDs, person-to-person experience, and other nonwritten materials. Common sense suggests and my reading surveys seem to confirm that people get more infor-mation from experience with nonwritten sources than from written ones. Popular media, say *Star Wars: Episode I,* or a friend's comments, perhaps recommending a concert at the union, have a strong presence and appeal. They involve more senses than writing, and they're usually more available.

Nevertheless, writing has several advantages that other sources normally don't. A piece of writing preserves words, providing a fixed text. It doesn't change from reading to reading, even if a reader's interpretation of it does, even if different readers interpret the words in it differently. Moreover, print enhances the fixity of writing. It makes identical versions of a text available to multiple readers in different places, at different times. You may argue with others about the reasons for Swift's proposal and analyze his way of presenting it. But you can prove he wrote "that a young healthy child . . . will make two dishes at an entertainment for friends, and when the family dines alone, the fore or hind quarter will make a reasonable dish" more easily than you can establish claims about the benefits of a burger your roommate brought from a fast-food shop.

The issue of fixity comes into sharp contrast if you compare printed texts with those on the Internet. It's relatively easy to change versions of digital texts. The speed with which the electronic word can be published, revised, and reposted equals the speed of light, or at least the speed of modems and processing chips. How often have you searched for a web page you'd once seen and found that it was no longer available: revised, relocated, or removed? Our society depends on a well-developed network of libraries and archives to maintain written texts. The network of keepers of electronic texts is relatively new and rapidly evolving.

Works you find in print usually have been reviewed by the authors' peers, editors, and publishers, and they've been refined by advice the authors receive from them. This vetting imparts a level of assurance about the information in a publication. It discourages offhanded, unreflective chatter. You'll frequently find statements in prefaces and introductions qualifying the text that follows. Publishers normally strive to build a reputation for printing only the most reliable works. University presses and professional journals routinely base the decision to publish a manuscript on reviews they solicit from specialists in the field the piece addresses. Unless you study the backgrounds of the people who maintain a site on the Internet, what assures you that the information it carries is reliable? Unless you closely examine and observe the popular media you encounter and the casual events you experience, don't they tend to wash by leaving imprecise memories?

When You Use Nonprint Materials, Convert Them to Written Form, and Examine the Texts Carefully

If you're writing about a film, TV show, song, or some other popular item that you've "read," develop a reference text for yourself. This step may involve transcribing sections of dialog that impress you—in which case, you may want to work from a recording such as an audiotape, videotape, or still photograph—or you may be able to find a published script or lyrics. After all, actors, singers, directors, producers, and other media production staff work from written references as much as, often more than, from instinct and impulse. To your transcription or script, add notes on any other sounds, sequences of action, and details in the settings you observe. Once you've written good notes, you can study them more critically than you can study shifting memories, and you can use portions of them in a paper for class.

What does Norman, the character Anthony Perkins plays in Alfred Hitchcock's *Psycho,* say his mother "wouldn't hurt"? His words are chilling if you connect them to the scene at the end of the film when he sits alone, watching. Does Norman repeat the lines and the behavior in the 1999 version of the film? Read the scripts. If you can't find printed versions, you can transcribe the dialog and note the corresponding action in videotapes. Once you have a printed source, it gives answers more quickly and reliably than memory or tape.

To draw on personal experiences in your writing, you transform your observations, recollections, and impressions into texts, don't you? Writing an interpretation of cultural events and processes falls in the realm of ethnography. Basically, ethnographers "read" cultures, seeking to understand through interviews, observation, and an analysis of cultural artifacts and texts how that group of people understands itself and the world. An increasing number of composition teachers use these techniques in assignments to generate interest. They generally find that it adds the excitement of cultural observation, exploration, and discovery to the routines that writers need to practice. *FieldWorking,* one of the most thorough books on the approach as it relates to composition, describes how an entire research course might be organized around ethnographic writing activities (Chiseri-Strater and Sunstein 1997). It includes sections on "Looking at Subcultures," "Reflective Fieldnotes," "Reading an Artifact," "Writing a Verbal Shapshot," "Describing Insider Language: Occupational Terms," "Analyzing Your Interviewing Skills," and many others that might help you develop a research paper based on a personal experience.

Ask Your Teacher About Her or His Openness to Various Types of Sources

Whether or not a teacher encourages an eclectic synthesis of sources, try it—unless she or he explicitly prohibits it. You owe it to yourself to make every writing assignment serve your own intellectual exploration and growth. Drawing from your experience outside class will let you integrate new ideas with old and advance your quest for knowledge.

If you have any question about whether it's ok, ask your teacher—in a conference before submitting the paper as well as in the actual text of the paper. She or he may have good reasons for wanting you to exclude certain types of sources on an assignment. For example, documents on the Internet may be too recent to include research on the subject you're addressing; informal conversation with your peers may not provide a broad enough opinion for your topic; or you may need practice finding printed documents and writing citations for them. Be prepared to sell your ideas for special sources—promote their benefits. I expect you'll be surprised at how often your teacher approves, and even if she refuses, she'll be impressed with your thinking and attitude toward learning.

I agree it's important for you to "get on with . . . life." You may even need to take some time off from classes. Just remember that your life—what you experience and "read"—is your best material when you return to writing.

Sincerely,

OL

Works Cited

Chafe, Wallace L. 1985. "Linguistic Differences." In *Literacy, Language, and Learning: The Nature and Consequences of Reading and Writing.* Eds. David R. Olson, Nancy Torrance, and Angel Hilyard. Cambridge; New York; Melbourne: Cambridge University Press. 105–123.

Chiseri-Strater, Elizabeth, and Bonnie Sunstein. 1997. *FieldWorking: Reading and Writing Research.* Upper Saddle River, NJ: Prentice-Hall.

Conference on College Composition and Communication. "Students' Rights to Their Own Language." *College Composition and Communication* (Fall 1974) 25.

Cox, Cynthia. 1999. "Taking the Comp Class 'Underground': First-Year Writers Become Publishers of 'Zines." Session A.1, Making Students Visible: Public Writing in the Composition Classroom. Conference on College Composition and Communication. Atlanta, March 24, 1999.

Houghton Mifflin. 1985. *American Heritage Dictionary,* 2nd college edition. Boston: Houghton Mifflin.

Lewes, George Henry. 1865. "The Principles of Success in Literature." *The Fortnightly Review,* 1 & 2 (May–November 1865). Reprinted. Westmead, Farnborough, Hants., England: Gregg International Publishers, 1969.

Stultz, Laura. 1999. "Portfolio Cover Letter." ENC-1145-25. April, 23, 1999.

Swift, Jonathan. 1729. *A Modest Proposal for Preventing the Children of Poor People in Ireland, from Being a Burden on Their Parents or Country, and for Making Them Beneficial to the Publick.* Reprinted (October 1997). Project Gutenberg. WWW: <ftp://sunsite.unc.edu/pub/docs/books/gutenberg/etext97/mdprp10.txt> (18 November 1999).

Zinsser, William. 1976. *On Writing Well: An Informal Guide to Writing Nonfiction.* New York: Harper & Row.

Sharing Ideas

1. As a counterpoint to Deborah Coxwell Teague's inside story of facing a high school class of readers in Chapter 1, tell your stories of being asked to read literary texts in school. How did your teachers' approaches help or hinder your reading pleasure and understanding?

2. Consider Deborah's active reading advice: Which activities do you follow and which not? Why? In a group, add to her advice.

3. In Chapter 5, you'll find Jennifer Ahern claiming that the books most of us remember as our favorites end up being some of those we were assigned in high school. Write a letter to your high school English teacher telling her how the books she was assigning could have been made more meaningful to the college reader you are today by using some of the suggestions shared in Chapters 1 to 4.

4. In their narratives, Deborah, Kirk, and Lysa mention *Cliff's Notes*. What are your experiences with these booklets? In a group, explore attitudes— as you know them—towards *Cliff's Notes* from the point of view of teachers, authors, and students. Are they study aids or cheat sheets, and so on?

5. Like Kirk in Student Narrative 1, write your own advice on how *not* to grow up as a reader; or like Chris in Student Narrative 3, write about a struggle you've had learning to read.

6. With your class, complete the same sort of survey of reading that Dan Melzer discusses in Chapter 2. Share the course descriptions contributed by the members of your class for each course they are taking. Analyze the reading and writing required in these courses. Draw some conclusions and compare them with the conclusions Dan draws in his essay.

7. How does the type of reading Lisa Albrecht describes in Chapter 3 connect to or differ from the type of required college reading described in Dan's essay?

8. Like Lisa Albrecht, make a list of all the journals you subscribe to or read regularly; as a class, pool your list. Now look at your class list and characterize yourselves as readers.

9. Write a letter back to Ormond Loomis (Chapter 4) *for* Jason Smith, or write a class letter response to Ormond.

Part II

Reading Yourself Reading

Assigned reading falls into two categories for me: that which may interest me and that which decidedly does not. For the first, I lay down on my bed with a Coke and some sort of chocolate and read for hours. I love making exclamation points and comments in the border. For the second type, I really have to push myself. Housecleaning, which I hate, may actually come first. I must read sitting up—again with Coke and chocolate—in order to attempt to keep my mind from wandering. It does anyway. Sometimes I may read a really boring paragraph forty times. Other times, I'll skim until I understand something or finally find something interesting. Still other times daydreams take over or, better yet, sleep. For this type of reading, I only have a twenty-minute attention span. I must get up, think, walk around, and return for however many twenty minutes it takes.

—Nancy

5

Why We Read (or Not)
A Class Discussion

Jennifer Ahern

All the reading I did as a child, behind closed doors, sitting on the bed while the darkness fell around me, was an act of reclamation. This and only this I did for myself. This was the way to make my life my own.
—Lynne Sharon Schwartz (1996, 119)

Honestly, I haven't read a book for pleasure in probably a couple of years. I read for school and I read enough for that.
—Kristina, writing student

My friend Stephanie and I were talking about the books she's been reading lately, and she ended the conversation saying, "Well, if you ever get any free time, add these books to your list." I've thought a lot about that statement and how jealous I am that Stephanie finds time to read novels. She reads what she wants. I read what I have to. In fact, it's been over a year since I picked up a novel, *Bridget Jones' Diary,* just because I wanted to read it. I find myself separating my reading life into three categories: student reader (what I read as a graduate student, studying composition and rhetoric), teacher reader (what I read to incorporate into the college writing classes I'm teaching), and pleasure reader (what I select to read).

At the time Stephanie and I chatted, I was teaching a class called "Writing about the X-Files." Class members were mostly freshman business and science majors, and we were reading a lot: "X-Files" episodes, The *X-Files Book of the Unexplained,* class E-mails, student essays, and fan fiction websites. I wanted to know what this class thought about reading and if they found themselves separating their reading life into categories like I did. In a class survey followed by a class discussion, we explored how college readers see reading, how our reading lives are similar or different from when we learned to read as children, and what we had to say about the value of reading.

Before I share what I learned, let me explain that I have always been a reader. The first book I can remember reading is *Where the Sidewalk Ends*. Then came *Mrs. Frisby and the Rats of Nimh, The Mouse and the Motorcycle, Tales of a Fourth Grade Nothing, A Wrinkle in Time,* and *The Lion, the Witch, and the Wardrobe,* as well as *Highlights* magazine. As I got older I progressed to Judy Blume books, *The Diary of Anne Frank, Flowers in the Attic,* and *Where the Red Fern Grows.* I remember all of these books and how they pulled me into their worlds, how grown-up I felt when I got to go to the public library with my mom, how accomplished I felt when I finished a book.

In high school I read the classics that everyone else did, but I was never obsessed with reading, never let it take over my life, until I encountered Tolkien. My stepdad had a ratty 1960s collection of *The Hobbit* and *The Lord of the Rings Trilogy,* which I happened upon by accident. I had forgotten to find a book to read for the next book report in my English class, was running out the door to catch the bus, and spied the four-pack on his desk. Once I started reading the first book, I was hooked. I couldn't wait to get home from school, so I could transport myself into the world of Middle Earth, of Frodo Baggins, Gandalf, and Gollum. I even ignored favorite TV shows, homework, and family time. That Tolkien experience was the beginning of my real passion for reading.

Then something happened in college. I started to dislike reading, and books became more homework than an escape. As an English major, I had to analyze the books I read, to rethink each novel and to try to unpack it. I couldn't read a novel without a pen in hand. What did the *Red Badge of Courage* symbolize? What's the significance of *Moby Dick*'s whaling chapters? Did Edna Pontellier show strength or weakness when she walked into the ocean in *The Awakening*? My job became: cull through the book, search for answers, pass the essay/test/class. I realized that reading was "good" for me, but not something that I could do any longer for pleasure.

It turns out, many of the readers in the X-Files class had similar experiences.

Surviving (and Thriving?) as Readers

* *Why do you read? Or do you?*
* *If you had to list everything you read today, what would that list include? Cereal boxes, CD jackets, people, TV, books, articles for class?*

I have always been interested in stories people tell about the way they learned to read and what they read each day, and I have done some research into the theories that try to explain this process. According to Frank Smith in *Understanding Reading* (1994), I, along with many readers in my writing classes, am a fluent reader. I have a large story repertoire because of the amount and variety of reading I've done. He would also say that I'm a member of the "literacy club" (217) because I'm a good reader, my mom and my aunt are readers, I received books as birthday presents, and I took trips to the library. While growing up, I was surrounded by books and reading. Lauren, a reader in the X-Files class, knows what it's like:

> I learned to read in kindergarten when I was 5, just like everyone else. My brother learned to read when he was 2—we're only 10½ months apart, so we've always competed with each other. I remember reading a lot of *Babysitter's Club* books and the whole Madeline L'Engle series. I *loved* those L'Engle books. Reading when I was young was something I did by myself, in my room, away from all the pressures of the world.

For Lauren, however, reading is now work. It's no longer the fun competition it used to be, nor is it an escape. "I used to read *so* much," she writes, "now all I read is basically crap." She mentions, too, that she likes to read, but adds, "I would never go to Barnes & Noble and buy myself a book. I usually only read what I am *given* to read (like how my mom gives me her 'Oprah' books)."

Another reader, Kathy, is proud of what I would call college survival reading. She hates to read, and reads only what she has to in order to get through a class. "Reading is not as crucial as most teachers make it out to be . . . I've made it through all of high school and one year of college without finishing a single novel." Kathy does not see reading as moving beyond the classroom and does not see value in the experience of reading; she sees only what she has to cull through to survive the class or test. In fact, according to class members, most admit that they don't have time to enjoy a text; they read what they need to because they're so busy and because they're often grade focused. In addition, I discovered that these college readers write very little in conjunction with reading, only writing about what they read in the form of an essay to be graded or a test.

Peter Elbow (1993), another reading theorist, argues that reading is privileged over writing in school. Even though "writing is *assigned* in a fair number of courses . . . it is traditionally meant to *serve* reading: to summarize, interpret, explain, or make integrations and comparisons among readings" (276). For me, and for many of the readers I talked with, it is this kind of school reading and writing that frustrates us and encourages the separation of school reading from pleasure reading, in much the same way that we learn to separate work from play.

Kathy has learned how to read for school very well, and reads only for school, and only because she has had to write in a way that tests her comprehension of novels, not her understanding of them. Kathy's reading history has made it easy for her to compartmentalize reading and to view it as separate from the "real" life she's leading. Frank Smith (1994) argues that "a person who has no purpose in reading can bring nothing to the reading, and the activity is bound to be meaningless" (3). For Kathy, that is certainly true.

So if reading is a form of thinking and a matter of making meaning, comprehension tests undermine the process of reading because they ask us not to think. Instead, they ask readers to repeat, to summarize, to tell the teacher what the teacher wants to know. For many of us, college reading experiences have more to do with the texts and with finding out what the teacher wants than with what *we* think as *readers.*

How and Why We Read—A Summary of Current Reading Theories

- How do your college reading experiences compare with those you had as a child?
- Make a short list of those books or other materials you liked to read as a child and those you've liked as an adult. What does that list say about you as a reader? Your school reading?

Frank Smith (1994) argues that reading is a complex, active process that is always in progress. He writes that "understanding is the basis not the consequence of reading" (3). Reading is creative meaning-making, a negotiation between writer, reader, and text, and it may seldom be the same experience twice. In school, my reading changed, however, from this interactive style to a more mundane, predictable process. The readers in my X-Files class followed this routine as well—read the article, underline a passage or two to mention in class discussion, look for what the teacher wants.

No matter what our early reading experiences, school reading plays a factor in how we see all reading. In their book *Enhancing Aesthetic Reading and Response,* Philip Anderson and Gregory Rubano (1991) argue that many times reading literature for the classroom becomes more about making sense of the text than about the experience of reading. Little attention is given to reading for the sake of reading because schools focus on comprehension. As a result, too often the study of literature has less to do with enriching student experiences and language background and more to do with "remembering and reiterating the content of stories, poems, and novels" (1).

- Think about your own reading and writing history in school. What kinds of tests did you take?
- What kinds of writing did you do with reading?

The comprehension model is used in schools for a variety of reasons. Teachers often have strict guidelines as to what they teach; they have to meet standardized test goals and prepare students for advanced placement exams. As you can

imagine, it's easier to test on plot, symbolism, and character development than on more abstract and varied reader responses. But it's not just the teachers. Perhaps you prefer objective tests and comprehension exams because you know exactly what's expected. Perhaps you've developed the habit of being a passive learner, learning for the test or the teacher, and you do not have to think about the kind of reading that you're doing.

I've never wanted to be the kind of teacher reader who makes students dislike reading, but it happened one day in my class. Toward the end of the semester, class members were working on developing their own stories for the "X-Files" series, and we were reading about other writers for the show and discussing how much background reading we'd have to do to create an original, yet appropriate story. To complicate our thinking, we read the article "X-Files and Ingestion: Or, How to Become A Vegetarian in Twelve Easy Episodes" (Wilcox 1997). I couldn't wait to discuss the article in class, but after several minutes of pained class discussion, Greg honestly said, "This article is too complicated. *This* is why we hate to read."

I wanted to dig a little deeper into that response because I suspected it had more to do with the way I read versus the way class members read the article and that it might provide some insight into college reading versus the reading we did as kids. Initially, I thought my students read the first few lines of the text, thought it was full of academic jargon, then skimmed the rest of the article because they didn't think it was worth their time.

After I summarized my thoughts on the article and what I thought the writer was saying, Jessica commented, "Then why didn't he just come out and say that? You tell us to say what we mean and not to hide behind words. How come he gets to?" Because I'm more experienced with the writing in this journal, I saw past the thick language to the clever argument, but the other readers in the class didn't. In this instance, I'd forgotten what it was like to read *through* the words, to see the words on the page, but not grasp their significance. Reading for school is often about learning the conventions and having a specialized knowledge—knowledge that the teacher seems to have, but that the students don't.

- Stop and think about a time when you read a class assignment differently than a teacher or a fellow classmate. Did you value both readings?
- Did one have more value as the "correct" meaning?

School reading, because it takes up so much of our time as children and as adults in college, inevitably affects all the reading we do. The challenge is to recognize the value of school reading (even if it's comprehension based)—how, for instance, it may connect to pleasure reading by introducing us to authors and to experiences. The real key, however, is to push meaning-making beyond one correct interpretation—to value the readings that all readers bring to the conversation.

The Joy of Reading?

- Wasn't there a point for most of us when reading (or being read to) was fun?

For Tracey, the answer is no. Even though she would be a bonafide member of Smith's literacy club because she has been surrounded by reading and readers all her life, she has never enjoyed it, and she has never seen it as a positive experience. She says,

> It's very odd that I do not like to read. I come from a background of English majors and even a Ph.D. in Philosophy. My family's also very artistic. However, I can't remember a time when I enjoyed reading—I'm far too impatient. A book is the only thing I can start without finishing. I don't know why, but I'd rather spend my time actually doing something rather than reading. If there is one thing I *love* to read, it's music and lyrics.

For Tracey, there's a difference between reading novels and "academic reading" and music lyrics. Perhaps she is resisting what she is expected to read and so finds enjoyment only in nontraditional texts.

Another reader, Jessica, notes ". . . I haven't read for pleasure in years, but I do read a lot of E-mail from friends and family and sometimes I even read the forwards." Jessica also believes, however, that there might be other reasons to read. She says, "I think reading is important because it teaches you and makes you a better person. There are, of course, some classes that you don't need to read a thing for, but I believe that if you really want to do well in a class then you need to read for it. It can only help you to at least review the material."

- Consider how/why reading makes us better people (or not). Is it the reading itself or the thinking about the reading that has the potential to make us better people?

Michael has had what he calls a "bad history" of reading. As he learned to read, teachers frequently told him he had the wrong answer to a question about a story. He writes:

> I could read good at about 5 years old, but most of the time I just said words fluently and did not understand. After that, I did not want to practice understanding. I got older and when the class had to answer questions independently, I never got the answers for the exercises because I did not take the same meaning from stories as everyone else did. Up to this point [things] have gotten worse. I [had to take] a reading course at the beginning of this year.

Frank Smith (1994) explains Michael's apprehension this way: "Poor readers often are afraid to take a chance; they may be so concerned about getting words wrong that they miss meaning altogether" (60). Michael and his teachers became so obsessed with correctness that he lost sight of the meaning-making that comes with reading. Ironically, Michael often had the most insightful responses to the texts we read in the X-Files class, to actual episodes, to the bizarre stories that inspired the show, and to his peers' writing.

I'm guessing that for Michael and for other reading-apprehensive students, the nonprint literacies that surrounded them at home may not have been valued at school. For instance, my grandmother constantly told me stories about her childhood in Guatemala, about her life in America during World War II, and about my father and aunt growing up in Connecticut. I came to love stories and storytelling because of her, but this oral literacy was not supported in schools I attended—only print texts were.

Everyone wants to get the meaning right, but that often comes at the expense of real learning and thinking about who we are as readers and what we truly think about the text. It's not surprising then, that when we realize there are many possibilities for interpretation, we worry about picking the best possibility, and we fear interpretive failure. That is, we may not see possibilities or we fear we'll choose the wrong ones. It's no wonder that nonreaders like Kathy who learn primarily the skill of comprehension are reluctant to read or to see beyond the plot of a book. She writes, "The only books I've read outside of class were the first two books of the *Chronicles of Narnia,* and my mom had read them to me when I was younger. I meant to read all of them, but I ran out of enthusiasm about halfway through the third book." The texts, to her, weren't full of possibilities, and reading was a mundane exercise.

School Reading: How Much Do We Read and Why?

- Think about your own school reading in college. How much reading are you assigned? How much do you actually read?
- How much do you think you need to read to do well in the classes you're taking?

Kathy explains her college reading this way:

> It all depends on the class you take as to how much reading is required. In literature classes, you obviously get assigned a lot more to read. In my lit class, I read half of one of the four books assigned, the one short story, and made by with *Cliff's Notes* on everything else. We never had to take quizzes, so I was able to make stuff up for the two papers and for class discussion. In my English class, however, the reading assignments were short and interesting, so I read those. Generally, you don't have to read everything assigned. Either get the *Cliff's Notes* or ask a friend about the main ideas. I've been doing that for the past 5 years and I graduated high school with a 3.7 GPA and am in the honors program here.

In *Textual Power,* Robert Scholes (1985) offers an explanation for Kathy's success in school as a non-reader: Kathy was not encouraged to be an active participant in the reading process, so she consumed a novel, then produced a text about it (reading, then writing). As readers we should, instead, be reflective and consider the part that we play in the reading. We should investigate the ways we are producing the text we read based on our own previous experiences, as well as our own race, gender, socioeconomic background, religion, and neighborhood. The focus, then, should be on you, the reader, not the reading. Try to let reading become part of your thinking as you explain your perspectives to classmates and collaborate with them to develop meanings. It's perhaps just as important, for example, to examine what happens to you as you read the whaling chapters in *Moby Dick* as it is trying to understand the significance of those chapters in the overall book.

For instance, it is difficult for Kathy to have an investment in reading when she knows she doesn't have to, and school reading for Kathy was based primarily on comprehension. So often little attention is given to the experience of reading a text for its own sake, to explore "unarticulated responses" (Anderson and Rubano 1991) and what happens to you as you read. Jessica writes that she is "assigned quite a bit of reading in [her] classes," but she "usually only read[s] what [she] think[s] is pertinent or . . . need[s] to read to better understand." She won't even glance at something unless she knows she'll be directly tested on it. However, the author doesn't necessarily know best, and, like Scholes (1985), I think we should work to determine not only what the author is saying, but to interpret and analyze, looking for the unsaid as well (32). You can complete this kind of analysis even if you are in comprehension-based classrooms, but it's up to you to move beyond the limited readings that sometimes take place in schools.

The key to college reading, then, is to make it pertinent to your own life. Readers in the X-Files class came alive when we had to collaborate in groups on our own "X-Files" episodes. To do this well, we had to be familiar with some of the writing on the show (we read articles about guest writers like Stephen King and William Gibson), to learn what it takes to be on a writing team, to explore what decisions we should make to keep within the show's mythology and the character development, and to discover what stories have been told already.

These readers began to approach articles and fan fiction as writers, looking for what they could borrow or explore when they wrote their own episodes. They read with enthusiasm, and their writing was the best of the semester. Some wrote parodies, some wrote fan fiction (which usually had Mulder and Scully ending up as a romantic couple), and some wrote series finale short stories. They read each other's ideas with interest, too, reinforcing the relevance of reading to writers.

Strategies for Reading in College

Because, inevitably, we will be asked to read what we don't want to, either in college or in the business world, we should develop strategies for reading what is required. Kathy has some good advice for getting the reading done: "If you do actually have to read something, pace yourself. You cannot procrastinate with reading. If you have 3 days to read 100 pages, read 33 pages per night before you go to bed."

Jessica has similar advice: "If you are planning to read, then read daily—don't wait for the test to roll around and then decide to try to read four chapters for content—the words won't mean a thing to you. If you want to read for pleasure, it's possible. You just have to set aside time in your day for it—even if it's just like 20 minutes." And Jessica also reminds us about other reading strategies, even reading rituals, that may help us get the reading done: "If you are reading a text and want to comprehend it, then I recommend finding a quiet place that you are comfortable in but not too comfortable in. Don't read on your bed in your room because you will end up falling asleep or getting distracted. If you are uncomfortable in the library like I am, then try going to Barnes & Noble or someplace like that."

These readers suggest that we make reading a part of our daily lives, even if it's school reading, to make the job of reading more bearable. If reading is thinking, we have to give it time. We have to think about what we are reading, have time to reflect and possibly write about it, rather than getting just the gist of a work.

Overall, readers in our class made the following suggestions for reading in college:

1. Don't rush reading. Give yourself time to get the reading done or you'll just hate the book, the teacher, and yourself.

2. Talk about what you're reading with other people. If you're confused, ask someone what she or he thinks.

3. Be an active reader. Make yourself either take notes as you're reading (writing question marks in the margin, underlining passages you like, passages you doubt or want to skim) or write a paragraph or short comments about what you thought once you finished. This activity gets you thinking about the text and helps when you go back to it later. Writing keeps you awake, too.

4. Try to read the article (or certain passages in a longer book) more than once. If possible, review the notes you made the first time you read. Don't assume you'll have the same reaction the second time.

5. Think about how you would have written it instead. Critique it; don't just accept it. You'll have more fun that way.

6. Try to imagine it outside the context of college and the classroom; some college reading could turn into pleasure reading; blur the lines between student reader and pleasure reader. (See Hint Sheet M for more student readers' advice.)

What college reading did for me, and high school reading did for Kathy and Jessica, was chip away at the joy of the process; because reading at that time was text focused, not reader focused, we tended to overlook the experience of it. Not all college reading will be like that, but some of it will. As a class, most of us were not able to pinpoint the moment at which reading no longer was enjoyable, but most agree that it probably began when we were assigned books, and then we were tested on them. We came to understand that reading and writing should be linked together in a positive, productive way that does more than prepare us for comprehension tests.

We came up with some solutions, too. To avoid comprehension-only reading, keep a reading journal, writing down what you think as a novel progresses (especially a who-done-it murder mystery), or write in the margins of an article or textbook what you're thinking along the way. Interact with the text. Think what you would tell the author if you could, what technique you may want to borrow, or what idea a passage gets you thinking about. This kind of writing challenges you to examine your perspective and to explore the process of reading, not just the product of the text itself.

Strategies for Reading . . . and Liking It

To return to the joy of reading, Jessica suggests, "Pick a subject that you are either really interested in or really entertained by and make some time to just sort of learn more about it. That way you won't get bored reading it, and you will sort of be having fun learning about your subject." Most of us in the X-Files class considered ourselves readers when we talked about reading outside the classroom (E-mail, letters from friends, nonprint texts like movies, TV, people), but, interestingly, many of our favorite books came from classes in which we were assigned to read them. *Lord of the Flies, Neverending Story, Tale of Two Cities, Like Water for Chocolate, The Diary of Anne Frank, Catcher in the Rye, The Scarlet Letter, To Kill a Mockingbird, Song of Solomon, One Flew Over the Cuckoo's Nest, The Bible, Where the Red Fern Grows, The Color Purple, Stranger in a Strange Land, Green Eggs and Ham.* We also liked Grisham novels, Dr. Seuss books, Stephen King, Ann Rice, Shakespeare, *The Babysitter's Club.* So, ultimately, even though we often dislike the school reading that we're assigned, we have to read a lot in order to figure out *what* we like. We decided on the following advice for liking the reading that you do:

1. Read in snatches of time if you have to (I have books, magazines all over the house); bring books or magazines you want to read when you travel, when you go to the beach.

2. Read anything; it doesn't have to be the Great American Novel, or an Oprah book, or part of a class assignment.

3. Recognize how much reading you do already (CD jackets, college newspaper, movie reviews, E-mail, billboards).

4. Remember that it's okay to read as an escape, to read without a pen in hand.

5. Put yourself in the story.

6. Talk about what you're reading; write about it in E-mails to friends.

7. Blur the lines between pleasure reader and student reader (and teacher reader).

But really, so much is up to you, the reader. Ralph Waldo Emerson wrote, "'Tis the good reader that makes the good book." It is the good reader who moves beyond the assignment, who plays with the text and imagines different ways to envision it, who can get lost in the world of reading. The readers in my class convinced me that I think too much about reading for academic reasons, that I need to get back to the fun of it. I'm starting a Stephen King novel, *Bag of Bones,* without a pen in hand.

Works Cited

Anderson, Philip M. , and Gregory Rubano. 1991. *Enhancing Aesthetic Reading and Response.* Urbana, IL: National Council of Teachers of English.

Cavelos, Jeanne. 1998. *The Science of The X-Files.* New York: Berkley Boulevard Books.

Elbow, Peter. 1993. "The War between Reading and Writing—and How to End It." *Rhetoric Review* 12.1(fall):5–24.

Goldman, Jane. 1995. *The X-Files Book of the Unexplained.* Vol. I. New York: HarperPrism.

Scholes, Robert. 1985. *Textual Power: Literary Theory and the Teaching of English.* New Haven: Yale University Press.

Schwartz, Lynne Sharon. 1996. *Ruined by Reading.* Boston: Beacon Press.

Smith, Frank. 1994. *Understanding Reading,* 5th edition. Hillsdale, NJ: Lawrence Erlbaum.

Wilcox, Rhonda V. 1997. "The X-Files and Ingestion: Or, How to Become a Vegetarian in Twelve Easy Episodes." *Studies in Popular Culture* 19.3 (April):11–22.

Student Narrative 4

Reading Rooms*

Dawn Maria Lieber

My father loves to read. Every night, you can find him sitting in the kitchen with a glass of milk filled with ice in one hand and a book in the other. An empty box of Vanilla Wafers is usually on the table, crumbs falling onto his book. This passion for reading that consumed my father skipped my generation. Looking back, I see I took a lighthearted approach to reading.

In fourth grade my parents made an imaginary line in the doorway of my room. The rules of the house said that I was not allowed to cross this border after 8:30 p.m., my bedtime. After I was supposedly tucked in bed, I sat behind the line Indian-style in the hallway of the living room. Sitting there, motionless, I "read" my parents' television programs like social texts, making sure that no part of my body crossed "the line." I saw some of the best episodes of "Kate and Allie" and "The Bob Newhart Show" this way. From religiously watching these shows, I learned how people live and relate to each other.

My bedroom, which is my favorite room in the house, is a little history museum for me because everything in my room is attached to a story. The story that sticks out in my mind happened when I was a third grader. I was extremely anxious to go outside that particular day. I remember how the kids in the neighborhood were on the street playing, and it made it difficult for me to concentrate on my school work. My class was to have a vocabulary quiz in English the next day and I had my flash cards prepared. I flipped through them quickly and ran to my dad who was reading the newspaper in the living room. He shuffled the cards and pulled out a word. I looked at him and said, "Skip that one. We'll come back to it." He picked out another card and I did not know the definition of that one either. Then he calmly told me to go back and study them. Five minutes later I asked him to quiz me again; the same thing happened. Unfortunately, I didn't know even one of those words. So, he sent

*The process narrative for Dawn's essay can be found in Hint Sheet A.

me back to my room four more times. The sixth time, he pulled out a word for which he had already asked me the definition but I still had a blank look on my face. He came into my room, picked up my chair from the desk, and chucked it through the wall. The hole remains.

When the teacher returned my vocabulary quiz at the end of the week, I brought home a perfect score. Instead of ceremoniously hanging the grade on the refrigerator, we hung the quiz over the hole in my wall. I learned quite a bit from that experience, including deciding to have my mother quiz me the next time.

Another room where I discovered myself frequently reading was the bathroom. To be honest, the bathroom is where I did all of my coming-of-age reading. It was in the bathrooms of my house that I found *Playboy* magazines. I remember how they provoked many uncomfortable questions for my parents. The pictures I saw had women in familiar places but stretched out naked. I felt strange about going to the dentist after that because I thought there would be naked women working there, flossing my pearly whites. I figured if naked women were repairing cars, then that could explain why my brother had so much difficulty with his 1978 Chevy. It was in the bathroom that I also learned a lot about the female body by reading the little pamphlets that fell out of every Tampon box.

Unlike my father, I never read novels or schoolbooks in my kitchen. Growing up, I had many rehearsals for dance, and I wouldn't come home until late, so I was often left to make my own dinner. Occasionally, I would get enough energy to prepare a respectably healthy dinner for myself. I read the labels on the different boxes and cans and prepared my feast. I loved improvising on the instructions. Not being the distinguished chemistry major I thought I could be, I figured I could cook food twice as fast if I doubled the heat. After one fiery dinner, my mother consistently saved me leftovers. Now I try to do most of my experimenting in the labs of my science classes. The only other reading I do in the kitchen is over the sink with a pint of Haagen-Dazs ice-cream. I always wonder how small the people were who concluded that Haagen-Dazs had a four helpings per pint serving size!

My teachers never thought of me as a reader, and in some ways they were right. I never read the assigned summer reading list, and "ye olde English" text was so stuffy and exhausting. However, considering everything I've learned from my daily reading as a child, they were also clearly mistaken. I read frequently while I was growing up, but this activity was not necessarily limited to textbooks. Reading materials other than schoolbooks have taught me more than any one encyclopedia ever could.

Student Narrative 5

It's a Gradual Thing*

Rob Adams

I can't actually remember when I learned to read. This comes as no surprise. After all, I was 3 or 4 years old at the time. Funny thing is, nobody remembers. If needed, my mother can tell you the dates that I first rolled over, sat up, talked, walked, and so on. The list is a seemingly endless treasure trove of dates of monumental importance. So where does reading fit in?

I talked to my mother on the phone yesterday and, thinking of this paper, asked, "When did I learn to read?"

"When you were 3—I think."

I pressed. "But when specifically, what date?" She had no reply. At this point, my confidence in my mother plummeted and I asked, "Why?" Her answer surprised me.

"Well, I guess it's because reading is such a gradual thing."

After ending the conversation by explaining that I would definitely need some money soon, I began to consider what she said about reading being a gradual thing. She was right (damn, how do parents do that?). From the time I first interpreted and voiced a printed word to the present as I struggle to comprehend information in college, I have been learning to read.

My first memories of the printed word involve me "reading" to my mother. I put this in quotation marks because it is actually a misnomer. More precisely, I memorized several of my favorite books and learned to recite them with an amazing degree of accuracy. It was through this process that I assume I slowly began to recognize and comprehend words—the first steps in reading.

I became a voracious little reader (if a 4-year-old can be voracious). I soon outgrew my first books, and then my older brother's. It was this that led our little family to the very Mecca of reading—the library. Although it is now

*The process narrative for Rob's essay can be found in Hint Sheet A.

completely remodeled, I still see it as it was long ago. A squat red brick building (it seems libraries just *should* be made of red brick) fashioned in very 1970s architecture (ugh).

The children's section was immediately to the right upon entering. But first, I had to pass through the turnstiles. This added to the excitement because I knew they only put those in really great places like amusement parks. The whole place had an intoxicating, musty odor. I invariably bypassed the big kids section (perhaps it was the high shelves). I did the same to the baffling monstrosity known only as the card catalog. All I knew was, it didn't look like any catalog I had ever seen, nor could I reach it. Its only redeeming quality was that it made an okay fort in a pinch.

My kind of books were farthest to the back. They were in a perpetual state of disarray. This was largely due to the fact that they were accessible to an age group not really into organization. I loved pulling out book after book, judging each cover, and picking my favorites. Of course, my favorites usually numbered into the twenties, of which I had to pick five. Temper tantrums at this juncture were not rare, nor were bloody fistfights with my brother Billy over books. Although we shared a bedroom, we'd fight tooth and nail over books. Blood and tears aside, we managed this ritual nearly every week.

Sometimes I would mistakenly check out a book above my reading level and face the taunts of my older brother (I didn't mispronounce his name as "Bully" for nothing). This may have been the biggest motivating factor for me, to prove to him I was as smart as he was.

This all paid off in elementary school when I was assigned to the smart reading group. This was the premiere status symbol of the day. I took great pride in this and always paid close attention when it was my group's turn to meet with the teacher to show it off. I was a good reader and never hesitated. Our softcover books always had titles like *Clouds, Impressions,* or *Expressions* and a workbook to match. We were allowed to write in the workbook and it came equipped with those handy perforated edges that almost worked. Occasionally, some poor soul would become confused and write in the real book, prompting a lecture to the entire class on "respecting school property." The stories in these books never failed to bore me. I always wanted to read ahead and grew tired of waiting for slow group members. In third grade I lobbied unsuccessfully for my own "supersmart" reading group.

Beginning in fifth grade, we read something called SRAs (I've forgotten what the letters stand for). These were short stories color coded by difficulty. Each one was printed on its own piece of thin cardboard, the kind that makes that neat sound if you shake one end. The only way to advance was to answer all the questions about a given story correctly. Naturally, this turned into a heated, class-wide race. Hiding stories was not uncommon, it was every man for himself—survival of the fittest in the jungle that is fifth grade. I thrived on this competitive reading. Without the contest, I would have been uninterested.

I can still see my teacher, Mr. Bazdar, standing in front of us: "People, this is not a race."

Junior high ushered in puberty and the age of literature. Both were equally confusing. We read lame plays, stuffy poems, and boring novels. This, combined with an uptight, pretentious teacher, drove me to abandon real reading. *Cliff's Notes* became my savior. Just as I had enjoyed the sheer challenge of reading, I began to love the challenge of not reading: *Don't read this book and see how good you can do on the paper. Don't read this play and see if you can pass the test.*

Unfortunately, this trend continued throughout high school. Granted, there were exceptions, but I essentially read none of what was the required reading. Three things I remember reading (and enjoying) were *Beowulf, The Inferno,* and *Brave New World.* It's not that I hated to read—I hated being told what to read and when to read it by. A rebellious teen, I was.

Despite my propensity for avoiding work, I somehow managed to remain in the honors English program. I was even exempted from half of the freshman English requirement when I entered college. You may want to have a talk with whoever makes those decisions. Looking back, I think the thing that really turned me off to reading was all the analyzing. As a kid I read simply for intrinsic value. Reading was fun. Somehow, once I entered seventh grade, I was supposed to be ready to analyze purpose, style, symbolism and the like. I don't know what to call all that, but I know what not to call it—reading.

I'm still learning to read. No, I don't struggle with Dr. Seuss anymore, but I still encounter things that I don't know how to read. Sure, I can literally read the words, but I use the word *read* to mean something more, something involving comprehension. Philosophy is one example of a type of reading that I'm just learning. The complexity of the arguments and the jargon sometimes make me feel frustrated, helpless, just as I did many years ago. But, I'm not worried. Like mom said, it'll happen gradually.

6

The (Reading) Literacy Narrative
A Limited Catalog of an Unlimited Resource

Wendy Bishop

Writing Prompt. Describe your reading process. What do you do when you read? How do you prepare for reading (if you do)? Under what conditions are you most comfortable reading? Has your reading process changed over time? What do you remember about learning to read? In what way are you the same or a different reader than you were back then?

> I don't *have* a reading process.—A 21-year-old first-year writing student who is mad at me for asking how he can be so sure, not once, not twice, but for a full term.

Here's how I responded: "Yes you do. You read the day, the classroom, the movies you attend, the way your family reacts when you return home from campus, as well as how I react to your not wanting to talk about reading in a writing class, to not wanting much to be in a writing class at all."

Writing Prompt. Make a list of all the members of your immediate family— those you lived with when you were between the ages of 2 and 10. After their names, write the occupations they had then and describe the locations and the scenes in which you remember seeing them most often. Now describe each as a reader. What did he or she read? When? How often? What feelings and beliefs about reading did he or she express? Paint a word picture of this person reading something—anything—to the best of your descriptive abilities (by the way, if you can't remember exactly, make up a reasonable description or work from old photos or join your memories to that of another family member, one you call up or E-mail and interview).

> No one in my family reads. I can't remember how I learned to read. It was all too long ago.
> —a 19-year-old first-year writing student.

At first, when asked to write a literacy narrative focused on early memories of reading, Corey resisted as much as the anonymous students I quote above. But through writing, he began to illuminate the past, to piece together memories; Corey realized his mother read the Bible regularly, his brother comics, and his father the coaching manual when he qualified to officiate. And Corey himself read popular magazines and—guess what—textbooks, all through high school. His family members, he finally decided, were all readers of sorts. If, like Corey, you close your eyes and visualize members of your family reading, pictures like these will come to you.

Writing Prompt. Walk through the children's book section in your public library (or visit a local elementary school library). I predict that forgotten and suddenly favorite books will call out to you from the shelves and reignite memories; you'll come to a literacy crossroads. Sit in a corner and reread several books and write a journal entry—what do you find different reading the book today? What memories of reading or being read to does the book prompt? If you have children, have you read this book with your own child? Why or why not? If you plan to have children, will you read this book—and what other books—with them?

> At the most basic level, the plot of a literacy story tells what happens when we acquire language, either spoken or written. But literacy stories are also places where writers explore what Victor Turner calls "liminal" crossings between worlds. In focusing upon those moments when the self is on the threshold of possible intellectual, social, and emotional development, literacy narratives become sites of self-translation where writers can articulate the meanings and the consequences of their passages between language worlds (Soliday 1994, 511).

I'd like to examine in this observation with you. *Liminal* means threshold, which you know in your house is the doorway between one room and another, the site where you leave one space (understanding) and enter another, connected but different space (or understanding). Now, think about crossings and thresholds in relation to language. We have all had complicated experiences with language. It is both omnipresent—crucial to our daily interactions with those we care and don't care about; entering our consciousness loud and long through ads, billboards, radio music, TV background drama—and subtle. For instance, we forget how we learned to use language and we tend to ignore how it initially shaped and is always still shaping us. We talk to others, we talk to the dog, we complain to the universe, we curse at drivers who can't hear us. We have names chosen for us and we choose special names. We tell stories, sometimes so they won't be told on or for us, and we're woven into the stories others tell. Sometimes we want to or are asked to write these events down. Sometimes we offer our writing and stories to others as pleas (love letters), explanations (contracts, directions), and entertainment (cards, jokes, tall tales, novels).

Specifically, the story of how we learn to use language lets us see familiar old selves in unfamiliar, but often productive new ways. The old self who didn't know how to read or write her way out of a paper bag, over time, may have become the new self. She's the woman who finds that her friends love to read (and perform) the skits she writes for fund raisers. The old junior high soccer player who never read a book unless threatened with dismissal from the team ultimately may be the man who finds he can explain a complicated psychology case study to his program peers. For most of us, life just leads us to these new places. For the writer who considers his or her literacy autobiography, these sites of self-translation can provide insights into the journey, sometimes speeding it up, clarifying it, putting it into better, or at least new, perspective. That happens because writing is a transformative act—it is the vehicle through which we can make liminal crossings. "We become what we write," claims Donald Murray. "That is one of the great magics of writing" (1991, 71).

Here are some claims about literacy narratives, presented to you in no particular order because certain claims will appear more compelling to you than others, and that's fine. The (reading) literacy narrative:

1. Provides a place where you can look at and critique your schooling and challenge your education (Fulcher 1996, Carey-Webb 1991, Franzosa 1991, Soliday 1994).

2. Encourages you to explore cultural and racial diversity (Anokye 1994, Stoddart 1991).

3. Can highlight gender and cultural issues that affect teachers and students (Hesford 1990, Donovan and Walsh 1991).

4. Can help you understand the literature you read (Hamann 1991, White 1995).

5. Can help you understand yourself and human-earth relationships (Wilson 1995).

6. Allows you to study their own writing processes and growth as a writer and reader (Sirc 1994, Sandman and Weiser 1993).

7. Helps you create public voices and identities and explore professional goals (Agatucci 1991).

I think several of these assertions are worth looking into. They argue that reading helps you to be a better consumer of your intellectual opportunities and think about who and what is helping you learn as well as who and what might be limiting your learning. Examining literacy as a subject can call formerly held beliefs into question or affirm your fundamental understandings of how readers and writers influence and are influenced by the world. For instance, many literacy specialists are exploring the ways home environments, local cultures, and gender construct us as literate individuals. It's pretty clear to literature teachers these days that who you are predicts to a great degree how you read. It may be a useful time to reflect on where you've come from right as you enter college because for many of us this is also a time of career decisions and complicated life-style changes. You are on a literacy threshold.

Writing Prompt. Draw the floor plan of the house, apartment, trailer, living space where you lived when you were first learning to read. On the diagram, label each room: kitchen, bedroom, bathroom, and so forth. Then number each room. At the bottom of the page, for each number, write notes for a story you might tell concerning you and reading and writing that took place in that room. Continue until you've completed notes for each room in the house. For some, numbering outdoor locations and making story notes also can be productive. Later, choose one story and expand it to two or more pages in length. Immediately you have an emerging literacy narrative. Here's part of my own:

> 1960. My sisters and I trade *Little Lulu, Superman, Donald Duck, Nancy and Sluggo, Scrooge McDuck,* and *Archie* back and forth in waves with other kids up and down Christmas Avenue. At 7, I find these child-sized magazines more pleasurable to read en masse. Arms full, I've hopped down the four concrete back steps from the main house to the colder, newly built den with its uncurtained windows that reflect a winter southern California sky: rain-grays and clearing blues. Once on the sagging couch, I fan my fingers across my treasures, stacking and sorting. They slide, from my knees to my feet along the familiar slope created by a plum-plaid wool Icelandic blanket that my father brought back from active Army duty in 1947. My sisters—Nancy 12 and Linda 11—and I each wrestle this blanket to ourselves whenever possible.

The immediate response I had to my own narrative jump-start was to question: "Why look at all the things I've forgotten?" I remembered comic books easily, but I had forgotten how often I went to the same spot to read them, how the plaid blanket was an important element in getting comfortable enough to settle down for a reading time in the colder-than-the-main house back room. And as suddenly as I get comfortable under the remembered blanket, along come my pesky sisters to take it away from me. How could I have forgotten how much I wanted to learn to read because they could read and would tease me with their superiority? Even in those years before Bart Simpson, it still sucked to be the youngest, to not be able to do what the older kids could do. Writing my literacy narrative, I learn, is like opening nested dolls—inside the big one is another one, and then another—but it's also the reverse because each story doesn't really get smaller: each is actually representative of another whole chapter in my reading life. The term *synecdoche* comes in handy here—part stands for whole—when I remember one part of my reading history, I shake out the memory, and it enlarges into a more luminous moment.

And oddly, the more I remember, the better I remember. I wrote my drafting notes 2 years ago with one of my writing classes. Reviewing them and rewriting into and out of them today, I suddenly reexperience the anxiety and desire I felt—that urgent sense of wanting to read just because my sisters could read. That alone was enough to make me thumb through comic books—and then the comic books themselves became their own beguiling mystery.

> *Archie and His Gang.* I don't really understand these buxom girls and car-mad boys but admire them, as I admire my older sister by 15 years, Judy, who is on scholarship at the University of Chicago. *Scrooge McDuck* is my favorite, and the nephews Huey, Dewey, and Louie, who seem like the antic, acting-out brothers I don't have but often long for. And *Superman*. The basic Superman. Chastely, stupidly going after Lois, who has to scheme all the moves; flashback scenes to his boyhood and his mild child-supporting parents on earth and his noble parents on the doomed planet Krypton. And particularly *Bizzaro World,* the place where everything is done backwards. Oh, I linger over that idea, turning my daily life inside-out with comic book-induced ferocity to see how it might be, if. . . .

To borrow Richard Rodriguez's image, writing autobiography makes one "a citizen in a crowded city of words" (Rodriguez 1983, 32; Dickerson 1989, 136). So I craved citizenship in an imagined city of words—the words of BAM, POW, SMASH of Batman, or the made-up words of Bizarro World, and I relished the lovely sound Krypton makes on the tongue. Trite but true, reading did open worlds. Reading comic books, you might ask? Should I dismiss that as just entering trivial comic book worlds? Not at all. One world leads to another world. Imagining gives the imagination energy to travel on alone or with other texts and allows the individual to crack open and explore the lived world, to step across thresholds. In those days, retelling a friend or a parent what I experienced as a reader of Superman allowed me to rehearse all my reader's moves. Maybe I was praised for reading, maybe scolded and told to read something else. Maybe I ignored adults entirely and just went to my neighbor Kit's up the street and borrowed more comic books and talked to him about what the stories meant to me.

> Ethnographic research shows that telling stories at home is a rich and complex social practice through which family members establish their identities as language users in culturally specific ways . . . More particularly, telling oral literacy narratives provides an imaginative, although not fully understood avenue through which children and adults develop a cultural sense of the literate self . . . Within our families we routinely practice representing, even fictionalizing, the nature of literacy to ourselves in ways that are probably culturally specific: parents tell stories of their children's achievements

> with literacy at school or of their own successes and failures in learning to read and write, and pre-school children tell literacy stories, for example by embedding literacy events within the plots of other stories they tell (Soliday 1994, 5).

Several of us in this book talk about ethnography—at its simplest, the act of systematically *reading* a culture through observation, analyzing its texts and other collected artifacts. Ethnographers read cultures far or near, in another country or down the block. Literacy specialists have spent time reading cultures to study in particular how reading and writing takes place for different individuals under different circumstances. For me as a child. For you as a child. For each of us as adults. At home, in schools, and in our communities, regions, and countries.

In any event, I do know that it wasn't long before I caught up with my sisters. I was reading. And our family narratives always cast me as the one they had to yell at twice in order to drag me from that stack of comics.

> On TV, Superman is in black and white—Jimmy the reporter and Lois Lane—and the convergence of TV and comic book realities are probably the reason I think I can read the more advanced comic plots. The colored comic books function as vivifying movies, livening the grainy gritty TV set Daily Planet and energizing the lame special effects of the classically plotted (disaster/resolution) weekly show that I watch whenever I can. Whenever I am good. And the TV shows provide me with voices for the comic book characters.

Okay—when should I tell these stories? I told them in class. But I really could only tell them in class because I told them sometime in the past to myself. When Superman movies were released in the 1970s and 1980s, I was already viewing them analytically by comparing them to the black and white TV versions that entranced me as a kid. I was performing the normal comparison/contrast action, developing a self-history, and doing the construcitivist self-making common to all humans. Every time I sit at the back of a writing classroom, observing teachers and students, as I often do as an educator, I hear similar self-construction going on. Sometimes two movies are being reviewed, sometimes two people, sometimes two parties.

> . . . [T]he approach I take to narrative is a constructivist one—a view that takes as its central premise that "world making" is the principal function of the mind, whether in the sciences or in the arts (Bruner 1988, 575).

Clearly we tell stories in order to share—but that sharing can include self-learning, self-defining, and self-shaping as well as entertaining, beguiling, and performing. We make and remake, calibrate and recreate, we move from one understanding to a new, more enlightened understanding.

> I like to read (or page through) the comic books in sequences—all of one type before moving on to another. That is, I read least favorite to favorite—the

same way I eat the crust on my cinnamon bread first, before the rich butter-spice-and-sugar center. I also travel in chronological order, oldest date to newest date. A pattern I still follow today. When I find a new detective novel sequence, I check out all the musty-smelling, county library-stamped earlier volumes from the shelves. At home, I open the books to check the publication dates, and stack them in reverse order, reading from first to last, in order to experience the flat, easy-to-like (romantic man or strong woman) detective characters who mature slowly and change only mildly over the years.

Until I wrote this, I didn't quite realize where this habit came from. Does it make a difference? Perhaps not a lot to you (although I suspect it may prompt memories of your own odd and personal practices and rituals), but to me it speaks forcefully, illuminating preferences. Examining these preferences suggests I might experiment with my habits (what if I were to read differently?) and sheds a new light on my self-history.

Reading specialists today discuss a writer's or reader's sense of self, proposing that while we talk of and often experience ourselves as a single, unified consciousness, our personality is constructed, over time, from a variety of influences. Our family, schooling, and general life experiences, our cultural affiliations and our racial and religious backgrounds co-contribute to who we are today. Our lived experiences continue to add up in varied and interesting ways to . . . us. In the same way, our life-long reading experiences have composed us as the readers we are today (and the writers we may be tomorrow).

Overall, questions about your reading past provide triggers for your own storytelling. Many times in this text you'll be offered encouragement and assignments, prompts and openings, and invitations to write in order to see what you know, that encourage you to remember in order to see what you remember, that urge you to analyze in order to see what you do well and could do better. Then you can exchange those writings with classmates because your memories will undoubtedly spark congruent and conversational memories from others.

> In writing autobiography, we hold conversations with ourselves to reconstruct and to mediate a present identity from the memories that emerge. We contain our pasts in language through the sounds of our voices. As we fashion our own voices within and against the voices of self and others in our culture and immediate lives, we create ourselves . . . By making ourselves public, we engage in an important exchange of knowledge (Dickerson 1989, 139).

Confession time. I've often been a little ashamed of my old habits. That's the way of the world. We learn new skills and think the new way is the better or the only way. You know that snooty way some of us get—thinking our way is the best way, thinking one skill or habit is higher or better than another. It's not really true—our pasts are imbedded in our presents. The academic writer that I am is composed of the small girl reading comic books that I was then and the adult woman who reads detective novels before she falls asleep. I feel better and more secure having learned why this is so; I feel more integrated and grateful for my literacy past and excited about my reading future.

> Print soap-operas. Saturday matinees. Movies that screen as soon as I want them to, as fast as eye and brain and hand can move. A serial, a superficial yet world-ordering and calming sequence, playing each night in my bedroom to help the older escapist me meet the younger escapist me, and—like Superman—leap tall buildings (and long nights) with a single textual bound.

Some individuals speculate that the narratives of men and women differ and that would hold true they suggest for literacy narratives, for your descriptions of how you learned to read, and for the meaning you make from such a description. Writing teacher Shirley Rose (1990) studied the narratives from her students and concluded:

> Once I acknowledged that differences in literacy practices could be related to gender differences, I was able to identify two distinct—perhaps contradictory, perhaps complementary—literacy myths which provided thematic content for the autobiographical literacy narratives . . . I have found the myth of literacy practice as a means to social participation represented in female students' narratives. Male students' narratives represented the myth that literacy practice is a means to achieve social autonomy. (250)

In short, she found women writing about their literacy as a way to enter their culture and men writing about literacy as a way of showing themselves as strong and independent, less interested in joining the social order. It's certainly true that my story tells of my wanting to be like my sister, to participate in our family literacy. It would be interesting to know what my nonexistent brother's experience would have been. Perhaps he would have rejected our fight over the readings blanket and sharing (stealing?) of each other's comic books.

If my comic story—only partially developed here (and sketched further in the notes I share below)—doesn't resonate for you, perhaps that's because your story is that of being a very different individual. Maybe, like the quotes from the students that opened this chapter, you feel you are without a reading process, or that you don't need a process. Perhaps that is your claim, and that claim is your story as it was for my student. It would be interesting to see how he tells the story now of his time in my class. In that class I was trying to direct him down the classic route, the same one I suggest you might take when finishing this chapter—to write about how you learned to read, to tell stories of reading and writing during your K–12 school years, and then to reflect here in your college years on what that means about you as a reader who writes. Shirley Rose (1990) sums up this trajectory:

> The first act the narrator describes is *acquiring literacy skills,* learning the

conventions for encoding and encoding written discourse. This act is followed by *practicing literacy,* actually reading and writing. The practice of literacy leads to the third act, *becoming aware of one's own literacy* (or illiteracy). And this awareness leads to the fourth act in the recursive activity, *becoming aware of the uses of literacy.* (249)

The literacy narrative is one powerful avenue to awareness. Perhaps you arrive on the narrative road by another route. That's fine. In fact, that's one of the lessons of literacy—it's different for different people. It reflects our experiences and involvement, our histories and beliefs.

Rough notes for continuing my literacy narrative:

- Reading and eating and sleeping—apples, waking, living in bed
- Not reading as punishment
- The library—working as typist, page, going with sisters, going after girl's club, working there after high school, working in college in the music library
- Visual texts—Chex boxes, newspapers, bound sets of *Reader's Digest* condensed books, making Christmas trees for the church bizarre out of *Reader's Digests,* folded and spray-painted gold, reading army milk cartons, 78 labels and 33 covers—Mary Martin, Sherlock Holmes with Basil Rathbone, Christmas letters (never matched reality)
- Reading more than one thing at a time—father with Perry Mason on TV and the Dodgers on the radio
- Borrowing—up the hill to get the *Wizard of Oz* books
- Making text—printing photos, the old typewriter (inheriting both)
- Carrying a book, a shield—reading while traveling, reading *The Rise and Fall* the first time I eat out alone
- Reading family (acts, photos, souvenirs, letters)—mother in the dark room, father at the recruiter's office, grandparent's house, cousins, sisters
- Not liking the phone—the phone dream, the sisters and phones

As my drafting list shows you, there are always other places to start. You may have started with any of the writing prompts shared in this essay. You might as usefully read reading memoirs—like those of Rob Adams, Dawn Lieber, Lysa Moorefield, Chris Olson, or Kirk Parrott, who like you were writing as part of a writing course. You'll also find these narratives in smaller and greater helpings in most of the chapters in this book: most of us couldn't write about reading without remembering our own reading thresholds. You also might try using any of the myths and strong statements and beliefs and advice about writing that you find throughout this book as meditation points.

Writing Prompt. Type a statement about reading from this book onto your computer screen, read it, and start talking to it, about it, against it, for it, beside it, beyond it. Eventually, you should develop enough starts (if you're not already plunging into a draft) to respond to your responses. Set up a second column and write about your writing. Be a teacher. Be a skeptic. Be a classmate. Be a parent. Be a second self. Be your younger self writing to your older self, and vice versa. Extend and explore your earlier exploration. Look for key phrases, repetitions, new insights. Take one of these, or a collage of all of this, and tell a story, a literacy narrative.

Now, accept the invitation to this textual dance and see where long ago meets today, where the passages between language worlds might continue to take you.

Works Cited

Agatucci, Cora. 1991. "The Lessons of Student Autobiography." *Teaching English in the Two-Year College* 18.2:138–45.

Anokye, Akua Duku. 1994. "Oral Connections to Literacy: The Narrative." *Journal of Basic Writing* 13.2:46–60.

Bishop, Wendy. 1998. *Teaching Lives: Essays and Stories.* Logan, UT: Utah State University Press.

Bruner, Jerome. 1988. "Research Currents: Life as Narrative." *Language Arts* 65:574–83.

Carey-Webb, Allen. 1991. "Auto/Biography of the Oppressed: The Power of Testimonial." *English Journal* 80.4:44–47.

Dickerson, Mary Jane. 1989. "'Shades of Deeper Meaning': On Writing Autobiography." *Journal of Advanced Composition* 9:135–50.

Donovan, Martha, and Marissa Walch. 1991. "In Search of Our Mothers' Gardens We Found Our Own." *English Journal* 80.4:38–43.

Franzosa, Susan D. 1992. "Authoring the Educated Self: Educational Autobiography and Resistance." *Educational Theory* 42.4:395–412.

Fulcher, James. 1996. "American Academic Autobiographies: Not Just Academic." *Interdisciplinary Humanities* 13.2:85–91.

Hamann, Lori. 1991. "Making Connections: The Power of Autobiographical Writing before Reading." *Journal of Reading* 35.1:24–28.

Hesford, Wendy. 1990. "Storytelling and the Dynamics of Feminist Teaching." *Feminist Teacher* 5.2:20–24.

Murray, Donald. 1991. "All Writing Is Autobiography." *College Composition and Communication* February 42:66–74.

Rodriguez, Richard. 1983. *Hunger of Memory: The Education of Richard Rodriguez.* New York: Bantam.

Rose, Shirley. 1990. "Reading Representative Anecdotes of Literacy Practice; or 'See Dick and Jane Read and Write!'" *Rhetoric Review* 8.2(spring):244–59.

Sandman, John, and Michael Weiser. 1993. "The Writing Autobiography: How to Begin a Two-Year College Writing Course." *Teaching English in the Two-Year College* 20.1:18–22.

Sirc, Geoffrey. 1994. "'The Autobiography of Malcolm X' as a Basic Writing Text." *Journal of Basic Writing* 13.1:50–77.

Soliday, Mary. 1994. "Translating Self and Difference Through Literacy Narratives." *College English* 56.5:511–26.

Stoddart, Kenneth. 1991. "Lifestory: A Device for Dispersing Authority in the Introductory Course." *Teaching Sociology* 19.1:70–73.

White, Brian. 1995. "Effects of Autobiographical Writing before Reading on Students' Responses to Short Stories." *Journal of Educational Research* 88.3:173–84.

Wilson, Ruth. 1995. "Ecological Autobiography." *Environmental Education Research* 1.3:305–14.

Sharing Ideas

1. Like Jennifer Ahern in Chapter 5, divide your reading experiences into reading categories. What types of reading do you do for each category? Share those categories with others. What is the broadest, yet most representative, set of categories you come up with? What types of reading have you all completed in each category?

2. Consider and tell times of intense reading in your life. Discuss times when you didn't read at all (if that's possible). Explore the reasons for your activity or inactivity at these times as a reader.

3. Describe one or more turning points for you as a reader. For Jennifer Ahern it was finding the writings of Tolkien (positive) and entering college as a reader (negative). Identify other turning points shared by authors in this collection and then by members of your own discussion group.

4. Tell some stories of reading as (a) medicine—you were told it was good for you; (b) punishment; (c) escape; (d) pleasure; and so on. How else and by what other labels do we characterize our reading experiences? Draw some conclusions from some of these stories you and others share about reading.

5. As a class, make up your own invention prompts that would help you explore your own reading past. Vote for the two you like most and write in response to those prompts. Share results. You may want to fold these writings into your own literacy narrative.

6. Do you (and how do you) feel your gender affects how you read and how

you write? What about your cultural or ethnic background? Your economic class—as you were growing up and then currently?

7. If the assertion by Frank Smith that reading is meaningless if you as reader don't bring purpose to your reading (see the discussion in Chapter 5) rings true to you, how can you work more to bring purpose to the reading you must complete to succeed as a writer, as a college student, as a citizen? You may want to think of the advice offered by authors in Chapters 1 to 4 and then move on from there.

———————————————

Part III

Writers as Readers

I find that each "reading event" is different, but there are patterns. With long fiction, I seek to become immersed and I am more forgiving of small-scale mistakes. With shorter fiction, I am less forgiving and seek to be entertained immediately and continuously. For plays, I'm working more with the pictures in my head, which is mostly entertaining. For poetry, it's like handling delicate lace with razor-sharp edges. For works that will have an impact on my life, I sit up like I'm in class and highlight. Reading that's good for me—for which I wish to develop an interest—often becomes so quite easily. The worst reading is that which is required and outside my interests.

—Ed

Chapter 7

Interpreting Poetry
A Song of Reading

Darrell Fike*

> Birds were talking.
> One bird said to Billy Pilgrim, "Poo-tee-weet?"
> —Kurt Vonnegut, *Slaughterhouse Five* (1991, 215)

According to *Backyard Songbirds,* there are over "645 breeding species inhabiting various regions of North America" (Schneck 1992, 12). It is no surprise that bird song is so ever present in our lives: drifting through an open window as we lie in bed and ignore the alarm clock, surrounding us as we dash down the sidewalk on our way to school or work, or accompanying the car horns and bus brakes echoing in the concrete canyons of a nearly treeless metropolis. Stop, be still, and listen sometime.

As we listen, often we connect emotions or feelings to the calls and songs, finding the chatter of morning birds jubilant, the lowing of the dove mournful, the ratchety bray of the crow angry. Given our culture's tendency to anthropomorphize animal behavior—that is, to bestow human qualities or emotions onto animals—it seems natural to think of bird song as happy or sad or mad. Although bird calls do serve a limited number of practical purposes for birds—prompting a prodigal fledgling back to the nest, contesting a territorial intrusion, or enticing a reluctant nest mate—our attachment of emotional content to bird song probably says more about what bird song means to humans than what bird song might mean to other birds.

Would a bird be merry, soulful, or angry in its singing? Since we are not the bird singing, how can we know what was meant or intended by the song? This same question of intention—what was meant or intended originally—can

*Poems in this chapter are the author's.

be applied to poetry as well. When we read what someone else has written in a poem, how much of the meaning that we get from the words is the writer's and how much is our own interpretation?

Consider the mockingbird. The mockingbird (*Mimus polyglottos*) is a frequent visitor to our yards and parks, a gray and white dandy wooing us from fence posts and tree branches. A long-tailed and short-winged fruit eater that favors berry-rich thickets and hedges, the mockingbird is, according to *The Audubon Field Guide to North American Birds,* at once a borrower and a bully (Bull and Farrand 1977).

As bully, the mockingbird defends defiantly the perch from which it sings. The mockingbird is so eager to protect the patch of yard or holly bush that it has claimed as home that it sometimes mistakes its own reflection for an intruder: "Mockingbirds are strongly territorial and, like a number of other birds, will attack their reflections in a window, hub cap, or mirror . . . Thus the boundaries of a bird's territory can be learned by placing a mirror at strategic locations and noting where the attack ceases" (Bull and Farrand 1977, 550).

As borrower, the mockingbird uses bits and pieces of other birds' songs to make its own. An expert mimic, the mockingbird weaves an opulent and varied wind-born tapestry of song from the tatters it takes: "Its beautiful song is richest on warm, moonlit nights in spring when the bird may spend hours giving amazing imitations of other species. The songs of 36 other species were recognized from the recording of one mockingbird in Massachusetts" (Bull and Farrand 1977, 550).

Thinking back to our earlier discussion about poetry and intention, we can use the mocking bird's use of other birds' songs as a way to explore and speculate about how meaning is affected by reading. As the mockingbird sings another bird's song, is the intent, or meaning, of the first bird's song preserved? Has a cardinal's cry of recognition or territorial claim been preserved as the mockingbird amuses itself and fills the backyard with a joyful noise using the cardinal's call? Or has the cardinal's song become the mockingbird's now, used perhaps to lure a mate or merely to sing for singing's sake?

And with a poem? As we read, as we sing a poem to ourselves, is the author's intention and original meaning preserved, or do we make of the poem our own song?

A Dictionary of Melody

I suppose that to accurately interpret bird song a dictionary of melody would be required. Hearing a call—a peep, a cheep, a woo-woo, or a whistle—we would flip to the proper page and find a transcription of the notes and the attached meanings. Even then, disputes would arise, no doubt, and we would be left again to the imprecision of interpretation, much as we are with poetry.

For even armed with our weighty unabridged dictionaries denoting every syllable of every word of a poem, often we cannot even begin to agree what a poem is supposed to mean.

Beyond a dictionary of melody, we would need a *hermeneutics* of bird song, or a set of assumptions to guide our interpretative activity of the calls and whistles we hear drifting about the lawn. But even then, we still may not agree on the meaning. Steven Mailloux, in a discussion of interpretation, says that to interpret is to argue; he suggests that hermeneutic, or interpretative, strategies, rather than working to ensure that a text's or poem's meaning is captured and caged in criticism, always continue the argument in an "interpretative debate" (1990, 133). That interpretative strategies are debatable is no surprise; indeed, looking back in time, contradiction seems to be the basis for many interpretive strategies. In fact, it would seem that traditional theories of poetry and interpretation are as fussy as birds chasing each other back and forth from a favorite spot at a backyard feeder.

As Mailloux would argue, each of these interpretive strategies encourages the reader to read and judge a poem in a particular way. Each of these reading strategies has its own characteristics or interpretive conventions that "provide a way of describing the process of interpretation" (1990, 124). So, it is possible to interpret the way that you interpret as well as the poem itself. Ah, what an enticing yet perplexing can of worms we open now!

Some Theories of Poetry and Interpretation

Theories of poetry speculate as to the nature and construction of poetry and, as a result, offer a set of assumptions to guide the reading and interpretation of poetry. These theories of poetry and their associated interpretive conventions can be seen to build upon the circumstances present generally when a poem is created or read:

- The poem is made from language.
- The poem has a subject.
- The poem has a writer.
- The poem has a reader.

The World of the Poem

Traditional theories of poetry and their interpretive conventions all, in one way or another, build upon and draw from these basic assumptions about poetry. Each, however, tends to place more emphasis on one aspect than the other, as we shall soon see. It is this varying of emphasis on writer, reader, subject, or poem itself that creates such a diversity of views about how to read and interpret a poem. Although in recent times the stability or ability of language to actually convey meaning has come into question, for our discussion here we will agree with the traditionalist view that language can convey meaning to a reader. We also, in terms offered by Mailloux, will examine both "the object of interpretation—the text [poem] and its sense" as well as the "activity of interpreting—the process of sense-making" (1990, 124). Resting upon this somewhat shaky basis—I am reminded of a hastily built jay's nest tossed about by a stubborn breeze—let's begin to examine some theories of poetry and see how these theories use the basic principles above in different ways in suggesting how to write and read poetry (see also the suggestions in Hint Sheet F). For simplicity, we will use categories of traditional theories first offered by critic and scholar M. H. Abrams. The categories are the mimetic, pragmatic, expressive, and objective.

Mimetic Theory of Writing and Reading Poetry

Poetry in general seems to have sprung from two causes, each of them lying deep in our nature. First, the instinct of imitation is implanted in man from childhood, one difference between him and other animals being that he is the most imitative of all living creatures, and through imitation learns his earliest lessons; and no less universal is the pleasure felt in things imitated.

—Aristotle, *Poetics* (1989 IV.1–2)

Basic Concept   The mimetic theory describes poetry as being an "imitation" of the world. This idea of the work of art as imitation seems natural, and indeed has been a key and influential way of viewing art and poetry for thousands of years. One of the earliest discussions of these ideas occurs in Aristotle's *Poetics* (1989), a treatise that discusses classical Greek drama and poetry. As seen in the quote above, Aristotle thought the activity of imitation to be an essential part of human nature and one of the principal ways that we come to understand the world.

Over time this idea of imitation, or *mimesis* in the Greek language, evolved into the mimetic theory of poetry. As such, poetry is thought not merely to describe the actual object, person, or event, but rather to use the particular instance to reveal a universal understanding. The mimetic theory urges us to regard the poem as a reflection or mirror of timeless and eternal forms evident to the wise and rendered beautifully by the gifted.

Figure 7–1
Mimetic Theory Emphasis

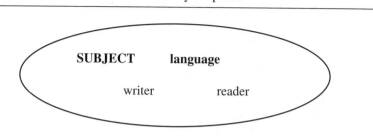

SUBJECT   language

writer   reader

This depiction of the actual, or *realism,* to reveal the essence, or *ideal,* grants to poetry a power to express truth and illustrate beauty that lurks beneath the surface of everyday experience. Aristotle describes the power of poetry to pull back the covers and give us a peek at the naked truth this way: "Since the poet, like the painter and other makers of images, is an imitator, the object of his imitation must always be represented in one of three ways: as it was or is, as it is said or thought to be, or as it ought to be" (Aristotle 1989, XXV.3).

Returning to our four basic assumptions about poetry, we can see that the mimetic view focuses first upon the subject of the poem, or what the poem is about—the world of human experience—and upon the making of the poem secondly. Little importance or attention is given to the roles of the reader or the writer. Some problems with this theory for poets or artists is that their efforts, of course, are doomed to fail and can never really offer us an exact and unbiased replication of the world. Some problems for readers is that although at times we may agree with a particular poet's vision of the world and even believe that an "ideal" representation may be possible, the mimetic orientation does not allow for the reader's own experiences or understanding to color the picture offered by the poet.

Reading Strategy   Test out the mimetic theory by reading the following poem, "Better Than Van Gogh." As you read, think about the "imitation" of the world that the poem creates. Is this imitation realistic or idealized? What universal ideas or symbols do the particulars of the poem suggest? Does the poem describe the world as it is or as it ought to be, or both?

Use the following poem to think about the mimetic theory.

Better Than Van Gogh

The field that rolls up towards heaven
is to the left on my way home,
a glimpse of green and blur of cloud
that catches my eye as I speed by,
a two-second paradise with a pond

and a solitary but satisfied cow,
a wedge of meadow pointed to the sky
and dabbed with afternoon light
better than Van Gogh.

Perhaps late some overtime Tuesday
after dotting every I and crossing one too many T's,
I will hang my tie from the rearview mirror,
checking one last time for what's
always coming up behind,
climb out the car and over the fence
and run madly through that landscape,
certain that when I reach the top
of the hill my foot will find a next step
to take me up into the starry night.

Pragmatic Theory of Writing and Reading Poetry

Poets wish either to benefit or to delight or to say things that are simultaneously pleasing and applicable to life. Whatever instruction you offer, be brief, for the mind is ready to pick up and learn things said quickly and to retain them faithfully.—Horace, *The Art of Poetry* (1974, 57)

Basic Concept   The pragmatic theory of literature demands that we judge a poem by the effects it has on an audience. In this theory, a poem is an imitation that is supposed to make something happen, to make the reader or listener react in a certain way. As we can see, the emphasis has shifted from the purely mimetic focus on the real and idealized depiction of the subject of the poem toward the reader's reaction. One of the earliest discussions of these ideas occurs in the *Ars Poetica* (*The Art of Poetry*), written by Horace, an influential Roman philosopher and poet. Horace felt that the role of poetry was to instruct and delight a reader or listener.

Over time, this focus on the effects of a poem resulted in a set of rules for writers to follow in creating their poems. Poems were viewed not so much as inspired visions but as something made by a craftsman of language. Because a poem was something that was constructed from the start with a purpose in mind—to achieve a specific effect—past poems that were thought to achieve a specific effect were examined. Because these poems had endured and were respected, it was thought that poets should imitate them to achieve a similar effect. This imitation would call upon certain images, language, or style to achieve the desired purpose.

Returning to our four basic assumptions about poetry, we can see that the pragmatic view focuses upon the reader of the poem in a limited way and chiefly upon the construction of the poem itself. Put simply, all the poet has

Figure 7–2
Pragxmatic Theory Emphasis

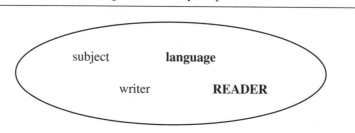

subject   **language**

writer   **READER**

to do is find the right words and put them in the right order, and *voilá,* like a hypnotist saying the triggering word, the reader will be moved to react in a specific way. As you can already tell, this theory ignores the individual disposition or personality of the reader or listener, and of the writer. Some problems for readers may occur when the images or language in the poem are unfamiliar and therefore do not have the effect expected by their use. Over time, cultures and attitudes change, so we might expect readers to react differently. Also, such emphasis on effect may encourage the poet to overdramatize or use clichés.

Reading Strategy   Test out the pragmatic theory by reading the following poem, "For Luck." As you read, think about the effects in the reader the poem might be attempting to create. What emotions—fear, nostalgia, affection, anger—does the poem seek to evoke in the reader? How and what kind of familiar images are used to produce an effect on the reader?

Use the following poem to think about the pragmatic theory.

For Luck

Luck is hidden in this handful of dry New Year's Day
peas, black-eyed and prim, waiting for a bath under the tap
then into the belly of the biggest pot in the cabinet
to simmer and toss all day, the aroma swelling through each
room of the house, as the peas grow tender and burst.

While the peas settle into their final flavor, the rich gravy
peppered again, I fix cornbread made to the long distance
recipe of my father, who lists the cups and measures, and offers
advice—what to do, and when, the secrets to success,
and my mother in the background, "Don't forget the sugar,"

only a little, but necessary to make the bread lighter than
without, both of them as excited as children by my call,
and I, who am older than my father was when I was born,
carefully list their instructions and promise to call again

and let them know if the bread rose and tasted like home,

and if the peas got done: heaped on a fork, nudged along
by a browned buttered wedge of the bread, framed by spring
onions neatly trimmed, these New Year's day peas are the best
I've ever had, and as I corner the last few I make a wish
for luck, and then remember the seconds on the stove.

Expressive Theory of Writing and Reading Poetry

Now composition is a kind of harmony of the words which are implanted in
man at his birth, and which affect not his hearing alone but his very soul
. . . moreover, by the blending of its myriad tones it brings into the hearts
of the bystanders the actual emotion of the speaker. . ..
                                    —Longinus, *On the Sublime* (1967, 150–51)

Basic Concept   The expressive theory proclaims that a poem is a piece of
the poet's very soul. In this theory, the poet's emotions burn purely and
brightly, and almost by magic find expression in words on the page. Unlike the
mimetic theory, which attempts to present an idealized version of the world or
truth, or the pragmatic theory, which judges a poem by how well its construction produces a desired effect, the expressive theory focuses its attention on the
poet's feelings and identity. One of the earliest discussions of these ideas
occurs in *On the Sublime,* written by Longinus, a Roman philosopher and
writer. Longinus, more than other critics of his time, speaks of the poet's passion as a source of poetry.

Over time, this idea of individual emotion as a source of poetry evolved
into various expressive theories of poetry. One of the most influential was that
of William Wordsworth, a nineteenth-century poet famous for saying that good
poetry was "the spontaneous overflow of powerful feelings" (1996, 157).
Because the poet's feelings and passion are now thought to be at the heart of
a poem, the poet's "sincerity" becomes an issue, or the notion of how well and
truthfully the poet has expressed her or his feelings. Whereas the mimetic and
pragmatic theories sought to maintain a truth to the nature of the outside
world, the expressive orientation examines the poet's truth to her or his own
human nature. The poet is thought to be perhaps more capable of experiencing
and explaining these powerful feelings than an ordinary nonpoet human.
Nonpoet humans, though, if they are worthy readers, may share the poet's passion and be moved by the words of the poem. If the reader is worthy, then she
or he might share the poet's privileged view of the world.

Returning to our four basic assumptions about poetry, we can see that
expressive view focuses chiefly on the poet and the poet's feelings, not the
world, or the poem itself, or the reader. This seems reasonable because it is an
individual of course who writes a poem. It seems reasonable as well to assume

Figure 7–3
Expressive Theory Emphasis

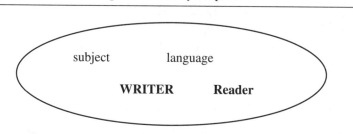

subject   language

WRITER   **Reader**

that an individual's feelings would influence her or his view of the world or be important enough to become the subject of a poem. Some problems with the expressive theory is the idea that the poet is overcome with passion and that the poem then almost magically creates itself. The theory seems to ignore the process of writing many of us are familiar with—prewriting, drafting, and revision. The notion of "sincerity" is tricky, too, because the expressive theory assumes that the poet is a stable, integrated self with special insight that the average person may not have, and then can express this insight with uniquely individual yet universal appeal.

Reading Strategy   Test out the expressive theory by reading the poem "Making Time." As you read, think about what feelings are expressed. Does the poet seem sincere? How can sincerity be judged? How do the images in the poem work to support the emotional content? Does the poem offer you any insight into your own feelings or thinking?

Use the following poem to think about the expressive theory.

Making Time

Slipping tire-high through the night
chilled loneliness of these North Alabama hills,

fifth-gearing along a road the headlights invent
in the moment before the tread grips down

the day old Christmas gifts in the back seat
are the only witnesses as I make time,

carefully calculating what remains ahead
and what remains behind, a road math

of memories, of short cuts and detours,
of exits missed and doubling back again.

Shouldering into the pull of a sudden curve
with regrets flung aside and tires squealing

I brake and swerve into the oncoming lane
face to face with another stranger going home;

for a moment, caught between, we stare,
the cold hills and dark highway anticipating

then he or I or fate looks away and we pass,
disappearing like the tail-lighted road

in the rearview mirror; trembling, I shake it off,
punch the gas, and once again make time.

Objective Theory of Writing and Reading Poetry

The whole idea that the "intention" of the author is the proper subject of literary history seems, however, quite mistaken. The meaning of a work of art
is not exhausted by, or even equivalent to, its intention. As a system of values, it leads an independent life.—Wellek and Warren, *Theory of Literature*
(1956, 42)

Basic Concept   The objective theory focuses upon the structure of the
poem as the source of meaning. What the author intended or what the reader
might feel is deemed irrelevant. The poem is viewed as a self-contained system that should be analyzed via close reading. This close reading will then
reveal the inner workings of the poem in such a way that it will demonstrate
once and for all the true meaning of the poem. Historically, the roots of the
objective view can be traced to Aristotle's nuts and bolts discussion in the
Poetics of various types of poetry and their necessary components. In the
objective view, the poem is a made "object" with its own unique system of
meaning-making.

Over time, this view of the poem as a system of components put together
properly by the poet grew into the objective theory. Some proponents of this
theory include the famous poet T.S. Eliot, as well as various literary scholars
whose way of thinking about poetry came to be known as *New Criticism.* For
the New Critics, the author's intention is not important, nor is it truly recover-
able. Neither is the emotional response a poem might bring forth in a reader
because this, too, is variable. Instead, the New Critics say that the poem should
be regarded as a system of words and images that work together in a unique
way to create the meaning of the poem. Although the poem may contain ambi-
guities, ironies, and contradictions, these components all work together to create the "meaning" of the poem, as revealed to a keen reader educated in poetic
conventions and sharing a common cultural vocabulary with the poet.

Returning to our four basic assumptions about poetry, we can see the
objective theory focuses upon the poem itself to the exclusion of the reader and
the writer. The subject of the poem has some secondary importance, because
its unique characteristics may influence the poem's structures and tensions.
Some problems with the objective view is that the poem does have a writer
with intentions and does have readers with their own ideas and experiences.

Figure 7–4
Objective Theory Emphasis

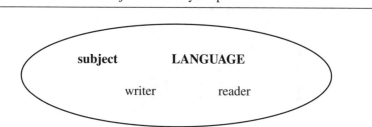

Also, it would seem that any act of interpretation is performed in a particular place and time, and this cultural influence would affect how a reader interprets a poem, regardless of what is said about the internal structure of the poem.

Reading Strategy   Test out the objective theory by reading the following poem, "From the Uncertainty of September." As you read, think about the poem's structure. How do the various images and elements work to support one another? Are there any contradictions or ironies? How hard is it to turn off your own experience and examine the poem "objectively"?

Use the following poem to think about the objective theory.

From the Uncertainty of September

The peewee swim class
lines up along the edge from smallest to tall,
pinching eyes and nostrils tight.
"Don't worry, you'll come back up,"
says the ruddy blonde college-girl counselor
as she tips them squealing, one by one, in.

Into it, head first,
for a moment paralysis, suspension,
then rising,
buoyed by the twin preservers
of their ballooning pink lungs,
shot back into the void
sputtering, arms churning,
swamped by their own turbulence,
struggling breath by squalling breath
for the tip-toe, chin-up safety of the shallow end.

The tallest gains a foothold in time
to witness the mothers—brushed hair
and lipstick, tan arms and legs—
pulling away in station wagons and vans.
"Don't worry, they'll be back soon,"
says the ruddy blonde college-girl counselor
as the peewees hug fast against the wall.

Shivering on the shady side of the pool,
goosebumps and Popsicle-blue lips,
the dripping, wrinkled peewees wait
for the lullaby-ride home
to lemonade and tuna salad sandwiches,
their tiny trunks and little one-pieces
tossed over the back gate to air and dry.
"Next week we learn to swim underwater,"
says the ruddy blonde college-girl counselor
and dips her French braid into the waves.

How to Read Like the Mockingbird Sings

Each of the four theories above offers an explanation for how poems work and how we are supposed to read them. None of these traditional theories recognizes the powerful role the reader plays in bringing any piece of writing to life. Although the pragmatic theory considers the reader's reaction important, it does so only as a response to the predetermined purpose of the poet and the use of prescribed and formulaic conventions and methods.

In recent years, even more theories of writing and reading have been introduced, including those that question the ability of language to communicate a single meaning and those which suggest that a reader, in a very real sense, rewrites a poem or other text as she or he reads, coloring the poem with her or his own experiences and knowledge, taking over the song of the poem much like the mockingbird does another bird's tune.

Wolfgang Iser, in *The Act of Reading* (1978), suggests that to read a poem is to necessarily interpret it, in that a reader brings to the poem a repertoire of literary and life experiences which influences his or her understanding of the poem: "Central to the reading of every literary work is the interaction between its structure and its recipient . . ." (20). Iser thinks that the reader, just like our strong-willed borrower the mockingbird, resists letting go of her or his own ideas and experiences when reading, defending her or his own "territory" just as strongly as the mockingbird: "Whatever experience each individual reader may have, he will always be compelled to adopt an attitude, and this will place him into a prearranged position in relation to the text" (217).

This "positioning" of reader and text is so powerful that, for Iser, the reader and author battle each other in a kind of ongoing territorial dispute:

> The convergence of text and reader brings the literary work into existence, and this convergence can never be precisely pinpointed, but must always remain virtual, as it is not to be identified either with the reality of the text or with the individual disposition of the reader (212).

Iser, then, locates the message not in any one place—not with poem, author, or reader—but like the mockingbird as it mimics a warbler in the next tree making of that bird's song one of its own, in the dynamic interaction of reader and text.

Allowing the reader room to maneuver, for Iser, is central to the success of a text: "[N]o author worth his salt will ever attempt to set the whole picture before his [her] reader's eyes" (218). It is in the gaps of the text that the reader is allowed to sing, to find her or his voice. For in causing the reader to assert herself in making sense of the poem, to fill in the gaps, to resolve the indeterminacy, to seek order where none might be apparent, the reader joins with the poem, becomes entwined with the poem, like an embrace or a counterpoint to a melody.

So the polite poet, gracious and eager to make the reader feel at home, will not bully, but rather will lead the reader gently into the garden of the poem's delights, so that she or he may enjoy the colors and fragrances, taking this path or that one, or perhaps even merely to rest on a favorite bench and listen to the birds.

Works Cited

Abrams, M. H. 1953. *The Mirror and the Lamp: Romantic Theory and the Critical Tradition.* Oxford: Oxford University Press.

Aristotle. 1989. *Poetics.* Translated by S. H. Butcher. New York: Hill & Wang.

Bull, John, and John Farrand, Jr. 1977. *The Audubon Field Guide to North American Birds.* New York: Alfred A. Knopf.

Horace. 1974. *The Art of Poetry.* Translated by Burton Raffel. Albany: SUNY Press.

Iser, Wolfgang. 1978. *The Act of Reading.* Baltimore: Johns Hopkins University Press.

Longinus. 1967. *On the Sublime.* Trans. T. S. Dorsch. *Classical Literary Criticism.* Baltimore: Penguin.

Mailloux, Stephen. 1990. "Interpretation." In: *Critical Terms for Literary Study.* Edited by Frank Lentricchia and Thomas McLaughlin. Chicago: University of Chicago Press (121–34).

Schenk, Marcus. 1992. *Backyard Songbirds.* New York: Crescent Books.

Vonnegut, Kurt. 1991. *Slaughterhouse Five.* New York: Dell.

Wellek, Rene, and Austin Warren. 1956. *Theory of Literature.* New York: Harcourt.

Wordsworth, William. 1996. *Wordsworth & Coleridge Lyrical Ballads.* Edited by W. J. B. Owen. Oxford, England: Oxford Univerity Press.

8

Extraordinary Readings of Ordinary Lives
Interpreting Personal and Cultural Ideologies

Kim Haimes-Korn

> My single, solitary and individual life is like the lives of the tribe; it
> differs in these specific ways, but it is a balanced life because it is
> both solitary and representative.
> —Toni Morrison (1990, 340)

Reading Culture

What does it mean when we talk about *reading culture*? We traditionally think
of reading in relationship to printed texts but as we see from the chapters in
this collection, reading can be seen as something more. When viewed as an
active collection of strategies, such as interpretation and analysis, the term
reading broadens to *process:* we can read everything. This understanding
widens our gaze when it comes choosing "texts to be read."

Raymond Williams claims that "culture is ordinary" (George and
Trimbur 1995, 1). His observation encourages us to ask, "What makes up our
ordinary lives?" In answer, we find that every day we are provided with many
opportunities for cultural analysis. We can study the ways we dress, the things

I would like to thank the following readers (student, general, and teacher readers) for sharing their
candid responses to this chapter during the processes of revision: Jill Davies, Cindy Gann, Bobbi
Henry, Shirley Hekimian, Larry Korn, Ashley Lawson, Jeff Orr, Nazim Rashid, and Nancy
Reichert.

we like, and the ideas we discuss. When we open ourselves to reading the ordinary, we can seek meaning in our popular media as well as in our literature.

However, it is easy to think of culture only as something that is loosely connected to us as individuals. We often hesitate to admit that we are somehow shaped or influenced by the weekly sitcom or the billboards we pass on the highway. In the United States we like to think of ourselves as a culture that values individualism highly. We might resist notions that our thoughts are somehow controlled by these hidden voices. If we consider ourselves as merely the products of the influences of a larger society, this perceived loss of control could create a feeling of powerlessness. But what if we instead view our reading process as one that draws together both the social and the personal dimensions of our experiences? As suggested by some cultural theorists, "People both are written by and write their language and culture" (McCormick et al. 1987, 35). With this position in mind, we can continually move back and forth between the internal and the external as we read and individually interact with culture and language.

> Language is the means by which people find their places within their world and by which they are defined. Although it is a continually changing set of words, codes, and symbols, language allows its users to articulate their striving for coherence, communication, and communion (McCormick et al. 1987, 34).

In this way, the reading of culture can give us a sense of context and connection to others and at the same time help us better understand ourselves. Although we all tap into a history of conversations and subjects that have come before us, we are still able to find our own meaning and communication within this matrix. Therefore, as readers of culture we need to remember the types of experiences and ideas we bring to our interpretations.

Ideology and Culture

Sharon Crowley, a contemporary rhetorician, discusses the ways in which language is more than a collection of facts. She says,

> Because facts are relatively mute when taken by themselves, rhetors [speakers and writers] seldom present a simple list of facts in support of an argument. It is the network of interpretation, the way people interpret and use the facts, that is persuasive. Some modern rhetoricians call this network of interpretation, ideology (1994, 6).

Crowley refers to the ways our ideas, language, and culture are influenced by context. Our thoughts and images always reflect a particular time, purpose, and situation. As people, we are involved in many of these "networks of interpretation" through our participation with others on many levels. Crowley continues,

Ideologies are bodies of beliefs, doctrines, even ways of thinking that are characteristic of a group or culture. They can be economic, ethical, political, philosophical, or religious. (1994, 50)

Although ideology might reveal particular cultural biases, it also can reflect our personal worldview. As Crowley points out, "Human beings need ideologies to make sense of their experiences in the world (1994, 8). These ideas help us construct our personal worldviews as we draw from the voices and images that surround us. We are continually influenced by cultural ideologies such as success, education, gender, class, and history. Although these ideas are often culturally situated through their history and dominant presence, it is in our unique ways of combining these voices by which we arrive at some personal meaning. Therefore, it makes sense that if we know more about our cultural ideologies, we will know more about ourselves.

Activities and Responses: Understanding Ideologies and Artifacts

It is important to understand the difference between ideologies and artifacts. Ideologies are the large, general ideas and assumptions in our culture, and artifacts are the language, things, behaviors, and images that reflect these ideas. Think of the ideology of convenience. We can probably safely say that the United States is a culture that values convenience. What is it that leads us to believe that this assumption is true? What are the artifacts in our culture that somehow reflect this ideology? Here is a list that some of my former students came up with during a class discussion:

ATM machines, computers, "doc-in-a box" (walk-in medical clinics), plastic surgery, cars, "drive-in-everything" (food, cleaners, photo shops, etc.), mail order catalogs, on-line shopping, cell phones, laptop computers, E-mail, the Internet, Quick-Trips, Mega-Marts, Superstores, correspondence courses, distance learning, microwave ovens, frozen foods, quick lubes, disposable everything (diapers, cups, containers, etc.), the lottery, HMOs, credit, "PC banking" . . .

This list was generated after 10 minutes of brainstorming. We obviously could take it further if given the time. Notice the range of artifacts represented in the list. Some are products, whereas others represent whole fields of thought, such as the lottery, which draws on the overall thinking of "get rich quick." Consider the larger implications of items like Mega-Marts, where shoppers can do "one stop shopping."

As you can see from these examples, culture is always situated in particular contexts and time. The language and artifacts reflect a current, specific culture. It is often easier to recognize the ideologies in your own culture when you take a step back and reflect on a different time and context. Consider some of the ideologies evident in ads and articles from 1950s magazines such as *Modern Screen, EveryWoman, Motion Picture,* and *Movie Life.*

When reading across these dated magazines, we might notice attention focused on relationships, with women generally portrayed in domestic roles. There are no career women to be found beyond Hollywood movie stars. Many ads directed at women (the primary audience for these magazines) offer solutions to body improvement such as girdles, "spot removers," and "cleansers."

The difference in ideological assumptions stands out to the contemporary reader. For example, one ad for Camel cigarettes features Donna Atwood, "dazzling star of the Ice Capades of '54." It shows her moving through a sequence of skating positions with the following copy: "She leaps . . . She glides . . . She dances . . . She spins . . . She *smokes* Camels." Here we have an athlete endorsing smoking as an energy source. She readily admits, "I started smoking Camels nine years ago" (*Modern Screen,* 1954). We would never see this kind of endorsement in a contemporary magazine because of our current ideas about smoking and athletes and what it means to be healthy.

Another article places women in completely subservient positions. In the article, "7 Ways to Charm Your Man," by Jane Russell (*Motion Picture,* 1956) we can reconstruct 1950s cultural ideologies through analyzing the language in the seven tips about charm:

> Charm—Do you:

1. Listen to his business problems but keep your daily problems to yourself?
2. Dress to please HIM . . . listen to his ideas about style and makeup? . . . 10 to 1 he knows about it.
3. Tell him he's WONDERFUL and really mean it?
4. Appreciate the little things he does for you?
5. Show an interest in his friends?
6. Cater to your man and make his favorite dishes?
7. Laugh genuinely at his humor? (*Motion Picture,* 1956, 56)

Today this list is almost laughable in the way it directs attention totally toward the man. The identity of the women of the time period is defined mostly through the ways men perceived them. Notice how the woman is expected to be a listener but must keep her own problems to herself in silence. Everything is about what she should do for "him." What does this tell us about the cultural ideologies of 1950s?

Now consider another related ideology that draws upon the culture's tendency to value the institution of marriage. For example, analyze this ad for Listerine mouthwash in which a woman sadly hangs her head in shame. The copy reads,

> Often a bridesmaid . . . never a bride! Most of the girls of her set were married . . . but not Eleanor. It was beginning to look too, as if she never

would be. True, men were attracted to her but their interest quickly turned
to indifference. Poor girl. She hadn't the remotest idea why they dropped her
so quickly . . . and even her best friend wouldn't tell her. (*Modern Screen*,
1956, 1)

We can assume that there is pressure in the culture for women to marry
because this woman is presented as if she has nothing else for which to live.
The culture positions her as a social outcast who is close to the end of her
marketable time frame. Ads like these surely influenced social and personal
relationships in the actual culture because readers of this magazine might have
felt a sense of inadequacy as they read this message.

When we read these cultural ideologies from another time period we can't
help but reflect on our present roles and expectations. In today's magazines we
might see very different images about the roles of women. Although there are
still images and language that portray women in subservient roles, contemporary magazines try to present an overall image of independent, self-defined
women taking on many different roles. The images come across as more
sophisticated and complicated, with multiple meanings and often contradic-
tory messages. In many cases, our interpretations might reveal that things are
often not as different as they seem at first glance.

Modern magazines provide many opportunities to explore a variety of
ideologies and artifacts. It is easy to come up with extensive lists because
multiple ideologies are represented in each image. As we read these magazines, we can begin to make generalizations about what we see and understand. We can begin to connect these ideas to our cultural and personal worldviews. When asked to participate in a similar activity, my students came up
with the following observations.

Consider Gillian's overall analysis of a 1998 *Cosmopolitan Magazine.*

What stands out to me is the blatant use of the human body to convey a
message. *Cosmo* shows a woman with purple eyeshadow in triangles around
her eyes who is wearing a sheer, silver, lycra evening gown with a split all the
way up the leg. Is this for real? Can a woman really expect to go out in public
looking like this? Are we supposed to dream about going to the fancy shindig
where we could actually wear a dress like that? Are we supposed to envy her
because most of us could not even imagine coming out of a dressing room
with that dress on? Are we supposed to be jealous because we know that even
if it could look good on us and we had somewhere to wear it, we couldn't
afford it?

Gillian's analysis clearly interacts with her personal ideologies and experiences as she questions her relationship to these ideas and the ways her behavior is influenced by these ideologies. She points out the contradictions between
the image in the magazine and her own ideas about her reality.

Note the differences in Deborah's response to a 1998 *Newsweek* magazine:

The ad for Microsoft uses the phrase "eyes peeled." I wonder what that phrase would mean to another culture? Amway placed facing ads paired with Junior Achievement. This could give the impression that their company is directly linked with Junior Achievement, implying that Amway offers the "opportunity" to "achieve" the American Dream. A dominant thing I noticed about the medical ads was that women and children peopled them. I thought that was interesting because it implies that women and children need medication more than men do and that women are the "caregivers."

Deborah reflects on the historical ideology of "the American Dream" and examines the subliminal pairing of two organizations. Her observations about the medical ads demonstrate the ways she searches to find deeper meaning and the reverberating effects of women as caregivers. Again, this reader opens the door for personal reflection as she considers the American Dream, her relationships with caregivers, and herself as a caregiver.

Bill analyzes *Reader's Digest,* which he says, "appeals to the World War II generation." He notes the sense of patriotism.

Readers Digest is a monthly periodical as American as baseball, hotdogs, apple pie, and Norman Rockwell. Although it is the most widely circulated magazine in the world, printed in 91 languages, it still portrays the ideology of America and the ideals for which she stands. Most of the articles are uplifting, "underdog" wins, can-do type of articles.

He discusses some of the artifacts:

The first thing I noticed was the automobile advertisements. The only ones represented were the Big 3 from Detroit: Chrysler, Ford, and GM. There were no Toyotas, Hondas, Volkswagens, or any other foreign manufactures represented.

Bill considers the ways a particular audience or generation determines the needs and artifacts of that generation. He points out,

- the Kellogg's advertisement shows an older gentleman running on the beach with a surfboard
- the ad for Ester-C, "Your Vitamin C for Life"
- the "Energizer Bunny" ad for hearing aids.

The messages in this magazine create a different cultural space for Bill as a younger reader. Images and references that might seem normal to an older person seem a bit out of place in Bill's network of interpretation.

All of these readers analyze these texts through their particular cultural lenses and individual networks of interpretation. Gillian reflects on her role as a woman amidst these societal expectations. Deborah opens up doors to question her relationship with the "American Dream," and Bill explores the concept of generations and his own place on that continuum.

Activity. Conduct a similar analysis of a magazine. Consider the time period of and the audience for the publication as you read across the text. First, generate two lists: one of ideologies and the other of artifacts. Next, read across the whole text and construct a cross-textual reading of the publication. In writing, analyze the patterns, themes, audience, and overall assumptions demonstrated. Consider the ways the individual artifacts work together to influence your thinking. Reflect, in writing, on the ways these ideas are connected to your personal ideologies or worldviews.

Coming Together: Collaboration and Culture

Analyzing magazines to determine ideologies is just a start in reading culture. Although somewhat telling, this type of observation represents only a small part of the whole picture. It is reductive to assume that our readings of these texts fully represent the people and attitudes around us. In order to gain a more complete understanding of a particular culture, we need to draw conclusions from multiple sources that include artifact analysis along with direct interaction with other people. Think of all the ways that culture and ideology might shape us. We draw ideas from the groups we associate with, the texts we read, and the relationships we form. We contextualize our experiences through the lenses of the media and other popular arts such as film, songs, and television. In order to understand a particular cultural ideology, we need to explore the ways it manifests itself in all of these forms.

One of the defining characteristics of ideologies is that we *feel* they are true. Although not always the case, this strong sense of truth often prevents us from seeing the perspectives of others. A close analysis of our own perspectives and the perspectives of others helps us to move away from our often self-centered views. These sorts of comparative readings allow us to see the ways different people process, negotiate, and understand similar concepts. It helps to understand ways we are all both similar and different due to our individual interpretations of our culture.

Many theorists speak to the importance of collaboration to reading and writing processes. The very act of reading depends on collaborative thinking as readers imagine themselves in creative conversation with ideas in a text. It makes sense, then, to find ways to extend the benefits of this conversation through inviting more voices into the cultural dialog. As we interact with others, we expand our notions and test our assumptions. This process encourages us to think more carefully about our positions as we change, abandon, or reinforce them.

Activity. Start by drawing together with others (your classmates, a group of readers, friends) and discuss the lists generated from the magazine activity above. Through discussion, notice the similarities and differences between people. In writing, explore the ways your personal worldview interacts with

the worldviews of others. Share these ideas and identify the networks of interpretation that shape your thinking and the ways they are interpreted by others.

Group Activity: Collaborative Project

Overall Project Description

Group members will work together to choose an ideology that is somehow
reflected in the images, words, things, and behaviors of our culture. Your
purpose in writing about this ideology is to discover more about how this idea
or group of ideas has worked its way into our culture and how it manifests
itself in our attitudes, beliefs, values, behavior, and language. This project asks
you to find your own direction and ways of interpretation and presentation.
The project should help you become a better reader of culture and give you
opportunities to closely examine both your group and individual perspectives
(see Hint Sheet F for full assignment and Hint Sheet G for a discussion of the
group process and evaluation).

Reaching Out: Gathering Data

Because culture involves the analysis of everyday life, this project asks you to
look at multiple dimensions and data sources. Your goal is to investigate both
the personal and social perspectives that shape and define your subject.
Consider the following data sources:

> *Observe and Report* on the culture around you. Go to public places and
> describe the ways you see people interacting and communicating. Pay
> special attention to language and artifacts that speak to your ideology. Do
> what you can to immerse yourself and analyze the cultural communities
> around you. Notice the ideas and representations that shape our ordinary
> lives.

> *Interview and/or Survey* the people around you. The best way to under-
> stand how people think is to talk directly to them. Generate a list of ques-
> tions that will help you get a better understanding of your cultural ideol-
> ogy. Using these questions, construct a communal survey (with your
> group members) in which you collect narrative perspectives. Interview
> people around you and share experiences, language, and ideas.

> *Collect and Describe* cultural artifacts that reflect your ideology. Look to
> popular media such as magazines, books, TV, films, clothing, music,
> bumper stickers, and images. Consider *anything* a source. Stretch your
> definition of reading as you search for creative artifacts to interpret. Work
> to understand the relationship between language and culture as you pay
> special attention to the ways your ideology is reflected in particular
> language (slang, sayings, advertising copy, etc.) and behaviors.

Interpretation of a Cultural Ideology

Obviously, there are many possible paths this project might take. I hope that sharing a particular example creates possibilities rather than limitations. Because ideologies and interpretations depend on particular situations, contexts, and individuals, the project is best understood through a close analysis of your particular culture and group assumptions.

Many readers have participated in this project, and all of their interpretations and presentations were different and challenging. Creative, innovative interpretation and presentation are part of the project. Presentations and papers have gone beyond the written text as readers experimented with techniques such as audio, video, art, websites, poetry, multimedia powerpoint (computer slide show), and drama. Readers have taken on subjects such as success, technology, greed, taboos, fame, authority, and escape. The artifacts and presentations have included popular media, traditional texts (articles, books), clothing, film, songs, sayings, gestures, and images. Due to time and space, I present only one particular group's response to the ideologies of *modesty* and *exhibitionism*.

Group Responses: Modesty and Exhibitionism

After much debate, this group chose the ideologies of modesty and exhibitionism. Although *modesty* was their main focus, they began the project grouping these ideas together when they found it difficult to talk about one ideology without the other. They hoped, in their research, to discover the range of extremes that would help people place themselves on a continuum.

They opened up their investigation with the following observations:

- We can only hope to understand each other and our personal ideologies. For me I wonder what causes a person to become totally uninhibited? Where and when do they go over that imaginary line that separates them from the rest of us? I mean, after all, we are what most people would consider nice girls. But does the image that we project to others really matter? Maybe this is what modesty and exhibitionism is all about (Nancy).

- I thought, at first, that this topic would be an easy one. I stop, however, when I think about handing out surveys to others. I was afraid of what people would think of me because I am asking such questions (Gillian).

- As I venture into this subject, I wonder where I fall on this continuum. I have nursed my child in a semi-public place, and have changed my clothes in an open dressing room. I would never even consider exposing myself to someone other than my husband (in a sexual manner), and I hate my gynecological exams (Amy).

- How did we ever get into this topic? I really like it and it has some sort of almost-naughty appeal. I am about the last person to choose a topic like this—I can't even say the words (Mary).

- The first time I remember hearing the word *modesty* I was probably about 10. I was trying on at Davison's (now Macy's) and I wanted my mom to wait outside the dressing room while I changed. She was tired and wanted to sit on the bench inside and called me "modest" for making her stand outside and wait on me. Since that time, I have become much less modest. I'm not ready to strip for strangers or anything, but I certainly don't care if my mom rests in the dressing room while I try on clothes (Ellen).

All of these statements speak to the initial assumptions shared by the group. Notice the ways each reader represents her ideas. Some tell stories, some ask questions, some are personal and some are social. Each writer examines her own relationship to the subject before moving out and collecting additional data.

Activity. Reflect, in writing, on your group's chosen ideology. Explain your understanding of the cultural ideology and your personal connections to the subject. Generate questions and speculate on directions. Write up what you know and understand about this ideology and what you would like to explore further.

Taking in some of the concerns listed above, the group made some decisions on the population and the scope of their investigation. They decided to question only women and to keep the responses anonymous (by providing blank envelopes for respondents to seal their answers). Each group member administered ten questionnaires and conducted several interviews. They worked together to generate the questions and ideas. In constructing their questionnaire, they tried to get at the extremes of their subject to get their respondents to tease out the fine details of this continuum. Here are some of the questions on their survey:

- Would you visit a nude beach?
- Would you dance nude at a strip club?
- Would you breastfeed your baby in front of your friends?
- Is Madonna a good mother?
- Would you pose nude for a group of artists who wanted to sketch you?
- Would you pose nude for *Hustler* or *Playboy* Magazine?
- Do you wear shirts that expose your midriff?
- Do you wear short-shorts?
- Would you wear "wonder-bras" to enhance your cleavage?
- Would you have a professional massage?

Amidst discussion, this group realized different aspects of the subject of modesty interested them. Although they saw some common issues such as the taboo nature of modesty, they found individual ways of interpreting the subject. They saw their subject breaking down into categories, and each chose a different perspective on which to concentrate.

Mary focused on undressing in front of others. Amy, who had been a nursing mother, concentrated on peoples' feelings about breastfeeding in public. Gillian was interested in the ways modesty and exhibitionism played out in appearance and clothing choices. Ellen focused on exhibitionist acts of "exposure," and Nancy chose to look at the ways context affects modesty and exhibitionism. In their group-authored paper, they shared some of their interpretations drawn from their research and observations.

One of the discoveries of the group was the importance of context. By asking questions designed to get at the subtle distinctions between people's actions and their contexts, they found out that the "situation in which the questions were set had a great impact on the answer." They cite the following examples,

> Some women were perfectly comfortable visiting a nude beach, but those same women would not strip in a nightclub. Is this a question of modesty or a question of Kairos? *Kairos* is defined as "a window of time during which action is most advantageous" (Crowley 1994, 13). Some women clearly felt there was nothing wrong with posing nude for a group of artists, but those same women would not pose for *Hustler.* The only real difference between these two situations is the environment.

Some of their work also caused them to revisit their initial assumptions and question the ways that they categorized certain people and groups:

> We have learned that it is impossible to guess what people are feeling about modesty until we ask them. For example, we learned that elderly women are not necessarily more modest than young women. Somehow it is more comforting to assume that grandmothers are more modest than their granddaughters are—we do not have the comfort of this assumption because it isn't true.

At times they worked more specifically with the artifacts, such as in this reaction to a "Dear Abby" column from the newspaper. Here they reflect on the ways gender differences might affect this ideology:

> Last week in the Dear Abby column (*AJC,* 1998), a series of letters was published in response to the "Whiz-zard's Wife," who wrote about her husband urinating in the yard. Although we did not survey men, we mention men in this portion because the women who responded to this letter were horrified that their husbands share "this age old tradition." All but one man defended the practice, but all the women were against it. From the responses

we received about this article, women do not want others to know this side of them. Even though women's public bathrooms have stalls in them (unlike most men's bathrooms), women still are very particular about their privacy when nature calls.(7)

They explore connections between artifacts of the article and the response letters and then the artifacts of the bathrooms themselves. They actively question the ideologies that create women's desire for privacy (the closed stalls) and men's relative comfort with openness (the lack of stalls). This example might feel a bit off-the-wall, but it shows the ways readers can experience the many layers and representations of this ideology. It is these readings of ordinary situations, such as bathroom stalls (or lack of them), that reveal ideas about our culture.

The group collected and analyzed many other artifacts in relation to this project. For example, their class presentation was framed with a colorful "clothesline" of artifacts such as underwear, bathing suits, nursing bras, lingerie, and " wonder-bras." They brought in magazine articles and advertisements that represented different levels of modesty and exhibitionism. They worked with film clips and songs that spoke to their subject.

The responses above represent the richness of their group knowledge. We can see the ways their responses complicate and investigate cultural assumptions. As a group they actively read across these contexts and different sources. The question remains, however: how did they individually interpret their findings? And how are they balancing the social and the personal in ways that help them grow as readers and writers? The following comments give insight into the ways that these readers understood their subject as individuals:

- Throughout this experience, my research and exploratory writings have forced me to consider my own feelings about modesty and how they are connected to society's views on the subject. In the past, "nice girls" didn't show too much skin in public. Society's rules about modesty were more clearly defined in years past. Today's "anything goes" mentality makes it okay for people do whatever they want (Gillian).

- I think that some of us learned things about ourselves that we never thought about before. This project made me pull from within myself to find answers and ideas rather than from exclusively scholarly sources. The survey taught me about myself, such as how I feel people should or should not think of me. The project made me more aware of modesty and exhibitionism in magazines, billboards, and in clothing (Ellen).

- When I was young, my mother used to talk about how we would do things when the house was clean or when she lost weight. I used to dream of what I would do when I was an adult. I saw adulthood as a time when modesty wasn't a concern. I now see that modesty and exhibitionism are very much creatures of the moment (Amy).

- Americans are showy creatures who like new cars and red lipstick. I mean, wasn't it modesty that drove us to manifest destiny? When talking about nudity, is anyone modest anymore? Yes. I can say that only because I know I am modest. I guess I have defined my parameters of my own continuum as: modesty—not changing clothes in front of your best friend after 18 years of shared experience; exhibitionism—mowing the lawn in a tiny bikini at rush hour (Mary).

- My personal modesty comes from within myself. My body image has a great influence on some of my beliefs. But let me point out that images of myself do not cloud my morals. Modesty comes from within and is something that we teach ourselves through our own experiences (Nancy).

This last comment speaks to the main reason that we should see ourselves as readers of culture. It helps us understand the ways our experiences—both social and personal—make us up as individuals. James Britton (1970), a language theorist, says that "experience is kaleidoscopic" (11). He uses the metaphor of the kaleidoscope to show that life does not happen in separate moments but all at once. We can direct our gaze to one facet or another, but we have to recognize that all facets are operating simultaneously. Reading also can be understood in this way: as an activity that is not about consensus or closure but about individual difference and the balance between the social and personal dimensions of our lives. Our individual ideologies are continually reshaped through interpretation and reflection on our culture and contexts. When seen as a way to interpret these multiple layers of experience, reading enables us to make meaning out of our ordinary lives.

Works Cited

Atlanta Journal Constitution. 1998. October 22.

Britton, James. 1970. *Language and Learning.* Miami: University of Miami Press.

Crowley, Sharon. 1994. *Ancient Rhetorics for Contemporary Students.* Boston: Allyn & Bacon.

George, Diana, and John Trimbur. 1995. *Reading Culture: Contexts for Critical Reading and Writing.* New York: HarperCollins.

McCormick, Kathleen, Gary Waller, and Linda Flower. 1987. *Reading Texts: Reading, Responding, Writing.* Lexington, MA: D.C. Heath.

Modern Screen. 1954. April.

Modern Screen. 1956. May.

Morrison, Toni. 1990. "Rootedness: The Ancestor as Foundation." *Black Women Writers,* 339–45. New York: Penguin.

Motion Picture. 1956. April.

9

Your Homework for Tonight Read TV!

Susan Taylor

The boob tube. The idiot box. The little box of horrors. Whatever you call your television, it is a fixture in the postcapitalist abode. Love it or hate it, you better be able to read it or you'll know nothing about the culture at large. Or worse, you'll have nothing to say at a party or be stuck eating your "chicken pot, chicken pot, chicken pot pie" by yourself because the average person watches 3 to 6 hours of TV per day. You, however, may not consider yourself average, and indeed, you have a point. You are reading this essay in response to a college teacher's request/assignment and are a college student. Also, you may—or may not—like to watch TV as opposed to reading it. Watching TV implies a passive mode of behavior, what you might term as "vegging out," an escape of sorts from the reading and writing required of you by your teachers, and from the hectic pace of daily life. Reading TV is another type of activity altogether.

To read TV you will need to utilize the reading strategies suggested in the other essays in this text, primarily the principles of a close reading. You will need to take notes on whatever type of programming you choose, perhaps videotape it if you are using the piece for research, and then analyze the visual and audio aspects within the text. Ultimately, you must synthesize—or make meaning—of the visual and audio within the text to have the piece be a credible source for your writing. In other words, you will need to break down the text into manageable parts to discuss in a writing assignment. If you try to use an entire news broadcast, sitcom, or commercial—although commercials and music videos are much shorter and easier to use in their entirety—you'll find that the source will not be considered credible because you haven't discussed it in depth and detail if you are using it for a primary source. You may make a casual reference to the text as a secondary source, or common knowledge such as quoting the "chicken pot, chicken pot, chicken pot pie" reference from the "Donny Episode" of the sitcom "Just Shoot Me" to create common ground, but unless you read the section of the episode closely where the quote comes from, your writing will lack substantiation. Therefore, use the following four steps to help you create a valid argument for using TV as a source:

1. Analyze the production values.
2. Analyze the images in the foreground and/or the background of the text.
3. Analyze the language used to facilitate the message of the text.
4. Synthesize the elements and question their meaning.

You may choose to use just one element to make a point that could not be made with just a printed text; however, moving to step 4 will make your reasoning appear much more thorough.

Keep a Commercial in Mind as You Read this Essay

Here's a brief demonstration of how to analyze the commercial for cotton. Although there are many variations of the commercial from the cotton industry, you will need to choose one, videotape it if you are using the piece to substantiate your thoughts so you may turn in the videotape to your teacher for source material, and take notes on the piece regardless of whether or not you videotape it. To analyze the production values, read and note such items as:

1. the colors used in each segment.
2. how the camera moves.
3. how the edits are cut.
4. the set.

Then ask yourself—and the text—questions that show your reader your purpose for using the commercial. For instance,

1. Is the commercial shot primarily in pastels? Bold colors? A mixture of the two?
2. Is the camera work clear? At an angle or angles?
3. Is it shot in extreme close-up? Medium close-up? A long shot?
4. Or is the piece edited, or put together, to combine several types of shots?
5. Can you see the camera or not?

To analyze the images in the foreground or background of the text, ask these questions:

1. What images do you see first? People or objects?
2. What objects are in the piece? How do the objects either enhance the characters or distract from them?

3. What is the purpose of the people in the text?

4. Do the clothes of the characters blend or stand apart from the overall color scheme of the text?

5. What is the gender of the characters? Their approximate ages? Are there primarily women, men, or children in the piece?

6. Does the age of each character work toward some message in the piece?

The common element in each commercial is the jingle, "the touch, the feel of cotton, the fabric of our lives." This would function as the language of the text. Ask yourself these questions about the language used in the text:

1. Does the language used—in this case, the jingle—complement or distract from the other elements in the piece?

2. How does the language used assist the viewer in synthesizing the message?

You may say to yourself, "The purpose of the piece is to sell the viewer on buying cotton products and it does so admirably because every element works together clearly—so what's the point to all these questions?" If you watch TV, this is the logical conclusion you will reach. If you read TV, you can go much further.

Production Values

You may have gleaned by now that the production values are:

1. how the piece in question looks.

2. how the camera is used.

3. how the piece is literally put together, or edited.

It is important to take notes on the "look" of a particular show because the look helps to set forth the purpose the writer or director wants to create. In terms of how a program looks, some TV programs that are shot with *high production values,* where the program looks like a movie and first may have been shot on film and then transferred to videotape. It is more expensive to shoot a program on film. [An interesting side note is that celluloid, or film, is made from cotton, and may just be the fabric of your life.] *Low production values* are either simple sets or footage shot on videotape. Examples of high production values versus low production values would be a local commercial, a local car dealership as a case in point, versus a national commercial such as the commercial for Ford or a national commercial with very high production values such as BMW or Mercedes. The set of a program will also have either high or low production values, and the value used enhances the look of a program. Think of a news program: what if there were flowered wallpaper in the background instead of a set that implied, "We're serious, so the background is plain." For example, many local news programs have pictures of the city in question in the background, as opposed to CNN, which shows the rest of the news room in the background. What's the difference in the message? That one program is serious and the other is more accessible?

How the camera is used is extremely important to reading a visual text. Bertolt Brecht, a German writer and performance philosopher, believed it was important to "show the means of production" to call attention to how a piece was put together to make a viewer question her or his view of reality (Brecht 1964, 212). Although a play is quite different from a television production, the point is that when a camera is shown, the producers and directors are "breaking the fourth wall," or letting the viewer in on how the message is reaching the viewer. Ask yourself, and the program, the effect that seeing the camera has on you. As you read TV, it is essential to address whether or not the camera is more than just a means to get the information to the viewer.

How the camera moves is another important facet of reading TV. Generally, in a news program the camera stays stationary and moves from a far shot of the entire set to a medium close-up that captures the upper body of the commentator. Rarely will a news program shoot the commentator, or the news broadcast proper, at various angles or in close-up. Close-ups are used in edited video segments for emphasis or other purposes.

> In categorizing camera angles, *close-up shots* are defined as a picture frame that includes an individual framed from the bust to the top of the head. An *extreme close-up shot* includes only the face and neck of the subject in the picture frame, and wide-angle shots, also known as *long shots,* include most of the subject's body in the picture frame. Camera composition will only include the identification of power and weak shot angles. A *power shot* is where the camera is placed below the subject looking up at the subject. This makes the subject appear more grandiose than at a straight-on approach. A *weak shot* is when the camera is above the subject looking down at the subject, making the subject appear small or weak. Another style of a weak shot is when the camera includes an excessive amount of head room above the subject. *Excessive headroom* is defined by the placement of the head in the picture frame. When the head of the subject appears near the middle of the frame, it is categorized as excessive headroom. This makes the subject appear small or weak in the frame. (McCarthy 1999, 30)

Use these categories of camera shots to help you read the difference between the segments cut into a program and the actual broadcast of the program itself. You also can use these categories of camera shots to help you read varieties of programming, such as a sitcom like "Just Shoot Me."

"Just Shoot Me" has fairly high production values. The set is fairly plain, with complementary blue and green walls on the main set, or office, of the program. There are large, rectangular windows with cityscapes in the background. Desks populate the set and are light oak. The characters, on the whole, dress in black or neutrals. Every aspect of the show attempts to speak "chic" or "simple"—in other words, how the New York fashion industry, the city and business satirized in the program, views itself. The camera is rarely used in an unconventional manner except to enhance the point of view of a particular character. Most of the edited shots are shot-reverse-shot, or moving from one character to another to simulate a conversation, or in close-up to punctuate a line from a character. The camera itself is never shown. The colors, set, and camera work together to offer the viewer a sense of verisimilitude, or truth, because the producers, writers, and directors want the viewer to believe they are watching "a slice of life" each week.

Dramas also use the same type of approach to be certain the viewer can identify with the program on some level. "The Practice," a drama about a group of defense attorneys, has either a courtroom or the office as primary sets. The courtrooms are not grand; in fact, they are rather plain and are largely white with just a few rows of seating for spectators. The office of the attorneys is quite small, boarding on claustrophobic, and is cluttered with gray institutional-style desks. The characters are generally dressed in neutral tones. This is a serious program. The slice of life in this piece is grim.

The camera work, however, is much more daring than in "Just Shoot Me." From time to time, the camera appears to shake. This is to simulate a technique in film called *cinema verité,* or truth/reality in film. In other words, it is the director's desire to call attention to the camera to simulate or enhance the action of a particular segment. Also, the camera may move from character to character quickly, blurring the other parts of the set in between edits. Generally, these types of camera movements are done with hand-held cameras and can be quite jarring to the viewer. It is meant to be so because although "The Practice" is a grim drama in both form and tone, it calls attention to itself as a drama by using the camera to jolt the viewer from watching the program complicity, or viewing the action as reality, to reading the action as contrived. "Just Shoot Me" must use dialog to shake the viewer from complicity, and it intends to do so with witty, silly plots.

The key questions to keep in mind when analyzing the production values of any type of programming are: What's the difference between the production values of each program, and how do the production values work to shape your reading as a viewer?

Background and Foreground Images

For purposes of this chapter, *images* refer to the objects and characters in a particular segment of TV programming. *Background* means what is farthest from the view of the camera, and *foreground* refers to background that is closer to the camera. Think of the TV screen as a painting—after all, the images seen on the TV screen are nothing more than a collection of tiny dots, or pixels, that connect in the view of the eye at a distance very much like a pointillist style painting such as the work of Georges Seurat. They are placed within the confines of the screen and camera deliberately and purposefully by the person in charge of the program. For example, the QVC channel exemplifies how the foreground and background work together. Surf to the channel anytime of the day or night and notice that the price of the object in question is close to the front of the screen while the object in question moves from the foreground to the background at any given moment. The images of the people are generally in the background, with close-up shots of the characters only done in a fragmentary style, such as a detail of a hand, ankle, ear, or neck. The characters, or show hosts in this case, are pleasant to look at but not breathtakingly attractive. They dress in TV-friendly colors such as blue or some other unobtrusive solid color. The female hosts wear dresses or skirts more often than pants, and the male hosts wear shirts, ties, and jackets, only occasionally wearing shorts or short-sleeved shirts and shorts. If patterned clothing is chosen, it is to emphasize a clothing style that is being sold or will be sold during the course of the day. The set decorations simulate the setting of a home or a storefront window. Nothing is extraordinarily colorful—unless it is a product—and nothing on the set is extraordinarily dull. The message here is to keep the viewer's gaze pleased, but focused.

TV news programs place the anchors in the foreground with video segments either to the side or placed over the image of the anchor. The anchors wear the same TV-friendly colors as the QVC hosts, with male and female anchors following the same dress code: shirts, jackets, and ties for men, and skirts or dresses for women. What's worn below the gaze of the camera is not known because the viewer rarely sees the anchor stand up, unlike the QVC hosts. The background of the news program is generally in neutral colors, such as gray, tan, or blue to highlight the anchor and not distract the viewer from the topic. If the background is a newsroom, such as the background on "World News Tonight," the images are blurred. Both QVC and news programming anchors are not old, but not children either. If objects are foregrounded in QVC programming, they are to be sold; if objects are foregrounded in a news program, such as papers on the desk of the anchor, they are an attempt to convince the viewer how serious the anchor is about the topic at hand because most TV anchors are reading a TelePrompTer, just like the hosts on QVC. The difference between the QVC hosts and TV news anchors is that the QVC hosts must ad-lib when talking with viewers: the TV news anchors rarely ad-lib, except on live broadcasts.

On QVC, female hosts dominate the airwaves, whereas on news programs there are more males. On sitcoms and dramas the ratio of male to female is fairly even, depending on the tenor of the show. The images foregrounded are always performing some action essential to the plot while the characters in the background serve to add ambiance.

For example, in "Just Shoot Me," if a particular plot line revolves around the character of Nina, the viewer knows that Finch is somewhere in the background because he is in nearly every scene. The viewer would not know he was in the production offices of *Blush* magazine without Finch somewhere in sight. In dramas, such as "The Practice," the images of the characters must be focused on one or two characters at a time because so many characters are in the show. Similar to "Just Shoot Me," the importance of the image/character is determined by how many times the image is shown and how close the character is shot. To read and analyze the significance of an object, person, or image, count how many times the image is shown to the viewer. If a particular program is read over a period of weeks, it is fairly easy to assess which images or characters are popular and which ones aren't. QVC hosts and TV anchors may not always be in the foreground, but they are essential to reading the program.

Remember to balance where the image is placed regardless of what type of programming you may be reading—either in the foreground or the background—with the number of times the image is shown in relation to the foreground (closer to the screen = greater importance) and you may find that a minor character or image is more essential to reading the program than upon a casual viewing.

The key elements to keep in mind as you analyze the images are described in the ensuing sections.

Language

TV programming is usually not noted for sophisticated word choice or usage. Clever, yes; intellectual, on occasion. What is fascinating to consider is that if a particular character is bright or intellectual, like Frasier or Niles on "Frasier," they are constructed to be pompous asses. The cranky, less cerebral father on the program uses much plainer language and is portrayed in a much less biting manner than the brothers, quite like the two central female characters, Daphne, the housekeeper/confidante, and Roz, Frasier's producer. Count how many and what types of "laugh lines" each character has. Draw a chart and decide how cruel or snide the line is in relation to the character that delivered the line.

One of the purposes of TV is to appeal to all types of viewers so the language should be accessible. But what about programs on PBS? Do they attract more intelligent or less intelligent viewers?

Investigate the demographics, or the gender and age groups, certain programming is geared toward—how do you think the language of an MTV VJ differs from Peter Jennings? How often are voice-overs used on programming that is geared to appeal more to younger viewers than to older viewers? Which requires a greater attention span? MTV or "World News Tonight"? Chart how many times the images on a music video actually speak versus lay the image over the sound. Watch a particular program with no sound. Can you still construct a read of the program or not? For instance, reading QVC is easy to do with the audio off; however, trying to construct a read of "The Practice" without the sound on can be quite difficult. Therefore, if the language used in a program is essential to the message of the program, and yet the language is not thoughtful, what is the purpose of the language? Just like good writing is clear and concise, so is good writing communicated via TV. The language does not need to be overblown; in fact, TV programming can—and does—make fun of characters with strong vocabularies; the language does need to serve the image in a delicate dance of purpose and meaning to provide a substantive read for the viewer.

For example, what if Peter Jennings started his news broadcast with the phrase, "What up?" The viewer may laugh but not find Jennings credible. What compels a viewer to read one news program over another? The language used? Perhaps. "World News Tonight" is meant for upper-class, college-educated viewers, whereas "The CBS Evening News," anchored by Dan Rather, is geared toward working-class, less educated viewers. Read each news program and see if you agree with these conclusions about class and level of education. What is the difference in the language used in each program? What if the opening line on the next episode of "Just Shoot Me" was delivered in a clipped British accent and Nina recited Hamlet's famous soliloquy, "To be or not to be" in a very serious tone? Then the rest of the program was delivered in the same manner and there was no laugh track? What would happen to your expectations concerning the language of the program? What if you tuned into "The Practice" and it began with a wisecrack reminiscent of a line from Finch on "Just Shoot Me"? How long would you read the program to see what the purpose of the piece was without having your expectation for the language used violated somehow?

The point here is that while language used is important, it works in conjunction with the other elements of your reading, which is why a simple plot summary of a program is a superficial read and not credible to use as a source.

Remember, when analyzing the language used in a production you must:

- take notes on what is said and how it is said, in the context of other information in the program.

- chart the level of language used to include the language in your writing.

Without breaking down the purpose of the language, you will accomplish little more than repeating the action of a program, and this is not a close read.

Synthesize Information

When you synthesize information in terms of production values, images, and the language used, you should "read against the grain." What this means is to not take the obvious message of the piece and use it for a source. Read harder. Read closer. You may think the act of reading harder or reading closer is an act of "reading too much into" a particular program. If you are not willing to synthesize, or bring together disparate elements of a program to make meaning for yourself and for your own for purposes of your writing, then don't read TV for a source. In fact, never attempt to write a research essay because "reading into" a particular piece is one of the qualities of analysis expected from college professors. That's why reading against the grain is such a fine practice to get used to performing. Here's an example of bringing several elements of TV programming together to make a point about our culture.

Think back to Columbine High in Colorado. What image stands out in your mind? How about the young student shot and bloody attempting to get out a broken window to safety? The wide overhead shot of the school from a helicopter works as a weak shot to make the student appear even more pathetic and frightened than he was. The school itself looked like many high schools in contemporary culture, a megalopolis. In other words, schools are not about quality education, they are about quantity, or how many students can be stuck in the minimum amount of space. News programs all over the United States chose to televise the young man's desperate attempts to save himself. Michel Foucault (1977), a French philosopher and "leather queen extrarodinaire," discusses the plan of the nineteenth century prison as a panopticon, or a single tower that is in the center of the prison so the keepers can constantly watch the inmates. The design was Jeremey Bentham's, a British nineteenth century philosopher who considered himself a reformer (Foucault 1977, 201). If you think of the classrooms at Columbine as a thousand cells populated with captives/inmates with the TV camera acting as the "watcher," it makes you wonder whether the purpose of our high schools is to herd or to control students instead of to educate them. The words used to describe the incident often included *tragedy* or a *tragic incident*. It is both a tragedy and tragic that high school is no longer a safe place. The political agenda of the camera was apparent. The editor of the piece and the camera worker chose to secure the shot of the young man to either secure ratings or make a point about our high schools. What color did the young men who committed the killings wear? Black. High schools all over the nation are now questioning young people and in some cases removing them from class for wearing black. Is this another example of institutionalized racism? When a number of young people commit-ted suicide under the direction of a man who had them wear white and Nike tennis shoes, did schools toss out students who dressed in white and wore Nike tennis shoes?

Think about the political agenda of "The Practice." The show is about a group of defense lawyers, supposedly ethical defense lawyers because of their tiny office cramped with low-rent desks. Think of the color scheme—grays, blacks, very little white except for the courtrooms and the occasional shirt. The colors attempt to communicate both seriousness and perhaps, sincerity. In the episode where the African American lawyer discredits an African American woman who is a rape victim, the language used worked to persuade the jury that she was not telling the truth. The episode read as an indictment of our legal system as well as an indictment of how whites (the defendant was a white man) are privileged over African Americans. The defendant was a rabbi. The writers of the piece portrayed him as guilty only after it was revealed he had raped another woman. Clearly, this an example of anti-Semitism.

"Just Shoot Me" is a comedy that is a scathing view of New Yorkers with attitude. The show is produced in Los Angeles and is about New York. What is so funny about making fun of people? The humor subtly communicates a mutual lack of respect for two sides of the country. Why do we need sarcastic humor to get through the day?

What does it say about our culture that empty, vapid programming such as QVC thrives while PBS programming struggles to survive? What does not reading TV, or not wanting to read TV, say about your level of curiosity? It's your little box of horrors—do with it what you will.

Works Cited

Brecht, Bertolt. 1964. *Brecht on Theatre.* Translated by John Willett. London: Hill & Wang.

Foucault, Michel. 1977. *Discipline and Punish.* Translated by Alan Sheridan. New York: Pantheon Books.

McCarthy, Colleen. 1999. Untitled Master's Prospectus. The University of Nevada Las Vegas, Las Vegas, Nevada.

I would like to thank sections 15M and 16M of ENC 1101 at Brevard Community College for their help and suggestions by workshopping an earlier draft of this essay. It would be less understandable without their careful and thoughtful suggestions.

Sharing Ideas

1. Get into groups and see what programs you like to watch. Chart which ones you have in common and which ones are different. Chart your age group. Investigate if the programs you watch are aimed at your age group.

2. Decide on one TV program or commercial and assign each group member an element of the program to read.

3. Over a period of days, watch the three major networks. Assign each group member a certain network and a certain element for analysis, then compare notes on what you find.

4. Record a commercial for class and be prepared to read it to them.

10

Go Back and Fetch It
A Method for Decoding Texts

Akua Duku Anokye, Jamie Barlowe, and Camille Cain

A text can be any object, including films, television programs, and music, as well as events such as the Oklahoma City bombing or historical conditions like slavery. Thus, reading is not restricted to the printed text, but includes any act of decoding and interpretation. Effective decoding (reading) of these texts relies on recognition of a set of conditions and circumstances—for example, laws, history, family, religion, education, and economics—that surround the text. These circumstances and conditions are referred to as *contexts*. One kind of context involves cultural biases and assumptions. Many of these biases and assumptions must be *unlearned* if we wish to accurately decode a text. There is also a kind of context involving common knowledge and practice. This common knowledge and practice must be *shared*. Still another context involves acquiring new cultural knowledge. It must be *learned*. For example, in the film *A Time to Kill* (1996), the white lawyer for Samuel L. Jackson's character was challenged to unlearn his racism and sexism. Jackson says to him, "You are just like the rest of them . . . Think like them." Jackson's character's provocation forces the lawyer to recognize his assumptions and biases before he can connect with the jury. Once he considers what he shares with the jury—biases—and what he shares with Jackson—fatherhood—he is able to create an effective closing that reflects his new knowledge and appreciation for an African-American father protecting his child in the same way that any father would protect his little girl.

Although many in our society consider film to be merely entertainment, it in fact plays an important role in reflecting and shaping our social values, beliefs, and attitudes. We apply critical analyses to film in order to decode it. In doing this we acquire visual literacy, a skill that is translatable and transportable to other situations involving writing and reading of texts. In this chapter, we take a close look at independent filmmaker Haile Gerima's film on slavery, *Sankofa* (1993), which is built around the tradition of orality and storytelling. Gerima creates new literacy practices by embracing and enhancing those oral traditions that were already present. We plan to show three strategies as a framework for decoding this film: unlearn, share, and learn.

Unlearn

The last frame of John Singleton's film *Higher Learning* (1995) shows a single word—*unlearn*. It is to this strategy that we turn our attention. Before one unlearns, one must acknowledge and examine those cultural, institutional, and theoretical biases and assumptions that are familiar to us and that are perceived as normal, for example, racism and sexism. However, it is nearly impossible to acknowledge and examine what is perceived as normal without a challenging oppositional *alternative narrative*. We must go back and fetch that alternative narrative: the lost history.

In order to decode *Sankofa,* we go back and fetch the lost history of slavery as an alternative narrative against the norms of sexism and racism. Racism, as it has been imposed upon African Americans, and racialized sexism, as it has been imposed upon African American women, are the direct consequences of slavery. Europeanized white cultures considered slavery a legal and social—even a theological—norm. Furthermore, white cultures did not easily, or in most cases, willingly end slavery. Once slavery was no longer the legal norm, white culture continued it as a social norm, believing deeply, generation after generation, in white supremacy—from its most overt forms (the Klan and other white supremacist groups) to somewhat less overt forms (such as erasing difference and engaging in stereotypes). Facing these internalized racist beliefs still remains controversial. White students carry this legacy of hatred, and black students bear its consequences.

When a group considers itself the norm and requires other groups to enter its domains and internalize its values—often forcing marginalized groups to identify against themselves—that dominant group can be said to have privilege. White privilege and male privilege are unearned. In other words one is born with them or without them, depending on social positioning according to race, gender, class, sexual preference, and physical disabilities. To those who are born with it, privilege itself is a norm, too commonplace, too familiar even to be acknowledged and examined. Peggy McIntosh argues that white privilege is "like an invisible weightless knapsack of special provisions, maps, passports, codebooks, visas, clothes, tools, and blank checks" (1997, 96).

Even today, racism and sexism are primarily perpetuated through visual representations and visual coding. Put simply, visual stereotypes through filmmaking techniques are oppressive. Mainstream filmmaking—the kind of films that most of us most often see—ensures that racism and whiteness remain the norms. In fact, whiteness almost always functions as the invisible and there-fore unmarked norm in mainstream filmmaking and blackness as the marked deviance from the norm.

Invitation

1. Try to think of five films that rely on whiteness as an invisible norm, in other words, that make whiteness the unspoken but assumed point of view or perspective. An example might be *Titanic* (1998).

2. Try to think of five films that attempt to challenge or expose whiteness as an invisible norm, for example, *Rosewood* (1997).

3. See if you can explain what you unlearned in order to recognize how these films work.

4. Consider, too, that some films appear to challenge the norms (for exam-ple, *Glory*) and actually rely on the invisible norm of whiteness as privi-leged and powerful. Although *Glory* (1990) purports to be about the history of the black Civil War regiment, the 54th Massachusetts, its perspective is entirely that of the white leader, Colonel Gould Shaw. Black history, therefore, is seen through the lens of white history and white film-makers. Can you think of other films like *Glory*?

Share

We use folklore in our daily lives. Each of us is a member of several folk groups, that reflect our cultural ways of knowing within those groups. Whether it is through our stories, sayings, customs, beliefs, songs, dances, dress, and so forth, we are surrounded by folklore and traditions that have been passed on from generation to generation by word of mouth or practice. They serve to characterize our culture. In addition to those features of our society that we pass on through the oral tradition, social and cultural groups also share unstated customs, beliefs, assumptions, and practices that must be recognized in order to understand and function effectively within those social groups. If you are a part of that cultural setting, your experience tells you what is appro-priate behavior. When you walk into a classroom, there are unstated expecta-tions of behavior. For example, it is common practice for students to leave a classroom if the teacher has not arrived after 15 minutes. It is a cultural norm not written anywhere in the university catalog, yet consistently practiced by students.

When we think of the social context of an event, we subconsciously exam-ine those *cultural presuppositions* contributing to its meaning. These cultural presuppositions not only underlie meaning, but they provide a means by which we can establish connections between one another. What do we have in common? What are practices that we share within our group that are also observed outside our context? What values, principles, motifs, designs, and music link disparate cultures? While we must unlearn negative stereotypes and assumptions, we must also fetch shared practices that connect our lives in meaningful ways.

As we examine *Sankofa,* we must remember the oral tradition that informs the lives of African Americans. However, African Americans are not the sole users of the oral tradition. Although the culture of African Americans is perpetuated through the oral tradition in every facet of their lives, it should be clear that we all maintain a folklore tradition conveyed primarily through orality. Thus, in the analysis of this film, we will use the oral tradition as an entry point for making connections.

Invitation

- Name a holiday that you celebrate. What is the purpose for celebrating that holiday? For example, why do people celebrate Christmas, Kwanzaa, or Hanukkah?
- Who is the most revered person in your family? Why? How do you show your respect to the person?
- How do you react to your parents' music? How do they react to yours?
- On what occasion is it most likely that you will tell a lie? A story?

Learn

The opening scene of *Sankofa* foreshadows the composition of the film through its use of the oral tradition, symbols, and storytelling. Throughout the film there are cultural presuppositions which underlie the meaning and provide connective intertexts for reading the social context. The film, set in Ghana, West Africa, at Elmina Slave castle, employs many motifs, sayings, beliefs, and symbols of the Akan people of Ghana. The Akan historically are one of the major groups of people transported to the Western Hemisphere during the years of slavery. Although a thoughtful reading of this film can be completed without exploring the underlying presuppositions, the wealth of meaning and inference comes from a careful explication of those motifs, symbols, and beliefs.

Knowing that Africans privilege the spoken word, let's consider the drum and consequently the drummer. The drum holds a sacred and secular place in African culture. Even in the making of the drum, spirits have to be propitiated. The drum must be consecrated before it can perform its duties properly, for not only is it a keeper of rhythm, but it is the keeper of the word. Talking drums come in many sizes and always hold places of importance in the drum orchestra. It is through the drum that dancers are called to dance, told what dance to perform, when to change, and so forth. However, the talking drum speaks to not only the dancer but the community as well. It gives warnings, brings news, and tells the story of the rulers and the village. It has the word.

On the other hand, the drummer in Akan tradition is referred to as *Odomankoma Kyeremaa,* the Creator's drummer—the drummer is a communicant with God Almighty and holds a divine place in the lives of Africans. It is the drummer who calls upon the spirits. He can be thought of as the divine storyteller.

Adinkra symbols similar to calligraphy were printed on funeral cloths in ancient times to tell the history of villages and rulers. Each symbol was accompanied by a proverb that, when placed together in patterns, conveyed a story. The cloth, worn by royalty, was an additional means for retaining that history. In the beginning was the word and in the beginning of this film we see Adinkra symbols of the talking drum (*donno*) and *Sankofa,* a bird with its head turned to its back. The proverb for *Sankofa* says, "There is no taboo to go back and fetch that which you have lost." For nearly two centuries the stylized symbol for *Sankofa* has been found in ironworks produced by African and African American blacksmiths in the American south. Other symbols have been popularized today, and we find them on fences, earrings, cloth, and so forth, but *Sankofa* is the most popular.

In the film we hear the words "Sankofa, Sankofa" spoken by the *Okyeame,* (linguist), who approaches Mona demanding that she "return to your source"—in other words, learn her past. The linguist, an important figure in this story, is the spokesperson for the divine drummer. In traditional Ghana, an important person, whether a chief of a village, a chief drummer, or queen mother, does not speak in public. The linguist carries the words of the important personage. In *Sankofa,* it falls to this individual to interpret and tell the story as told by the drummer on the drum. He is Sankofa the linguist.

A crucial figure in the film is the bird. Not just any bird, but a vulture, *peta peta* which plays an important role in Ghanaian culture. The vulture and *Sankofa* are synonymous. The flight of the bird throughout the film represents going back to retrieve—learn—its history as well as to return home. Look at the many mythological references to Africans in flight in African American literature and folklore to recall the significance of this act: Toni Morrison's *Song of Solomon* (1977), Julie Dash's *Daughters of the Dust* (1991), and Virginia Hamilton's *The People Could Fly* (1985). Even the popular song by R. Kelly "I Believe I Can Fly" (1996) uses this age-old theme of the flying Africans usually returning to the continent or home to safety.

We are reminded in the opening of this film of the unabashed ancestral worship. In African culture the memories of the past are kept alive by calling (re)calling those spirits. "Spirit of the dead rise up and . . ." (Sankofa 1993). This ancestral worship is not unlike that of the Western world. Don't we print the faces of "dead" presidents on our money, or build memorials with statues of past heroes, or celebrate holidays in their honor? In fact, this is one of those intersections that we share in most cultures. Throughout this film we see faces of those who are looking on in the fields. These are the faces of those now on a spiritual plane looking on and giving support to the actions of those still living. This represents the monument of Africans to their ancestors.

Another use of folk culture is seen in dress. Clothing, costume, dress, and adornment are significant methods for expression throughout our lives. As we observe Mona's transition from denial to conscious recognition of her past, we see also a stripping away of the veneer of Western dress that represented the barrier between her and new cultural knowledge:

1. She begins with a stylized leopard skin swimsuit with heavy makeup, long talons for nails, grotesque orange hair, and lewd posture.

2. Next is a contemporary stylized machine-made kente cloth outfit stereo-typically resembling the dress seen on the organ grinder's monkeys.

3. The following costume includes less adornment and makeup with loose-fitting clothing that is worn as she goes down into the dungeon.

4. Moving into the past, she is forcibly stripped and branded.

5. In the past she dons the dress of a slave without adornment, but as the film progresses you notice a transition to white as she moves closer to self-actualization and truth.

6. Her return into the present after her ordeal of "return to your past" shows her naked and reborn as traditional African women clothe her in the style of a young girl with a single blue and white cloth.

7. The blue and white cloth is reserved for special, spiritual occasions. Even the design on the cloth, the state sword, represents her recognition of her past, her history, and the placement of that history in a privileged context among others of the African Diaspora.

8. Given this new cultural knowledge, we can read—decode and interpret—the meaning found in the film.

Invitation

*   Name three activities that you participate in to remember those who lived many years ago.

*   Do you have a keepsake from someone in your family who has died?

*   If you had to leave home suddenly with the foreboding possibility that you may never return, what single item would you take with you? Why?

*   How do you dress for a party? A sad occasion? When you want to impress someone? For sacred occasions?

*   Is there a customary dress for your school? What is it based on? How do you rebel against it?

Decoding *Sankofa*

Sankofa, unlike many mainstream films, has already decoded film techniques that unmask and deprivilege the white norm. The film immediately establishes its perspective—its "I"—through the voice-over done by Oscar Brown, Jr. He asks those whose ancestors were enslaved to "step out of the ocean" and "tell your story." He says to "possess your bird of passage" (the *Sankofa* bird) and "claim your story." He refers to the realities of slaves' lives: tortured, time-bound, whipped, shackled, raped, castrated, and burned. He also covers the geography of slavery, naming states in the United States and countries like Cuba and Jamaica, where slavery existed for centuries.

The film also immediately makes visible and marks whiteness, denormalizing its privileged claims. In the film, the white tourists are considered intruders by the linguist, and they are noticeable and noticeably uncomfortable, even afraid. We also see very quickly the white photographer's utter disregard for the slave castle as sacred ground. As the linguist interprets the drummer, he says to the whites, "What do you want here . . . Go back. It is special ground . . . blood has been spilled here." The tourists react, but the photographer's sense of privilege as a white American man makes him blind to his desecration of the ground and of Mona. The drummer and his interpreter say to Mona, "Go back to your past. Return to your source." And, as we see, she does.

Sankofa's perspective attempts to articulate primarily the black female experience of slavery. Even in scenes where women's bodies are exposed, for example, the scene of Mona/Shola's branding, there is an attempt not to replicate traditional, sexually objectifying uses of the camera. By that we mean that *Sankofa* avoids close-in body shots or long camera pans of female body parts—you know such camera shots well, since they are everywhere. Instead, in the instance of Mona's branding, the camera pulls way back to shoot the scene, even shooting downward both to distance viewer's from the fact that her breasts are exposed and to allow viewers to see the white patriarchal savagery of the act of branding, which was commonplace. Such nonmainstream filmmaking as alternative cinema uses the camera in direct, frontal, analytical ways that avoid, as much as possible, sexual objectification.

Except for the ending, the rest of the film depicts slave life on a Jamaican plantation. Mona becomes her ancestor Shola, who must first face a series of incidents that strip her of her denial. Shola must eventually face her own memories of rape and humiliation, and, as a consequence, she participates in the uprising. At this point, the film transports characters and viewers back through the canefields and across the ocean to the slavery stronghold. In all these scenes on the plantation, whiteness remains the marked case—the slave-owners and overseers take on those characteristics they projected onto Africans (and white Americans continue to project onto African Americans): savagery and brutality. In the final scenes of the film, after Mona's/Shola's rebirth, whites are absent from the cinematic frame.

An accurate decoding of the film *Sankofa* relies heavily on our ability to unlearn, share, and learn about new or different cultural ways. It is a literacy that relies on our appreciation for the connections between orality and literacy in such cultures.

Orality and literacy have been debated issues for many years, and the plethora of articles, essays, and books written on the subject are testimonials to this fact. Many argue that the spoken word only exists in the moment of its being spoken or that writing is a permanent record that is constant and everlasting. Needless to say, these critics favor literacy. However, for cultures that did not utilize literacy, there was another method used to make records such as history, events, and all other types of things we write today permanent. This information was made constant and everlasting, orally.

Patricia Gillikin says, "One way the distinction between orality and literacy can be useful is in its ability to question the ways of thinking and looking at the world by which literates are limited: literates assuming that without writing, nothing of any importance can be done or thought" (1993, 90). This assumption is biased in that it favors and privileges one culture over another.

The privileging of literacy over orality is the initial problem with the communicative differences between African Americans and European Americans. According to Akua Duku Anokye in her article "A Case for Orality in the Classroom" (1997), it is a cultural trait of African Americans to meander around a point that causes problems with Anglo Americans, who want to get to the point and be direct. The differences in these communication styles create problems in decoding one another (Anokye 1997, 230). Meaning conveyed by a text—in this case the film *Sankofa*—is a meaning to be interpreted by making inferences using the cultural, social, or linguistic connections underlying what is said.

Reprise: The Go Back and Fetch It Method

1. *Unlearn:* Acknowledge and examine cultural biases and assumptions.

2. Go back and fetch lost histories that work as alternative oppositional narratives.

3. *Share:* Embrace and enhance common cultural knowledge and practices.

4. Go back and fetch through dialogue, music, folktales, family history, religious practices, food, myths and legends, fairy tales, genealogy, community practices, festivals, holidays, rituals, dance, art, artifacts (quilts, pottery, instruments), design motifs, drinking, and folk remedies.

5. *Learn* new cultural knowledge. Fetch through research—on-line, libraries, interviews, biographies, autobiographies, ethnographies, and filmographies.

Possible Writing Assignments

1. Compose: response journals, free writes, exploratory and personal narratives, family narratives, community histories.

2. Choose a film and apply the "Go back and Fetch It" method. Write about your experience as you unlearn, share, and learn while decoding the film.

The following films also are recommended: *Rosewood* (1991), *Like Water for Chocolate* (1994), *Smoke Signals* (1998), *Mi Familia* (1995), and *Higher Learning* (1995).

With this method, we can ask ourselves, "What can be made of a visible text, a culture, and its symbols?" Without the underlying cultural presuppositions, we cannot learn new cultural knowledge. When we acknowledged traditional symbols, explored the history, and made connections between the culture and its visual texts, we decoded a text through new eyes. We have seen how a prize-winning filmmaker was able to use African culture, symbols, and beliefs to tell a story of universal appeal. We too can use traditional modes to recall ways of knowing the story and creating richly textured texts. In essence, we can go back and fetch that which is lost in order to unlearn, share, and learn new knowledge.

Works Cited

Anokye, Akua Duku. 1997. "A Case for Orality in the Classroom." *The Clearing House.* 70.5:229–31.

Daughters of the Dust. 1991. A Geechee Girls Production. New York, NY: Kino Video.

Gillikin, Patricia. 1996. "Problematizing Orality/Literacy: A Brief Survey of Critiques." *College English* 58:89–94

Glory. 1990. Tri-Star Pictures. Burbank, CA: RCA/Columbia Pictures Home Video.

Hamilton, Virginia. 1985. *The People Could Fly: America Black Folktales.* NY: Knopf.

Higher Learning. 1995. New Deal Production. Culver City, CA: Columbia TriStar Home Video.

Kelly, R. 1996. "I Believe I Can Fly." BMG/Jive/Novis/Silvertone

Like Water for Chocolate/Como Agua Para Chocolate. 1994. Arau Films International S.A. Touchstone Home Video. Burbank, CA: Buena Vista Home Video.

McIntosh, Peggy. 1997. "White Privilege: Unpacking the Invisible Knapsack." In: *Race, An Anthology in the First Person,* 96–101. Edited by Bart Schneider. New York: Crown Trade Paperbacks.

Morrison, Toni. 1997. *Song of Solomon.*

My Family/Mi Familia. 1995. New Line Cinema. New Line Home Video.

Rosewood. 1997. Warner Bros. Burbank, CA : Warner Home Video.

Sankofa. 1993. Negod-Gwad Productions. Washington, DC: Mypheduh Films.

Smoke Signals. 1998. Miramax Films. Shadowcatcher Entertainment Production. Burbank, CA: Miramax Home Entertainment.

A Time to Kill. 1996. Warner Bros. Monarch Entertainment and New Regency Film.

Titanic. 1997. Twentieth Century Fox and Paramount Pictures.

Sharing Ideas

1. What metaphor might your group choose to substitute for Darrell Fike's metaphor of bird song, bird-reading-bird in Chapter 7? Play out a new metaphor for the different definitions of reading that he examines. The theories he discusses apply equally to fiction and nonfiction. Apply them to a favorite short story or to an essay written by one of your group members.

2. To what degree do you already see yourself as a reader of culture? Of TV? Of film and video? What does each chapter in this section add to your reading strategies for each? Which type of reading (text, culture, TV, film) do you prefer to do and why?

3. Choose one of Lisa Albrecht's radical rags listed in Chapter 5 and read it using the processes described in the first part of Chapter 8 by Kim Haimes-Korn. Then try using Kim's method to read TV or film.

4. Add the technical analysis questions provided by Susan Taylor in Chapter 9 to the "Go Back and Fetch It" method described by the authors of Chapter 10. Use them together to deepen your reading of a favorite film, to see it in new ways.

5. Several authors in this book mention the way assigned reading has sometimes taken the pleasure out of the act of reading for them. Do you feel this is as true for assigned readings of TV or film? Why or why not? Write a letter to one of the author's in Chapters 7 to 10, explaining your thinking on this question.

6. Together with a group draw up a list of other stereotypes besides whiteness that could usefully be decoded with the unlearn, share, and learn method described in Chapter 10. Then prioritize your list. Which of these stereotypes are crucial for citizens of your community to address? What films would you use for illustration and examination of each?

7. How do you respond to/interpret Camille Cain's analysis of her class in Hint Sheet 4 at the end of this book? Write a letter to her from a student's point of view, discussing her educational experiment.

Part IV

Reading to Write

My own reading process? Well, hell, that's a dumb question (only because I haven't thought about it!). There is no single process that I employ. It's as varied as the texts, contexts, and purposes are. I mean, take a short story. If I'm reading it for the first time, for a class that I'm taking, I'll approach it slowly, lovingly, and relaxed but alert. On the other hand, if I'm rereading it for the same purpose, I will then underline, highlight, asterisk, etc. various areas that I consider crucial to my understanding. Thirdly, if I'm reading it after a class discussion or lecture, my approach will be to read quickly the parts not discussed in class while slowing down for areas that had drawn critical discussion.

—Greg

11

Making and Examining Strong Statements About Reading
A Journal Inventory

Wendy Bishop

What we think about what we read—what we read at all—is deeply connected to our beliefs about reading (and writing). Writer and teacher Donald Murray (1991) ends an essay titled "All Writing Is Autobiographical" with this observation:

> I suspect that when you read my poem, you wrote your own autobiography. That is the terrible, wonderful power of reading: the texts we create in our own minds while we read—or just after we read—become part of the life we believe we lived. Another thesis: all reading is autobiographical. (74)

Murray's final observation suggests that to better understand who we are as readers, we should take stock of our reading beliefs in order to:

1. decide which are strong beliefs and which are weak ones.
2. compare these beliefs to what reading specialists can tell us about current understandings of readers and reading processes.
3. examine what the strong-false (not verifiable) and the strong-true (verifiable) beliefs say about our own reading lives.

In an earlier chapter I talked to you about writing your reading autobiography, your own literacy narrative. In this chapter, I encourage you to examine your strongest feelings and beliefs about reading, which might illuminate that story as well as function as an important step in the process of using reading to improve your writing, a subject the following chapters take up in even more detail.

Playing the Game

First, stop right here and—alone or in a group—list ten strong statements about reading: things you think you believe, things you've heard others say that you agree with, and observations drawn from your own history of reading and from your reading so far in this book. If it helps, use statement starters like "Reading is . . ." or "Readers are . . ." or "X kind of readers do Y . . ." or "X type reading is Y . . ." and so on.

Recently, several writing teachers and I undertook a similar project. Using journal writings in a seminar based on reading theory, we examined our own reading beliefs. Our assignment, more or less, was the same as yours: To list the assumptions, myths, and beliefs we held—or saw discussed—about reading and to respond to that list, looking at each item, arguing for or against it, exploring what it meant to believe or not believe. We did this to investigate those statements, to contextualize them using our past experiences and our current readings. As you read some of our statements and our responses, I trust you'll be prompted to argue for or against our assertions. There are no right or wrong responses to these statements—think of them, rather, as thoughtful, thought-filled musings that may help you interrogate your own beliefs about reading and readers.

For instance, Dan Melzer, who wrote Chapter 2, explored some of his strong beliefs in this manner:

> *If it's in a book it's true.* This is one of the "myths" some students have that makes it harder to get them to challenge texts. And finally, a last myth—Reading fast is reading well. It's no wonder our students pick up on this myth since there are so many commercials for speed reading. It seems like there's a happy medium between getting caught up in individual words (as reading specialist Frank Smith [1981] pointed out) and skimming so superficially you have little comprehension.

Also interested in investigating the idea of reading speed, another teacher, Joe Chapman, argued for and against speed reading in this way:

> *When it is useful:* As Frank Smith says, fast reading means paying attention to the minimal number of signs necessary to get the meaning. It's good because the reader doesn't get locked into tunnel vision, paying such close attention to every letter and word that he/she loses the overall meaning. *When it's not useful:* For me at least. I read just a tad faster than my speaking rate. When the material is difficult, I have to go slower, sometimes rereading sections several times. I find my pace picking up when I can breeze over sections because I have a rough idea of what they're going to say anyway. *Conclusion:* The more familiar you are with a text and the easier the material—i.e., when you can make more predictions—the faster you can read.

Reading Joe's and Dan's journal entries, you get a feel for how to play what Peter Elbow (1986) calls the doubting and believing game and to do it with your own strong statements about reading. In the sections that follow, I've compiled some of our statements and responses. You might find it useful to keep your own journal handy as you go over them; copy down arguments you want to respond to, and then do so. You might:

1. Change statements, tinker with them, match them to your experiences and beliefs. Then explain your changes, explore your own strong responses.

2. Consider how teacherly these statements and arguments might be and ask how others might see this issue in a similar or different way.

3. Consider the stance you—as writer—take on a reading statement and whether that differs or agrees with the stance you hold—as reader.

4. Where you see one side strongly argued, try playing devil's advocate— take the other side, just to see what that feels like.

5. Finally, when you see an argument you can no longer refute, consider what that now predicts about your future relationship to reading.

"Reading Is a Linear Process"

Pro: When you read, you read from left to right, not randomly skipping down the page; in that way, I suppose reading could be "linear." *Con:* However, you don't read one letter at a time to make meaning, but read more in clumps. Also, making meaning from reading is more complicated [because you are] bringing in prior knowledge, making reading not only nonlinear as a process, but also in time. —Holly

Pro: Educated Western people read from left to right, top to bottom, beginning to end, decoding strings of coded grapholytic symbols. *Con:* I sometimes start at the end of a book or magazine, and I frequently jump from section to section in serendipitous order, from a second or subsequent use of a key word to an earlier use of the word; and from a sentence to a note and back.—Ormond

Con: As we move to valuing computer hyper-text, I'm moved to think more and more about how the act of reading is active, physical, and messy. I consider myself an active reader. I rarely read a text front to back. I rarely read a complete text in one sitting. Often, I'm not sitting when I read. I move through the house and back to a stack of readings. I read more than one text at a time. Reading one thing may prompt me to stop and go read something else (especially if I'm researching and trying to compare/connect others' ideas and further develop my own). I continue to read after I close the text, put down the page. I might ponder while exercising and driving to work and then return to a text to check that reading off the page with an idea on a page. I reread a text at various stages in my life and compound my understanding of it—savoring or favoring different parts of it.—Wendy

"Active Reading Is the Act of Revising/Rewriting the Text"

Pro: I think my students are starting to get the idea of the importance of revision, but they never seem to catch on to the importance of rereading.—Dan Melzer

Pro: I wonder if I believe there is such a thing as passive reading. I guess there is. Reading that isn't read? Text passed before eyes? Words mouthed but not considered? Eye movement without comprehension? Interaction without interest? It does seem to me that when I'm actively engaged with a text, the moment is luminous, charged (actual brain chemistry?). It's like I'm sculpting, painting, rewriting the text of my understanding. It's like those pop up 3-D cards or story books—the text itself feels energized, something I want to hold and grapple with. And when I fold down that text, refile it into my schema, I have rewritten it for myself and for the conversation I can hold about it. That is, when I just watched *Gone with the Wind* again with my daughter who was watching it for the first time, I was writing it into a new version for myself and watching her read it with very different questions than I now have. But I recognized her reading—I had experienced that text once and she allowed me to, in part, reread it (write it again) in the way she was reading it. Back for a minute to reading as active and oral—when we borrow others' questions/readings, read together, interpret orally and communally, aren't we helping each other revise and rewrite new texts?—Wendy

"Reading Is a Solitary Activity"

Pro: You are the only person making meaning in your mind when you read. Also, the act of reading is often a literally (and literary—ha ha) solitary activity. *Con:* Theorists would argue that reading is a social process—that your schemas are constructed socially, and therefore, how you make meaning is highly influenced by others. Also, much of the act of learning to read and developing reading skills is done with other people—being read to as a child, being in reading groups, etc. —Holly

Con: Physically, there is often someone present. I read something aloud to a friend. To myself. I read outdoors. I read with others in the room or in the airport waiting lounge. Critically, there are often a number of influences—the book review, the movie review, the mention of a text on an E-mail list, the question from a child or a friend about whether I know of or have read a text. Beyond pleasure reading, professional reading is highly social—I have to assess the value of the text not just to me but to others. I may have a problem with the text and choose others' readings, verbal interpretations, writings on/against the text to help me create my own text. The closer my writing is to my reading—the closer I am to sharing my reading with a community. When I allude to a Gerard Manley Hopkins poem in my poem, I'm being social. When I explain the derivation of my ideas in the introduction to an essay, I'm situating myself in an imagined community of discussants. I like to read newspapers at the breakfast table with the newscast offering its countertext. I read in coffee shops. I feel whole reading in a bookstore, browsing and sampling while others do the same. I stay in school because doing this houses me with other interested readers.—Wendy

Pro: Good comprehension and reading speed requires concentration which is enhanced by some level of separation from society to minimize distractions. "The fact that writing is a lonely activity whereas speaking typically takes place in an environment of social interaction causes written language to have a detached quality that contrasts with the involvement of spoken language" (Chafe 1985, 105). *Con:* I share favorite texts aloud with friends, sometimes spontaneously, sometimes in ritualized social "readings."—Ormond

Con: I don't think the reader completely creates the text, but neither is the text completely dependent upon reader response. However, I don't believe that it's the writer's fault if you can't understand the text. This is a common student statement that I disagree with (usually). Students like texts that require as little effort as possible, and this also ties in with their reluctance to reread. They get angry at the writer if they can't understand a complex paragraph or sentence. Sometimes they're right; there is such a thing, I think, as poor writing. And this will cause poor reading.—Dan

"English Majors Love to Read"

Pro: They certainly do read a lot, so they must like it. Also, English majors are the type of people who loved to read as kids. *Con:* Actually, there are some English majors who have never loved to read; they got into the field because they liked other things about it. Also, others have been turned off of reading because it has become nothing but work and obligation, and much of the pleasure of reading has been lost. English majors don't necessarily love to read; they just happen to be good at it.—Holly

Issues in Goodness and Reading: "There Are 'Good' and 'Bad' Readers"; "Good Writers Have to Read a Lot"; and "Women Are Better Readers than Men"

Pro: When most people are in school, they are placed in a reading group which lets them know what kind of reader they are, from the "good" reading group to the "bad" readers. They learn early on that there is a distinction and that that one is a value judgment. People who are in families who read a lot tend to read a lot themselves. Also, abilities and strengths can be genetically determined.

Con: The environment you are raised in can be more influential than genetics. Reading and making meaning is a skill that improves through practice. Maybe one could be born with the potential to be a wonderful reader, but if that person is never taught in their environment that it is important to read, then that "natural" talent could atrophy or shift to other skills. Frank Smith distinguishes between "experienced" and "nonexperienced" readers in any given reading experience. There are no value judgments to label and discourage individuals. Again, "experience," or practice is an important consideration. Reading is a skill, like tennis, where some may need more practice than others, but no one is essentially "bad" at tennis, or reading.—Holly

Pro: Writers must gain a sense of language by lots of reading. Expand their vocabularies, use the language more skillfully, learn about the manipulation of meaning, etc. They also have to have a strong reading skill so that they can apply it to their own writing when revising. *Con:* There comes a time when the writer has to become the artist himself/herself, stop reading, and start composing. Writers are creators with the freedom to do whatever they want, more or less. And there are other ways to gain a command of language, such as speaking, [having] experiences, learning foreign languages, building relationships, etc. *Conclusion:* Good writers may have to be good readers, but that doesn't necessarily mean they have to read a lot.—Joe

Pro: Girls do learn and use communication skills quicker than boys when babies, and then continue to do better at reading and reading-associated fields than males. Males also have dyslexia more frequently. *Con:* Girls and women are more socially rewarded for their language skills than boys and men are (think of the "strong, silent" male archetype). Boys and men may stifle their abilities and not work to better them because they may fear being seen as not "manly." Boys are expected to be good at math, while girls are supposed to be better at English. Expectations can be very powerful. As for dyslexia, some theorists doubt its reality. Also, it is more "acceptable" in boys and more frequently diagnosed.—Holly

Issues in Processing Written Text: "Reading Is to Gain Information" and "Reading Is (Should Be) for Correct Meaning/Comprehension"

Pro: A whole lot of times! Look at the books and essays we've read in this [reading] course. I've learned a lot of things I didn't know before. *Con:* Maybe it's incorrect to say "gain." Maybe reading is to weigh information. Again look at what we've read this semester. I've learned a lot, but I wouldn't necessarily say I've adopted it all as fact. *Conclusion:* Information is awareness of other theories. You read to be exposed to them so you can decide to what extent you want to revise your own.—Joe

Pro: Texts have a right interpretation; good readers find that meaning; groups of good readers can agree on core meaning(s) of a text; standardized tests provide an objective measures to confirm how well a reader comprehends a text. *Con:* I often see that competent readers disagree on the interpretation of a text; depending upon when and how I read, I frequently find different meaning in the same text; reader-response theory suggests that there is no absolute meaning of a text.—Ormond

Con: As soon as I sit and read, I want to write. As soon as I write—I think of things I might read, or I read/imagine texts that are influencing my thinking and incorporate my response into the growing text. Sometimes I have to write and read myself to know myself. Other times, I have to write myself and offer to be read to be sure others can see some aspect I can't articulate at the point of utterance with the accuracy (real or imagined) I'd desire. Writing lets me rehearse myself, my thinking, my writing, my reading—it lets me examine a reading from all sides, to cube it and consider it. When I write I often subvocalize. When I read, I stop and talk to my writing voice, considering whether I can keep that thought in short-term memory or need to share it in saved conversation by writing it down.—Wendy

Issues in Print Literacy: "Reading Is (Should Be) Only Associated with Written Texts" or "Reading Is (Should Be) Associated with Print"

Con: When reading, I'm casting about, much as I am in speech. I'm trying. I'm throwing out an interpretation and returning to get it right or better or enjoy it again. When I speak, I'm often casting about too; both speech and writing feel like a "two steps forward, one step backward" process. As I remember and analyze what the person(s) I'm conversing with is(are) saying, I'm "rereading" what I just said and "writing" what I will say next. The process of shuttling seems much like the internal process of reading—I do have less control of the direction and the voices but not really—I can stop the conversation. I can go backward. Just as I can in reading. Of course, the conversation partner can walk away—but so can my reading attention.—Wendy

Pro: Educated Western people read words—handwritten or printed—on paper, words that are strung together for meaning in sentences, paragraphs, sections, chapters, books, volumes. To take meaning from anything else is not reading; it's looking, scanning, observing, or something. Educated discerning people put texts that have achieved a minimal level of social approval into print to ease standardization, distribution, and consumption of the words; print has a satisfying aesthetic quality for competent readers. *Con:* I find words on a diverse array of material—boxes, graffiti, notes, rolling movie and TV announcements and credits, signs, stickers, etc.; all of them convey meaning. Furthermore, I "read"—that is, take meaning from— pictures, three-dimensional nonverbal artifacts, and human behavior. Some of the most beautiful texts I know are rendered in handwriting; some of the most exciting ideas I encounter are communicated with illustrations, arti- facts, and behaviors, without any reliance on written words. —Ormond

Continuing to Play the Game

Now that you've got a feel for the doubting-and-believing-strong-statements- about-reading game, continue to play it in your journal, in a reading or a writ- ing group, in a class discussion. I'll leave you with some of the statements we continued to discuss: "Good readers are born, not made"; "To read well, you have to be smart"; "Reading is difficult and unnatural, and reading is irrelevant to life"—I'm pretty sure you've already come up with a better list of your own, based on your own reading experiences.

Revisit that list. Doubt the statements, believe them. And continue to test them as you go on into your reading life.

1. Are you a better reader of videos than of books? What does that mean to you?

2. Do you find yourself liking or disliking different types of reading at different points in your life? What does that predict about you as a reader at ages 20, 30, 40, 50, and on?

3. Do you think books will still be stacked up on any reader's night stand in the year 2050?

4. At one time, reading was restricted to the upper class and to scribes and a limited set of individuals who read and wrote books. Books were not available to every person. Will that time return again and what will that mean for your culture and society?

In short, stop reading our statements and questions about reading; it's time to investigate your own.

Works Cited

Chafe, Wallace L. 1985. "Linguistic Differences." In *Literacy, Language, and Learning: The Nature and Consequences of Reading and Writing.* Eds. David R. Olson, Nancy Torrance, and Angel Hilyard. Cambridge; New York; Melbourne: Cambridge University Press. 105–123.

Elbow, Peter. 1986. "Methodological Doubting and Believing: Contraries in Inquiry." In: *Embracing Contraries,* 253–300. NY: Oxford University Press.

Murray, Donald. 1991. "All Writing Is Autobiography." *College Composition and Communication,* February. 66–74.

Smith, Frank. 1981. "Myths of Writing." *Language Arts* 58.17 (October):792–98.

———. 1994. *Understanding Reading,* 5th edition. Hillsdale, NJ: Lawrence Erlbaum.

12

Discovery Reading Conversations About <u>Trifles</u>

Karen Schiff and Art Young

Dear Students,

In composition classes, it's so easy to get caught up in reading a text with an eye toward the-paper-that-is-to-be-written. We have been concerned about how that approach to reading short-circuits whatever wonder and joy you might have gotten out of that text for yourself. Thus, we developed an idea to encourage a more discovery-oriented approach to reading. Our idea is for each student to write a letter to another student about a course reading. Because everyone will write a letter, everyone will receive one too, and then each person will write a letter back as well. In both letters, it will be possible to explore thoughts about the text (or a particular part of it), though the conclusions may not be predictable at the start. You may not even come to any conclusions by the end of the letter; it's simply a tool to give your reading discoveries a place to appear.

Ironically, we're suggesting a structure for a writing assignment that aims precisely to get away from structure! Actually, though, our proposal outlines an open door through which thinking can pass, and every door needs a frame. We are not building a labyrinth through which there is only one way to walk, nor a maze in which you must choose the one correct path. If you walk through this door, you are the only one who will chart the territories of your reading. The door is truly open; we cannot predict what lies on the other side.

In keeping with the spirit of this assignment, we will write this book chapter as a series of E-mail messages to each other about the letters Karen's students have written in her English 102 (second semester composition) class. After all, these students' letters are the "class texts" that we ourselves hope to make discoveries about. Karen made two photocopies of her students' letters, and then she and Art each read them several times as they wrote E-mails back and forth. Although we have edited and rearranged some of our words, we have preserved our surprises, uncertainties, and even some asides. We also found that our written messages couldn't substitute for live conversations (and therefore, by analogy, for class discussion), conversations that we had regularly over coffee during spring 1999.

When you read our E-mail exchanges and the excerpts from the students' letters, you will get a glimpse into how we as teachers think about writing that comes from students who are in a course like the one you're probably taking now. In addition to letting you see what issues are important to us, we hope to raise issues that are important to you and on which you might further reflect on in class discussion or in brief letters or E-mail exchanges with your classmates.

Warm regards,

Karen and Art

Karen: I find I'm needing some clarification, Art. When we talk about "Discovery Reading," are we focusing on the kinds of discoveries that students can make when they read each others' writing about the class texts, or on the discoveries that students make when they're reading the class texts directly?

Art: Both, and more. That is, students make discoveries as they read the literary text, more discoveries (possibly) as they write about it, more discoveries as they read each others', more discoveries as they listen to class conversation, more discoveries as they reread the text after the written and oral conversations about the text, more discoveries as they read additional texts and hear other conversations. In many ways, I think this is the way that scholars develop knowledge no matter what field they're in—but often students do not experience the process this way. Often they are asked to produce an insightful academic essay about a literary text after only one or two private readings of it and maybe a teacher's lecture. To me, this traditional process alienates students from reading, from writing, from literature, and from animated conversation.

Karen: That makes immediate sense to me—often I can't even articulate what I *think* about something I've read until I've talked about it with someone else. So in Friday's class, I asked students to write letters to each other about a play we had just read (and performed in class), Susan Glaspell's *Trifles*. The assignment was very open; they could write to their partner about anything they were thinking, feeling, or wondering about the play. On the following Monday, their partner was to bring in a letter that they'd written back, and I had the students exchange their letters. After they read their pen pals' replies, I asked them to write and hand in some responses to questions about what they were hoping for and surprised about in the letters, etc. I thought this information might help me "read" their letters.

Art: I'm not sure I know the play *Trifles*. What's it about? If we're going to use this play in our case study, I'll need a copy myself, and we'll need to write a summary for our readers. Will you do that, Karen?

Karen: Sure, no problem. You know, I wrote an expository-style summary when we were still thinking of writing this book chapter in the usual essay form. After we started writing letters instead, I reread it, and I was appalled at how clunky and boring it sounded. Much less engaging ("juicy"?) to read than our E-mail messages or the letters that the students wrote. So now I'll put the old one aside, take a deep breath, and dive into trying to describe the play from memory, to *you* instead of to some anonymous sea of potential readers of this book. I hope it will reflect a more "discovery reading" mode of thinking and writing.

What's *Trifles* about, you ask? It's essentially the story of how two women figure out that a third woman has killed her husband. They don't ever say it out loud, nor do they have any "hard evidence"— they work by finding clues in the woman's domestic "trifles" such as drab housekeeping, unfinished canning, erratic quilt stitching, and the final clue: a dead canary in her sewing basket. (They figure out that her husband killed it by wringing its neck, and that this must have been the last straw. Mrs. Wright had loved singing when she was younger, but we get the picture that Mr. Wright had killed that spirit in her, and now that he'd killed the last singer in the house, that was it.)

Well, the women don't even really "work" to find clues—they just discover (!) these things as they wait for three men (who include the town sheriff and one of the women's husbands) to complete their official investigations. The men don't find a motive, but they do scoff at what they think are the insignificant things the women are occupying themselves with as they wait. The women decide to conceal what they've discovered, again without saying so out loud.

All of this mirrors the situation that the murderess had found herself in—belittled by her husband (who presumably wouldn't let her sing anymore) and silenced by the power he presumably held over her. (This reminds me of how the Sheriff, I think, says to one of the women that she is "married to the Law." Since the play is set in the early twentieth century, men did hold many legal powers over women.) I keep saying "presumably" because we never see these main characters, who are named Mr. and Mrs. Wright. Their absence means that the questions they inspire must be solved by us; the Wrights are not available to give any "final word" on the story. The letters of their surname inspire the question: was Mrs. Wright *right* to get out of the situation by getting rid of her husband, or *wrong* to murder, regardless of the circumstances? What are alternatives (a question which requires examining the situation in greater detail, becoming conscious of the emotional and social contexts in which it exists)?

Art: Thanks. Something interesting happens when you say, "This reminds me of . . ." and then you talk about a line in the play that happens to reveal an important underlying dynamic that comes from the social context of the time. If you hadn't done that, how would I know that the play was set in early twentieth-century America?

Some of your students, in their letters I've been reading, do similar things in their letters to each other. For example, I like the way John/Lisa make connections to other events in society—when John writes about the murderer Charles Manson on a TV special and Lisa writes that she "discovered" the fact that "most murderers probably have a story similar to Mrs. Wright's background." Does she really believe that? Do I believe that?

Karen: Well, I'll leave that question to you . . . I don't know that it's actually possible to answer it, anyway. How can you know the "truth" about the backgrounds of "most murderers"? But here's another example of a student drawing a great connection between the play's plot and a larger social dynamic. This student, Susan, takes a little while to get to her specific idea, but I think that's part of the process. We warm up to our thoughts as we write, *n'est-ce pas*? Thinking seldom follows a direct path, anyway. Here is Susan's letter:

LeToya,
Although I didn't get to see the live performance, this play made me think of how many common injustices we have in our society. They seem to just run rampaging through the streets. I am not too sure exactly what Mr. W did to Mrs. W, but it certainly caused some form of mental trauma. She should have left. . . . but now he's dead and she is going to have to pay the price. It makes me think about women who are in abusive relationships and eventually kill their abuser. Even if they had reported it to the police time and time again, they still go to prison on murder charges. That is so unfair. They will even get a longer prison sentence, without parole, than a man who brutally raped and murdered a woman for no apparent reason. It just isn't fair. Why are men so demeaning to women? They think we can't handle ourselves, or have no brains. I would like to really show them up. I have writer's cramp. Oh well. I suppose I don't have too much more to say.
Later, Susan

Art: Yes, that's an interesting letter. Susan brings up several complexities of justice and gender. And though her mind wanders, it stays close to the task at hand. But what about when students go completely away from the assignment? What's the limit? Or how do we as teachers help students to find a good balance? Should we provide any guidelines?

Like what about Meredith's letter to Jeff? She writes, "I think that you are a dork and your feeling sucks." It was at the end of a paragraph. Jeff had written in part to Meredith that "Women should know their place and not get involved in men's jobs." As you know from our conversation last week, Meredith's comment amused me as I watched both Meredith and Jeff spar about feminist issues in the play.

On the other hand, I question my own amusement. Calling another student a "dork" might lead to even more crude personal attacks. What if she had called him a "bastard" or a "prick"? This is very far from academic writing, indeed, and it might be even further from what classroom conversation should be all about. So, should the teacher step in and say to Meredith that this kind of language is not allowed in these letters?

Karen: I think that her "dork" comment and Jeff's comment about women "know[ing] their place" which precipitated it are, knowing them, actually just good-natured and off-the-cuff. Jeff writes, "I'm just kidding" and both of their "attacks" end with incomplete sentences or words. They could even be flirting, or simply trying to spice up the writing assignment somehow. Who knows? I've been amazed to find out sometimes that there have been romances stirring among people in class. Strange, though, that I should be surprised; I remember when I was in college that romance, or even the possibility of flirting with someone, played a big part in classroom dynamics.

But I'm concerned about your questions about whether these sorts of attacks demand some teacher intervention. Although I just wrote that Meredith and Jeff are writing in a good-natured way, how can I be sure that that's what's going on? Maybe they're really pissed at each other, or grappling with some gender issues that the play is bringing out, and they can only address it by *seemingly* harmless jokes about each other as men or women. But the thing is, we (as teachers, or as readers in general) *can't* know. So I think it's pretty dangerous to start saying things like "this kind of language is not allowed in these letters." Especially if we want students to free up their writing.

In any case, I'm more concerned about what I as a teacher should do when students are clearly *not* writing frankly to each other. It's much easier to deal with words on the page than words not on the page. I think it's hard to tell when students are really writing frankly.

Tell me something about your point that the gender issues in the play perhaps make the gender of the student writers more important; I remember from our conversation last week that this was neat. You might consider the exchange between Stefanie and Josh. I like how they're writing to each other, but then I start to wonder . . .

Art: I like the "discovery" Stefanie makes about the canarie (misspelled!) at the bottom of her letter—and the connection to Minnie Foster, Mrs. Wright's maiden name.

Dear Josh,
The canarie to me was a symbol of life for Minnie Foster, and later a sign of death for Mrs. Wright. The bird, while it was still alive, was similar to Minnie Foster—they were both pretty and cheerful and possesed the gift of song.
Stefanie

And then I find it interesting the way Josh makes a "discovery" that I didn't see in any other student letters—that the real guilt belongs to the two women—because it was all their fault—they could have "prevented this misfortune" but did not.

Stefanie,
The ladies thought that if perhaps they had intervened in Mrs. Wright's life, then perhaps she would have found something to live for. For as it must be observed, the killing of the canary signified the end to all that Mrs. Wright wanted from this world. Murdering her husband in punishment for murdering her life so long ago was a springboard for her to exit this world, which she viewed as cold and bitter. The ladies were aware of this domino effect and held guilt in their hearts because they knew they could have prevented this misfortune. Josh

In one sense he is blaming the victims of society's sexism, but in another sense, what he says complicates the play and the actions of the women in ways I had not thought about before. Thanks Josh! I think it is interesting that Stefanie agrees when she writes Josh: "I agree with your opinion that the greatest crime committed was the ladies' inability to help Mrs. Wright break free." Good God, does she really believe that that was "the greatest crime"? Or is she just trying to be agreeable and say something nice back to Josh? Is Stefanie being silenced or allowing herself to be silenced on this matter—by Josh, by social conditioning, by (heaven forbid) the nature of this letter exchange assignment?

Karen: I'm not sure how to interpret Stefanie's agreeability. It could be some veiled type of flirtation, as we've been talking about it, but it could be that she's just plain trying hard to push herself to see the new point of view that Josh is suggesting. The question you raise—that maybe she's pushing the idea too far—could have to do with a general wish to do the assignment well. She was quite earnest about her work. I am concerned, though, that she's playing a stereotypically submissive feminine role by being so agreeable. But I found that most of the students, no matter what gender they were, said they were trying to affirm each others' ideas.

Art: So what? What does it mean to say that most of the students were trying to affirm one another? To write that they "agree" with opinions that they don't really agree with? But then I can't help noticing the irony in our discussing gender issues about when men and women converse. Are we flirting? Let me quickly return to our subject—the student letters. I thought I detected a different kind of affirmation in the letters of two women students, Susan and LeToya.

Karen: Maybe all intellectual work is really just flirting with ideas. I mean, a good conversation in class or over E-mail can be pretty zippy. But about Susan and LeToya—they did some serious female bonding; they earnestly explored the details of the play and discovered that they were allies in indignation.

Because LeToya had been in class on the day we performed the play, she filled Susan in on what happened. Her letter got more daring in terms of interpretation toward the end; I think that she was also settling into the writing (because her grammar gets more lax, which indicates to me that she was relaxing and letting things flow more).

Susan,

The play itself was good. While we were talking and the questions came up as to why the ladies didn't tell the men that they found some information. Well what I thought was that the women felt that the men didn't feel that women should get involved in things like murder investigations or things of serious matter. Men in those days felt that women should be in the kitchen and handling the children, which is not so. Men just haven't discovered yet that women are smarter than they are and just settle with it. The women didn't say anything because they didn't want to hurt the men's ego.

I just think Mrs. Wright was fed up with Mr. Wright for a long time and when he killed her bird she just snapped and kill the man. I think he deserve it but she should have tried and cover it up and then just move on with her life. She can always get another bird. LeToya

LeToya's position resembles Susan's—the woman should not be punished for the murder because the man had been causing her too much pain for too long. But her closing comment, "She can always get another bird," is startling—it looks into a future moment that isn't included in the play. It could also be an argument for why Mrs. Wright *shouldn't* have killed her husband over a dead canary, but that's just my further interpretation of the play based on riffing off of LeToya's letter. Also, after I read the play, I'm not convinced that she could just get another bird—at least not one that Mr. Wright would let live.

Susan's response is immediately affirming . . . and it gets back to the play! She again asserts a connection with contemporary gender dynamics, and even engages in some male bashing that she might not have dared to do if her pen pal had been male. Here's the whole letter:

LeToya,

I agree completely with your point of view of men vs. women. In that era, and even today, the majority of men felt that a woman's place was in the home and that a woman had no form of societal brains. In all reality, women are probably smarter than men just because they have the ability to look at more than just one possibility or look at a situation from more than just one angle. In all reality, the ego that the women are always trying to prevent hurting is the only thing a man really grasps and feels. If you impact their ego, you make a connection. If the women were to have done the men's jobs, the crime would have been revealed in detail much sooner.

I don't have much more to say.

Later, Susan

Of course, the idea that the women were aware of the details of the crime more than the men was a basic and obvious point in the play. But Susan gives it a twist when she phrases it in terms of the women doing the men's jobs—this is where the reading of the play starts to come from an original, or discovery-oriented, angle.

Art: I like the way LeToya and Susan get into identifying with the woman and thinking she should not be punished—and giving their reasons for it—and also the way they stereotype men (which the play does also). But as I read this exchange I thought of the broader issues of teachers and students as readers: where else in traditional classrooms would students read this kind of writing with such frank honesty—and from peers? Where else would teachers get a sense of what students are "really thinking"? What perspective does the teacher gain on the classroom community by reading these letters from all 22 students—some of whom radically disagree with each other? Once the teacher knows about the radical disagreements (Mrs. Wright should not be punished; she should be punished), where does the class go from here? Is expressing opinions enough?

Is LeToya black? Does she regularly leave the endings off of verb forms? If so, should the teacher point this out to her?

Karen: Well, I think some of the point is that not all the radical disagreements will get settled. Maybe some of the unique positions could be aired in class, so that everyone will get a chance to see a point of view that they did not originally have.

On your other topic, yes, LeToya is African American. But I must say, my first thought is to ask, why do you want to know? I mean, what difference does it make? I mean this seriously or curiously as well as defensively, because I have an impulse to protect LeToya from whatever negative stereotypes might be lurking. (And I wonder: where does that impulse come from? What does it imply?) I know you're a kind and open person, but I'm concerned that our readers won't know you—I'm learning that much of this letter-writing exercise depends upon knowing the person you're writing with so you can get a general sense of how to judge their tone and underlying meaning.

Art: Okay—and I'm also concerned that our readers won't know LeToya—so maybe we should correct all surface errors before publishing this piece? And yet, our bumblings and mistakes make writing conversational—a felt sense of personal engagement with other unique human beings—a sense not always found in formal academic writing. However, in every class I teach, some students don't think I'm doing my job unless I give them lots of criticism on everything they write. I guess I'm asking that when we assign letter writing for the purpose of discovery reading, are we only doing it to help students make discoveries about the reading? Aren't we also doing it to help students become better academic writers?

Karen: I think it's tricky. I mean, as writing instructors, we're supposed to be teaching students about writing "properly," but this letter-writing assignment won't work if we're correcting them at every turn. I mean, if we're always making it seem as if they've done something wrong, they won't feel as free to write what they're thinking. It's a question of which skills to focus on.

I'd say the same thing in response to your pointing out Stefanie's spelling mistake ("canarie"), by the way. For this kind of writing, it's best to let it go. I mean, I didn't correct the spelling mistakes in your messages until it was time to go to press! True that we're peers, and that I'm not trying to teach you spelling, but we *are* trying to learn something from each other, and calling attention to each other's mistakes would take away from more interesting stuff—just as it does in oral conversation.

But I'm also amazed at how the identities of these student writers have become so important. Gender and race are turning out to play a big part in how they're writing, or how they're interacting with each other about what they're reading. Makes sense—I mean, they're *people* writing these letters! And so are we; I mean, I had quite a little quandary going about whether to say anything about the errors I found in your messages. Since you're older than I am, and in a higher rank in the profession (and maybe also because you're male?), I found myself hesitating. Sexism, racism, agism, classism—it's all a way of saying that who we are has an impact on other people and on what we do. That sounds so wishy-washy, though. Do you know what I'm getting at? The "conditioning" that you wrote about in the message about Stefanie's response to Josh can be insidiously invisible and can have an immense influence.

Art: Do you mean "ageism"? Oh, that hurts! But what about when two men discuss the gender dynamics of the play? So far we've only talked about two women writing or a woman and a man.

Karen: Okay, so I'm not immune to spelling mistakes either. In terms of two men writing to each other, I discovered stuff in the letters that students wrote to me about the letter-writing activity that I found quite troubling. It didn't occur to me until we were putting this book chapter together that it might be connected to gender dynamics. Two male students from different pairs wrote to me about how their male partner seemed to be dense about something in the play. But when I read the letters that they wrote to their partners, they were full of praise and affirmation—they gave no indication of their intellectual disappointment or even frustration. Here is an example:

Brad and Gene are writing partners. Brad writes to Gene (in part) about the feelings he gets from the play. ("I also thought about how sad Mrs. Wright must have been in that house. She had nothing real important to do. There was no noise, [no] nothing and maybe she knew that her husband was the cause of it so she killed him.") Gene writes back about how the police "become so obstinately cemented into the 'proper' way that things are to be done." His letter starts out with the word, "Yes," but that's as far as he goes in actually addressing the things that Brad is saying. In his letter to me, Gene confesses,

1. I was hoping to find some affirmation of the lack of attention paid to the women in the play.

2. In writing Brad back, I took the message that I thought he was trying to portray, and added onto it.

3. I think that several of the key elements were lost on him.

I read (3) and I think maybe Gene himself could discover more about the "key elements" in the play if he read Brad's letter more thoughtfully. In fact, Gene would find "affirmation of the lack of attention paid to the women in the play."

In writing this, I realize that I actually do think this letter-writing assignment does have an agenda. As a teacher, I'm hoping that students will consider each others' opinions seriously and then write back with their own opinions that have been inspired by reading the student's letter in some way. Gene just uses his response letter as an excuse to go off about the thing he thinks is important, kind of like making a journal entry or doing a freewrite—as if interaction with a partner is a waste of time. Is he resisting the assignment or the opportunity for collaborative learning, or have I been unclear in my goals?

Art: I don't know, but I'm interested in this idea of resistance. Is it resisting the process of reading for discovery, or resisting the writing assignment (and aren't they the same thing)?

Karen: Here's another kind of resistance that I found fun (because it totally breaks the bounds of propriety). In her letter to Mike, Raechel is getting away from the assignment, but I'm secretly psyched that she has bucked the system. I'm intrigued by her sentence that questions the worth of the entire assignment. You might call this "resistance," and it might be . . . but it also contains some creative thinking. On the other hand, I can't believe she's suggesting a better murder plan—this could be another example of what Stefanie was doing: affirming without being critical. Isn't this just another type of resistance, along the lines of what Gene was doing (or not doing) with Brad?

Mike,

I hope that you had a fun weekend and remembered to write me back.

I agree with you about coming up with a better or, at least, a more creative way of killing her husband. If she (Mrs. Wright) would have had a better way of handling her situation, she may not have ended up in jail. Mrs. Wright could have gotten rid of the dead body and no one would ever have found it. She could have bought as many canaries as she wanted and decorated her home more cheerfully.

This was the weirdest assignment I have ever gotten. What's the point? Guess what? We (my sorority) is still going to have the Jimmy Buffett party, but I do not know when. I promise I will tell you when so that you can come to it. Raechel

Art: So, Karen, we want our students to "own" their letters—does this mean they can "flirt" about sorority parties on class time when they are supposed to be writing about *Trifles*? (I'm also thinking about the exchange between Scott and Bill: Scott writes: "The play should be taken as it is written. I believe this short play was not meant to be picked apart like some kind of great work. I think we have spent enough time on it already." And Bill responds: "You are totally correct in your analysis of the discussion of the play. It does not have as deep a meaning as Dr. Schiff would have us believe.")

So, each in their own way—Gene, Raechel, and Scott—resist your letter-writing assignment. Although as teachers we are disappointed when students appear not to take our assignments seriously, maybe this is a healthy thing. Maybe we are misreading these students' letters. It would be nice to get student perceptions on these questions. I wonder if the students who read this book chapter would be interested in giving us their point of view on these issues.

Or maybe this letter-writing assignment is just not a good one altogether! Is it too manipulative; that is, just playing games with students as a captive audience?

Karen: I think all assignments have an element of manipulation in them; we'd like the students to think in some new way or about some new thing. I don't think that it's a problem in general. The main problem, as I see it, would be if students try to psych out the assignment; it might result in their not actually writing freely (i.e., in the spirit of discovery that we've been discussing).

Art: Students—maybe all of us in school situations—have a difficulty "writing freely." We want to know how our writing will be assessed. Here's another way to put it: when students write a critical essay or a term paper or a book review or an essay test to me as the teacher, or vicariously to some unknown (except for me) academic audience, I know how to read it, to grade it, to criticize it for grammar and content. In one sense, although a student essay may be several pages long, it is "easier" to read than these letters.

Karen: So then, how *do* we "assess" these letters? I think that we *respond* to them, same as we're asking the students to do.

Susanna who also teaches 102, asked me the other day, "How can you tell a student that you're giving them a good grade because you can feel their mind churning in their paper, even if it's not very well written?" I told her, "You can just tell them that you can feel their mind churning. They'll know what you're talking about, because they felt it too." So I think the same thing is possible in terms of telling "good" from "bad" or "mediocre" letters.

Art: That makes sense, but if I were to ask students to write letters to each other in order to help understand the play *Trifles* and how different people might interpret it, I'm not sure I'd know how to read those letters or tell my students how to read them. I say read, learn from each other, express your ideas in an informal, conversational voice, and develop knowledge about this play collaboratively. "Great," they say to me. "What the hell does he want?" they ask each other. "How are you going to grade it?" they ask me. I say I'm not going to grade it—just count it as part of your "class participation" grade. So then they say to themselves, this kind of writing mustn't be very important, so why should I put thought and energy into writing these letters. And if the students don't put thought and energy into writing them, who, for God's sake, wants to read them? Certainly not me.

Karen: I was tickled when you wrote, "'Great,' they say to me. 'What the hell does he want?' they ask each other." I think I try to maintain an illusion that students will see the inherent value in this kind of writing without my having to be a cheerleader for it. But just because it's fun to buck the convention (of writing with a formula) doesn't mean that the utility or the unique fun of writing to discover more in reading is clear.

Art: I think some cheerleading needs to go into it. I also think students have a right to know why we ask them to do the things we do. What interests me is that when I assign a long book report or a term paper, students don't question it—they know that's the way things are supposed to be—even though they may not know why a particular teacher is asking them to do it.

On the other hand, ask students to write letters, or E-mails, or freewrites, and they think you are piling on extra work, or busy work ("playing games" with them), and this isn't their fault—the system encourages this attitude. So I try to explain that I've "discovered" in reading this kind of student writing over the past 30 years that there is more value in it than many of the term papers I've read. Most students, I'm afraid, are very skeptical when a teacher talks about "the unique fun of writing to discover more in reading." The only way to have such resistant students understand the concept is to give them opportunities to experience it. With the experience, we hope, comes understanding, appreciation, and proficiency in using language as a thinking and communication tool.

Dear Students,

We have learned a lot from reading Karen's students' letters and then writing about them to each other. This experience is what we try to capture in our title, "Discovery Reading: Conversations About *Trifles*," a title that did not emerge until very late in the process of preparing this book chapter for you to read. We learned more about our teaching; about our students' perceptions; about ways of reading our students' writing; about ways of interpreting *Trifles*; about the issue of gender, race, and status in our classrooms, in literary texts, in our lives; about the importance of social context in learning. For example, Karen knew all her students by their first names; Art had never met any of them; so Art and Karen were reading from different perspectives and asking different questions of each other about Karen's students and their writing.

Of course, we hope that you learned some things too in reading our chapter and discussing it (either orally or in writing) with classmates. If you would like to consider further some of the issues our chapter raised, we'd be happy to receive letters from you. We know we have much more to learn about the concepts of discovery reading and discovery writing, and you can help us. Just let us know some things about yourself as well as what you're thinking, and we'll plan to write you back.

Best Wishes

Karen and Art

P.S. If your teacher asks your entire class to write us letters, please coordinate with us ahead of time and send them as one package. Then we'll respond with one letter that addresses your class's interests and concerns. You'll find us at: Department of English, Box 340523, Clemson University, Clemson, SC 29634-0523.

13

Angles of Revision
Using Purposeful, Dramatic Reading for Revision

Devan Cook

Jenny writes her parents because she has run out of funds 5 weeks before the end of term. She thinks she's said what she wanted to say: thanked her parents for their call on her birthday but relayed the sad information that her card (with check) must have gotten lost in the mail; asked how her dog Baffles was doing; and made sure to remind them that she is now working fewer hours at WalMart in order to concentrate on school—catching up with schoolwork after her spring trip to Mardi Gras has been tough.

To her, the letter is sweet and charming, written with just the right touch. But Jenny decides to let her roommate read the letter first. Her roommate reads carefully, then tells Jenny that if *her* child sent a letter like this, she wouldn't send a dime. Jenny's letter is a lot like the one she sent her parents last year, her roommate says, and her parents were amused and annoyed—mostly annoyed.

So Jenny and her roommate rewrite the letter. After a few days, money arrives with a stern but fond little note.

Jenny shares 10 percent of her check with her roommate.

Let's look at connections between reading and revising: in particular, how reading can improve and ease revision. I'll talk about whys and hows, give you some hints and plans, tell you what's worked for me. Please remember that reading processes, like writing processes, are highly individual, while sharing contours, a set of experiences: prewriting, drafting, and the activities that make up revision—rereading, perhaps more research, rethinking, response, reading aloud, additional drafting or redrafting, more response . . . and so on.

Here's a point of interest and clarification that you'll want to keep in mind as you read this essay, which contains many references to writing as well as reading: Separating reading and writing is probably impossible. In fact, it's been suggested that writing and reading are different physical manifestations of the same cognitive process (the construction and reconstruction of meaning and sense from or in inscribed cues) (Berlin 1990, 220). Of course, what our bodies do when we read and write seems about as unlike as cooking and eating, but in our minds, reading and writing don't look that different. In both, there's the stab at meaning, the slippage between what we're trying to say and what we write, between what the author thinks she wrote, what she actually wrote, and how we read those words (Harris 1999, 117–22).

Purposes for Reading and Revising

Our purposes for revising determine how we revise—to meet the expectations of an audience (like Jenny's parents); to get a better grade in a class where revision is required; to satisfy ourselves that we've said what we wanted; to further explore our subject, to twist and pull and shape and map or metaphorically look under rocks, just to see what's there.

Similarly, our purposes for reading determine how we read. When Jenny reread the letter mentioned above, she read as herself, aware of what she needed—how hard she'd tried to budget, all the things that had come up unexpectedly like car repairs and impromptu trips to the beach—as well as how easy it is to pull the wool over your parents' eyes. But her roommate, whose purpose was to read as if she were a parent, poked holes in what Jenny thought was a perfect appeal and then helped rewrite her letter so it would say more of what her parents might expect to read.

Not all reading is alike, nor is there *one* way to read. But based on the episode above, we'll hypothesize that our point of view when we read helps determine how we could incorporate reading processes when we write. Unfortunately, we don't always have a helpful roommate. What matters, though, is that just as Jenny's roommate provided a valuable service by role-playing a parental viewpoint, thus giving her the benefit of a different perspective from which to revise her letter, it's clear that this matter of viewpoint or angle of vision is important in both reading and writing.

> It has often astounded me how a piece of writing by someone we don't know can immediately transport me back to a place in the past (Kim).

Personas in Reading and Revising

Kim's comment (above) reveals how closely related place and reading and writing can be: in fact, the word *topic* comes from the Greek *topos,* meaning place. A topic, then, is a location of meaning. But what then? Topics are fairly dull ideas, something we all had to do in third grade when we wrote reports about weaving or China or copper mining. But a topic also suggests perspective, a point of view, an angle of vision—and all those ways of seeing suggest a person. It's clear that we may find something extra by imagining people or personalities when we read, rather than simply places to stand while looking at a text. In other English, literature, or writing classes, you've probably heard references to a piece of writing's "speaker" or "persona" or "voice," implying not only a position but also a role, a set of beliefs, something that brings the point of view in question home and gives us enough information to try it on for size.

Reading to write is role-playing. In a play, characters are people who occupy positions on stage: "from where *I* stand . . ." In reading we try on different voices and personalities, which Douglas Wells (1998) calls "masks": "Readers, like actors, do a sort of oral interpretation of writing by imagining its vocal quality, tone, speed, volume, and pitch based on the written symbols" (50). As Wells points out, *persona* is the Latin word for *mask*.

So we wear personas—masks—as well as take positions when we read and write. In this way, reading and writing resemble acting. How can we use this information to make our reading and revising processes work more smoothly?

The persona we adopt—the role-playing we do—when we read and write is one major aspect of the drama of rhetoric. In composition classes we are likely to hear or talk about writing from a rhetorical perspective: its audience, purpose(s), speaker, and subject. But we rarely talk about the fact that skilled readers-who-write read that way, too—conflating these two concepts, perhaps unconsciously. That is, skilled readers-who-write read rhetorically, and in doing so are engaged in processes—imagining voices, trying on roles, assuming positions—that are very like those they engage in while writing.

Rhetoric provides what may seem to be a new and different way of looking at—reading—anything, including your writing. More than likely, though, you already engage in rhetorical readings of the sea of text—billboards, TV commercials, music videos, websites—in which we are all afloat. Rhetorical reading is one way we swim through this sea. For instance, perhaps you are not the target audience for the current Viagra commercial. But because you know how to read cues in the ad, you can also read the audience—male, married, World War II generation. And from the actor's (politician's? veteran's?) attitude, you also read the ad's purpose: honest, courageous, caring men take Viagra when a physical need arises (or doesn't arise!).

Daily we sort through tides of text, swimming semi-consciously, in just this way. Items that land in my mental "keep" file, for instance, I then reimagine to see how they might fit in with my life, my personal subjects and purposes, creating my own little scenarios or playlets. Can I eat that breakfast bar while driving 70 mph down the interstate? Does the on-line bookseller take American Express? Are those chocolates filled with Idaho huckleberries? Am I really the audience the creator of this text has envisioned?

Rhetorical (role-playing) reading like this is just as efficient and effective when we write, in or out of school, as it is at other times. It helps us explore our ideas more fully, mark out our discursive territory with more authority, clarify and order our thinking, and gives us other thinkers to talk back to and word-play with. And because it does those things, reading rhetorically—adopting the masks that speaker, subject, audience, and purpose wear—gives us suggestions about how we might revise our writing: think of Jenny's letter home.

Fine, you say, but that sounds like English teacher talk. (It does, too—see how easily you stepped into that persona?) How is all this going to help you do something with the paper you wanted to do a better job on, the one you liked, the one you hoped would earn a good grade? It still seems to be missing something, but you're not sure what. You like it pretty well, but it's got no flair, no zing, no sizzle, no voice (okay, no life), and nobody—including the polite people in your peer response group in class, including you—knows how to improve what you've written. You could, of course, turn it in as is. You had higher hopes for it, but how can you read like a teacher, or like an audience you don't know?

Role-playing reading—as speaker, subject, purpose, and audience—can help.

Speakers in Reading for Revision

You've probably had the experience of reading something so strongly voiced that you heard it. You had no trouble putting on the character's mask, playing the role, speaking for the character in your mind. Holden Caulfield in *Catcher in the Rye* does that for many people—he did it for me. The first time a voice from a piece you're reading enters your head uninvited, it may be kind of creepy; yet for many people, it's one of reading's greatest pleasures.

You want your writing to have a strong voice. As Kate Ronald (1999), an experienced writer and writing teacher, says, "I worry that I'm responding to something in my students' writing that I'm not telling them about—their style, the sound of their voices on paper" (171). She calls such writing "'writing where somebody's home,' as opposed to writing that's technically correct but where there's 'nobody home,' no life, no voice" (171). So voice, persona, is very likely something the particular piece you're working on needs: that's why it may not sound alive. And yes, researched essays are no different from short stories in that they too have voices readers carry around in their heads like Holden's—try reading Maya Angelou or Gloria Anzaldúa or Richard Rodriguez or Edward Abbey.

The Voice in the Text, the Voice in Your Head

You get something of the voice from reading that you hear in your mind's ear into your writing by reading and rereading after you've written a draft. I often reread sources just to get the voice right before I start to revise. Pick sources for voice: don't be satisfied until you find someone whose writing "sounds" the way you want yours to, and immerse—soak, drown—yourself in reading that person's work. If you want to sound like an expert in your field, read an expert whose writing you admire.

If you read with focus and concentration for several hours before you revise, that voice—its pauses, rhythm, phrasing, vocabulary, tone, breath—will begin to be part of you, and some of it will begin to be part of what you write. You aren't copying, plagiarizing, or pretending to be someone else: you're role-playing but still yourself, just as a great Shakespearean actor does not become Shakespeare but makes his characters his or her own and with performance adds something unique to them while following Shakespeare's script and stage directions. Reading in this way is easy and natural; it's reading to hear your voice, your knowledge, and the voice of the text's speaker talking, blending together in your mind. Of course that happens often, but here you undertake this reading purposefully: your voice and that of the persona you're adopting by reading will also blend in your writing and revising.

Reading for Form, Sound, and Rhythm to Shape Meaning

Urk, grunt, bang, hissssss . . . Sounds have meanings; when we talk, when we write.

So read your draft aloud. How does it sound to your ear? Find yourself a patient friend or spouse or roommate, and read again. Both of you should listen. A hard, clipped rhythm comes from lots of clanging consonants and short choppy words; it conveys urgency, force, tension, or drive. A soft, slow pace from vowels or aspirated consonants like "p" and "t" can give a dreamy feel. How does that tie in with what you're saying? Surfeits of esses whisper something sinister and sneaky, and a grillion gobs of greasy gees gag nearly every reader.

You can prevent this—or take advantage if that's what you want—by getting there first: read aloud. Make sure the voice mask your readers will hear is close to the one you think you've constructed in the writing.

Reading, Writing, Talk

Good ideas and excitement and pleasure in writing all come from talk, whether with a text or a person.

> [Tracy] Kidder writes with a realness—nothing phoney to me. I felt like I was sitting and talking over a cup of coffee, not trying to stay awake in a boring lecture (Jan).

When I have a writing problem I want to solve or an idea I want to explore or a game I want to play (like playing the dozens, talking's a game), I talk to lots of people. One conversation, one source, or one triggering event is rarely enough.

Revision is recursive; that is, we look from a new perspective, a different mask, and when we do that we keep, in a sense, starting over, rethinking, reviewing, rereading, rewriting. So as we revise we continue to need the conversational triggers that reading provides. Author Nathaniel Hawthorne thought of his reader as "a friend, a kind and apprehensive, though not the closest friend, [who] is listening to our talk" (quoted in Tompkins 1999, 384). And like Jan, essayist Jane Tompkins writes that she too considers the reader/writer relationship a friendly and generative one:

> I feel I'm being nourished by [readers], that I'm being allowed to enter into a personal relationship with them. Then I can match my own experience up with theirs, feel cousin to them, and say, yes, that's how it is (Tompkins 1999, 383)

We verify our ideas by trying on those of others, do reality checks, touch base, and see where we or others stand when we talk. We try out ways to say things: read, talk, revise.

Subjects in Reading for Revision

My single largest problem as a writer is that I write before I know what I'm talking about. This also may be my greatest strength: getting started isn't a problem. I begin drafting to sketch out where I am in a particular project and what I know about that place: this gives me direction. When we write, we need to map out borders: the territory occupied by other writers and thinkers, the shape and size of our own piece of writing, who we're writing to and why.

As I draft, I begin to find holes. It's like working a jigsaw puzzle only to discover that a rambunctious 2-year-old has hidden puzzle pieces all over the house. I can tell what's missing, and I can make educated guesses about where I might find pieces, since I've often played detective behind this 2-year-old. More often than not, I find the missing puzzle pieces when I reread material I first looked at before I began writing, or when I read related material that I hadn't found before I started writing. I can take the new piece and complete the puzzle. Or I realize that the new piece changes the whole shape of what I'm working on. It's not a rock, it's a zebra, and it's going someplace!

This process may sound nutty to you, but it's what many writers actually do—you may do this yourself. On going back and rereading material, I always find new things, sometimes even new main points. As Gertrude Stein said about writing, "You can't say the same thing twice. The second time it sounds different precisely because it is the second time" (quoted in Padgett 1997, 45).

Refining Subjects

First readings have already shaped my thoughts and changed my behavior because I've done some writing that has further changed my thoughts.

So I go back to my sources: reading and writing have revised me. Books, poems, and articles I've read many times are marked up red, black, green, pale blue, dark blue, lavender—a different color denotes a different reading, and during most of them I've underlined or argued about or vehemently agreed with a different section, or found a heretofore unremarkable section especially useful. My perspective on my subject's shape changes because I'm not who I was, because my mind's eye alights on different features of a text: that's what I find out when I read to revise. When we do this we are, in a sense, reimagining or recreating the subject.

Reading to recheck fact is also useful if not nearly so high flown. When we read, we—in renewed guises or updated and changed personas—are not only looking at our subjects or topics or locations differently; we're revisiting the subject, maybe even reconversing with it as we nod our heads or sigh and scrawl a rebuttal in the margins. We garble, confuse, and misread: reading for revision helps us straighten out facts and not be embarrassed by silly mistakes while giving us a chance to unsnarl our essay's threads of thought and argument.

The Value in Reading Off the Subject

It's 2 a.m. Your problem-child essay shivers neglected on your desk, while you snuggle in bed reading the latest mystery or romance or thriller. You need to go to sleep; you needed to be asleep 2 hours ago; you have a big test early tomorrow morning. But you can't put the book down. At least you're relaxing.

And suddenly you know exactly how to make your essay perfect. You're not exactly sure what happened, what you were reading to fire synapses in a uniquely productive way. You get up, rummage in your desk, scribble down your ideas. The next morning you are proud to see that this new approach or addition to your essay will do the trick, amaze your friends, and make you proud.

Of course this happens at other times, too: for me, it's when I'm running or showering (and one friend swears she gets her best writing ideas when taking her trash to the dumpster!). But it happens to me more often when I'm reading.

> Everything that I read makes me think about the subject that I just read (John).

If only we knew what we'd done so we could do it again! I love the way the mind makes connections without my having to do much work, so I've learned how to take advantage of the process:

1. I work hard on first drafts—research, prewrite, draft, reread, fill-in-the-blanks, start over, and so on.

2. During this time and after it, I read whatever I want—something highly entertaining—for a minimum of an hour a day.

Perhaps this works because it gives my brain something to do, something to occupy or even anesthetize it, while it's also working on the problem essay (our brains multi-task). Perhaps it works because it puts a different mask on the subject, covers a discussion of writing or reading theory with a mask of English mystery or alien invasion. Perhaps when I read I adopt a different voice, and therefore a different perspective on the subject. Perhaps none of these is true.

This procedure is effective if you allow enough time for it. Usually after about 24 hours, I will have an idea. It may not be the solution to problems with my draft, but reading will point to a pathway, show me where I need to go.

Or as Donald Murray (1999), a well-known teacher of writing, suggests, "[R]ead widely as well as deeply . . . The best ideas . . . come from connecting information from different disciplines. We should also be bottom feeders, gobbling up everything that comes our way" (354).

Purposes in Reading for Revision

Usually, when we read and when we write, we have more than one purpose. Jenny, the impoverished letter writer with whom this chapter began, needed her parents to send money. She also wanted to send her love and let them know that even though she'd had a temporary setback, she was growing up and becoming more independent.

But her first attempt at satisfying these potentially conflicting purposes in one short letter failed: lack of clarity about purposes (or trying to oversimplify them, as we do when we say we're writing only because we have to, because we need a loan or a grade or to fulfill a requirement) often causes writing problems. Here's how reading can help.

Act It Out: Read Your Draft Aloud

Your voice will let you know what your purposes are. Does the tone of your writing support what your voice is saying? What do your listeners think? Though she herself didn't see it, Jenny's tone—too jovial, which made her sound as though she had something to hide—undercut all her reasons for writing by making some of them seem false.

Read to Discover How Other Writers Achieve Purposes

What are they doing that you can do, too? How are these writers envisioning the part you wish your writing to play? Even seemingly small matters in a text, like syntax and punctuation, help writers achieve purposes—they give directions, show readers how to read. From my reading, I've learned that phrases set off by dashes and colons tell readers to pause, breathe in a conversational way, and expect some explanation. So I've used them: I want this essay to sound informed, yet informal. And I've tried to keep subjects and verbs close together, so that the main point of the writing sounds direct and clear—despite all that explanation. As you read, you'll decide whether the signposts constructed by my punctuation and syntax have worked for you.

Reading also helps me to refine and expand my ideas about purpose in other ways. When I became dissatisfied with my personal journal's shallow whininess, I read the published journals of others—Joan Didion, John Cheever—to see what journals could do, what they talked about, what effects they achieved and how. A journal, I discovered, is a lot more than a place to blow off steam: it's experience and reflection, history and personality, murder and food. So now I have other options, although I still write journal entries in which I complain about my commute or my colleagues.

No one may be able to clarify purposes better for you than other writers in your class, especially those in your peer response group who've read your work often and know something about you—and not just the official version, but what you really think, feel, want to say or are likely to say. They've been reading you and can probably point you toward a clearer presentation of a piece's aims and goals.

Audience in Reading for Revision

In reading for audience, you role-play your piece's intended readers or listeners so you know what will appeal to them. This may sound more dishonest and manipulative than it is: we consider audience (usually automatically or unconsciously) when we talk, and would never think of making a class presentation in the same language we use to explain something to our very bright 2-year-old nephew.

Purpose and audience are very closely related. It only makes sense that our reasons and goals for a piece of writing depend on who we're writing to, and vice versa. Like writing, reading is social: as Frank Smith (1994), a Canadian psychologist who has studied reading extensively, writes, "Language does things for *people,* and its particular conventions—the way it does things—are matters of social contract and social identification" (45). So the conventions of language that we learn and practice when we read can be thought of as audience-related reading.

> The only time my interest was peaked, in fact, the only section I remember, is when she is talking about Idaho. Maybe I'm selfish and only like to read things I can relate to (and I'm not even Idahoan) but isn't that the purpose of reading? (Katie, writing in Idaho).

Reading as a Social Act (Language, Conventions, Styles, Manners)

Although it's true that these days people usually read alone, silently, to them-selves—front-porch reading aloud of novels to others while everyone sips lemonade in the cool evening has almost died out, though it shouldn't have—reading is intensely social. This is partly because texts, readers, and writers share common conventions, everything from spaces between words (a Renaissance innovation), to punctuation systems, to what sorts of expectations a given structure for writing sets up in readers. We expect something different when we read a poem than when we read a pamphlet explaining how to use the new battery cables to jump-start the car. Obvious surface conventions (bullet lists, illustrations) usually cue us to other conventions embedded within a text. Poems are usually more rhythmic than instructions, for example; that's one way we recognize each one, understand that one piece is a poem and another instructions. (Of course it's always possible that a piece of writing can be both!)

Frank Smith says that "Knowledge of written language conventions is essential for readers and writers because conventions are the basis of under-standing and communication" (1994, 44). Smith believes readers must be able to "predict" what conventions the writer will use. While you've read this piece, for example, you've expected that I would write in complete sentences with subjects and verbs and objects, that I would use English rather than Spanish or Tagalog or Latin word order.

You've also expected some other conventions of textbook writing to be employed: that I would tell you where I was going next; provide a clear, infor-mative introduction and conclusion; make sure that each paragraph begins with a topic sentence so you can skim; and give you some suggestions that can be accessed through subheads so you can glean through the text for what you need. That's often how I read, although as a writer I shudder at how cold-blooded and lazy this process sounds.

Reading for revision allows you to check on conventions for the particu-lar sort of writing you're doing, just as it allows you to check and double-check facts. Writing conventions are tricky. When Wendy Bishop read the first draft of this essay, for example, she suggested even more subheads and using different fonts to make the hierarchy of subheads clearer. That's a convention, how academic writers guide readers. She also suggested—among many other things—that I change "2-year-old" to "2-year-old nephew," honoring the audience-oriented convention that college students aren't likely to have children (although many of mine do since I teach at an urban, commuter campus). Given these two small examples of how conventions can operate in reading and writing, it's not surprising that it usually takes students several years to get a good grasp on how a personal essay in the English department or a news story in Communications or a report of observations and findings in Botany is "supposed to sound."

You learn this by reading, writing, and reading again, verifying that the conventions you follow are the same ones employed in successful examples of the genre in which you're writing. Your audience expects it, and you read to get inside their expectations (that's what Wendy was doing, too). In time, if you continue with this sort of writing and reading, the conventions will become "natural" to you; then you'll continue reading to see what sorts of twists and fillips have been added to the conventions. You may create some yourself: then students will be reading your work to construct you as "the perfect audience." (See Hint Sheet K for more ideas.)

"Reading," Frank Smith reflects, "is a thought-full activity" (1994, 20). In this essay I've indicated, suggested, and struggled through some kinds of thinking that we do when we read, and explored rhetorical reading—reading in different perspectives, for different roles—as a valuable time-saving strategy for revision.

Reading in this way is creative and imaginative. Wendy Bishop writes, "Creativity involves risk taking" (1999, 195), and reading as the voice(s) of speaker, subject, purpose, and audience is certainly that. It sounds so off-the-wall, so impractical.

But maybe it's what we do when we read. Maybe we haven't exactly thought of reading before as something so close to writing that the processes are truly inseparable, or considered reading as a way to blend our voices and thoughts with the voices and thinking in the texts we're reading and writing, a chance to think with imagination *and* logic, a place to make and say something new.

Consider:

> I have never been able to read a single book to which I give myself over entirely; at each step, always, the incessant commentary of intelligence and imagination interrupted the thread of the narrative. After a few minutes, it was I who was writing the book—and what I wrote nowhere existed (Pessoa, quoted in Padgett 1997, 4).

Consider:

> Reading is a change of state, a change of state of a very particular sort . . . [W]e find ourselves instantly and implicitly changing our apprehension of the meaning structure of the world (Birkerts 1998, 50).

Pessoa says we write when we read, Sven Birkerts that when we read we change, even the ways we think about how and what the world means. (We also, of course, read and change when we write.) And maybe that's why we haven't consciously and strategically used reading as part of our processes of revision. Maybe that's why our reading hasn't been particularly helpful when we revised—as when Jenny first reread her letter asking for additional funding—so we tended to discount reading as part of the revising process.

We rarely make it a point to read systematically as part of our revising. Yet reading and writing—both processes—involve the imaginative reworking of experience from a new standpoint, wearing a different mask. The next time you read, remember that you are reseeing, reviewing the ordinary meanings you assign experience: reading as revision. It's how we read. Use it purposefully, dramatically, rhetorically: in writing.

Works Cited

Berlin, James. 1990. "Writing Instruction in School and College English, 1890–1985." In: A Short History of Writing Instruction, 183–220. Edited by James J. Murphy. Davis, CA: Hermagoras Press.

Birkerts, Sven. 1998. "States of Reading." In: *The Best American Essays of 1998,* 49–58. Edited by Cynthia Ozick. Series editor, Robert Atwan. Boston: Houghton.

Bishop, Wendy, ed. 1999. "When All Writing Is Creative and Student Writing Is Literature." In: *The Subject Is Writing,* 2nd edition, 192–202. Portsmouth, NH: Boynton/Cook Heinemann.

Harris, Jeanette. 1999. "How Writers and Readers Construct Texts." In: *The Subject Is Writing,* 2nd edition, 117–122. Edited by Wendy Bishop. Portsmouth, NH: Boynton/Cook Heinemann.

Murray, Donald. 1999. "One Writer's Secrets." In: *The Fourth Genre: Contemporary Writers of/on Creative Nonfiction,* 351–357. Edited by Robert L. Root, Jr. and Michael Steinberg. Boston: Allyn & Bacon.

Padgett, Ron. 1997. *Creative Reading: What It Is, How to Do It, and Why.* Urbana, IL: National Council of Teachers of English.

Ronald, Kate. 1999. "Style: The Hidden Agenda in Composition Classes or One Reader's Confession." In: *The Subject Is Writing,* 2nd edition, 169–183. Edited by Wendy Bishop. Portsmouth, NH: Boynton/Cook Heinemann.

Root, Robert L. Jr., and Michael Steinberg, eds. 1999. *The Fourth Genre: Contemporary Writers of/on Creative Nonfiction.* Boston: Allyn & Bacon.

Smith, Frank. 1994. *Understanding Reading,* 5th edition. Hillsdale, NJ: Erlbaum.

Tompkins, Jane. 1999. "Me and My Shadow." In: *The Fourth Genre: Contemporary Writers of/on Creative Nonfiction,* 382–395. Edited by Robert L. Root, Jr. and Michael Steinberg. Boston: Allyn & Bacon.

Wells, Douglas. 1998. *Stretch: Explore, Explain, Persuade.* Upper Saddle River, NJ: Prentice Hall.

14

Making Peace with the Research Essay
One Teacher's History

Gay Lynn Crossley

Here's what I remember: After spending 10 or so weeks of spring semester 1983 writing what my teacher wanted to hear about assigned literature, she introduced the research assignment—and introduced the topic that every member of the class would have to study: Alaska. Then, each of us was given a slip of paper telling us what we would have to research, specifically, about Alaska. The fates were not smiling on me that day. My slip read: the economic repercussions of the Alaskan pipeline. A minimum of ten pages, with a minimum of twelve sources, on the economic repercussions of the Alaskan pipeline. Yes, the economic repercussions of the Alaskan pipeline.

I assumed that I was supposed to report on them somehow. Not that I knew why, or who would care—that is, until the class before the essays were due. Our teacher was moving to Alaska that summer, and students in her composition class were to provide her with a crash course on her new home. I imagine that explanation helped some students, those lucky ones researching the settling of Alaska or the impact of the gold rush. For me, though, her explanation felt hollow as I read transcripts from the state legislature and any article I could find on the Alaskan pipeline, so desperate I no longer cared if they addressed economic repercussions. I had to find twelve sources on a topic that seemed a last ditch effort on my teacher's part to come up with as many slips of paper as she needed for the number of students in her class. The essay I submitted was the biggest cut-and-paste job you've ever seen. I threw together the outline and note cards *after* I'd given a handwritten copy of my essay to a typist (in the days before the personal computer). Then, friends took me out (it was a Thursday night, I believe) so that I could forget the last few sleepless nights, the stress and strain. The next morning, I dragged myself to class (late) and turned in the assignment, remembering as I did that I'd never written the conclusion. To this day, as you may gather, I resent that teacher.

When I began teaching, I was determined to handle the research assignment differently. Everything I was learning about the teaching of writing confirmed what I had intuited as a student. The outline and note card routine was flawed in that it imposed a linear "think-then-write" process on student writers, and was motivated more by a need to police us than a desire to teach us anything about writing. By throwing a ten-page, twelve-source minimum at writers, teachers encourage a hatchet job since we are understandably more concerned with finding a source, any source, than with learning from that source. If we are limited to citing books, reputable magazines, and academic journals, we experience only one narrowly defined version of research. Furthermore, if we are not encouraged to think rhetorically about researched writing, we'll more than likely produce "schooled" writing, just as I did. And Alaska as the assigned topic, not to mention the economic repercussions of the Alaskan pipeline? Bad, just bad. The student I was, the student you are, should be encouraged to research topics that are important to us, or to find our own reasons for researching an assigned topic.

During my early years as a teacher, it was my mission to persuade writers to find something worthwhile in research and, simultaneously, to prevent them from remembering me with resentment (or at least the same kind of resentment that I felt). With the zeal of a used car salesperson, I emphasized the freedom to choose topics and purposes for research that grew from their own interests. I argued passionately that research was not about reading the index of a book in order to find the few pertinent pages, that research was not about pasting together quotes, that research was not about masquerading our personal perspectives in the name of objectivity (all the things I thought I had to do). Research was about learning, and discovering the joy of learning. Let freedom ring.

And that's what it was about for me: freedom. It makes sense; it's the very thing I wished I'd had. Freedom to write without faked note cards, without the obligatory references to books I hadn't read, without that horrible, stilted feeling of quoting for the sake of quoting. Freedom to write about anything but the Alaskan pipeline. Still, during my first years teaching, I found myself reading stilted essays, butchered prose, awkwardly placed quotations. Over time I realized that these students were teaching me a lesson: encouraging writers to use their freedom isn't enough. They showed me that I was spending so much time teaching what research wasn't that I never got around to teaching what it could be. The freedom to choose our own topics, to consider alternative sources, to find our own reasons for researching a topic matters little until we learn that research, first and foremost, is about reading—about reading fully and actively, in both the most traditional and the broadest sense. Here's what I've learned.

Reading Your Topic to Life

At its root, research (it's a verb, too, you know) means to *re-search*—to search again, within ourselves and in the company of others. It's the work of a reader searching into—questioning, challenging, qualifying, borrowing—what others have to say and a writer searching for words that will shape what has been discovered. However, for many of us, our work as a researcher takes a back seat from the get go. The "topic" sits squarely in the driver's seat and with it the perception that the success or failure of a research essay hinges on the topic. I've found this perception to be not only largely untrue, but also harmful. The topic is important in that it should somehow inspire us, but it's our questions, interest, passion, and inquiry that drive a research essay. A writer makes or breaks a topic, not the other way around.

But how do we "make" a topic, especially if we didn't get to choose it? We read life into it by reading ourselves into it—our interests, questions, passions. Rarely do we find ourselves researching a subject that we know nothing about. (How many subjects do we know absolutely nothing about?) Yet, it never dawned on me to consider what I knew about the French Revolution when my history professor assigned the term paper. It didn't seem to matter, in my mind, that my favorite novels in high school were Dickens' *A Tale of Two Cities* and Hugo's *Les Miserables*. Or that, like many adolescent girls, I was captivated by biographies of Marie Antoinette. Or that I had sought out every film and mini-series related to the French Revolution. I didn't consider what I found compelling about the French Revolution, so my research essay for that history course was basically a string of quotations from historians, rehashing what I pretty much already knew about the causes of the Revolution. Had I considered what fiction had already taught me, or the very reason I was drawn to novels and films about the French Revolution, I could have come up with a much more interesting, focused essay about ideas that I'd found exciting since childhood. Maybe I could have explored the romanticism associated with the French Revolution and why it resonated so powerfully for me growing up in the United States. Maybe I could have learned something.

From what I gather, my experience is not unique. Take some time to think about your own past as a researcher:

1. Do you recall a time when you were encouraged to share research for an audience other than your teacher? If you do, what kind of research did you do? Was that research experience different from others you've had? How or how not?

2. What have been acceptable sources for your research projects? Have you been free to draw on alternative sources that were perhaps more familiar to you? What value did you find in working with those sources?

3. Have you *ever* researched a topic that started out interesting to you but, in the process, became dull and stale? Why do you think that happened?

4. Did you ever learn what your classmates were doing for their research projects and find them more interesting that yours? What made theirs different?

If our teachers assign a topic or limit our choice of topics, we're not doomed. Perhaps a topic does seem foreign and unfamiliar at first, but once we read ourselves into it, we tap into the potential of that topic to motivate writing that is worthwhile to us and to our readers. So consider when you first heard about that topic, who you've heard talking about that topic, where most of your knowledge about that topic comes from, the questions you had about it, how your interest in that topic has changed over time. Connecting ourselves in these ways to an assigned topic can help us personalize it, give us a chance to do something interesting with it.

We often think that an "open topic" assignment would solve all our troubles. If only we could choose to write about what we want. However, choosing our own topics can lead to writing just as stale as my essay about Alaska. We can feel the pressure to choose a weighty, significant topic; it is for an academic research essay after all. Again, we are not reading ourselves into our research projects. If you are able to choose your own topic, make a list of topics that interest you, the concerns that have been occupying your mind lately, the questions that run through your mind as you watch the news, talk to family, and think about your boyfriend or girlfriend. Don't dismiss any possible topics on your list, and more importantly, don't edit your thinking as you're jotting them down. Once you have your list, then read yourself into each topic. That is, beside each pose the specific questions that make that topic alive for you or note the particular motivation to learn that each holds. In my experience, few topics are trivial or inappropriate. More likely, they have been treated in a trivial or inappropriate way. If you aren't sure about a topic, or how to research that topic, talk with your teacher, who can help you discover how to pursue that subject appropriately for the assignment.

Writers in Context:
Reading Our Purposes and Audiences

Even if we've found a topic, a focus for our research, that reflects our sincere interests, the essay we write can still seem forced if we see no real reason for sharing our research other than to complete a requirement. Without a rhetorical context for research, we can be just as unsure about our role as research writers, about what we're supposed to do as researchers. Transforming the research process from a passive process of quoting to an active process of reading requires a transformation in how we see ourselves as writers. And again, this transformation requires us to read—this time our goals and intentions as writers. Rather than students trying to get an assignment "right," we are writers with a job to do—a job that's important to us.

Once you've identified some topics you are interested in researching, list your possible answers to the following questions:

1. What do you want to research about this topic? (Your answers to this question can help you focus your project.)

2. Why are you interested in researching these specific areas? (Your answers to this question can help you imagine a purpose for your research and name possible audiences.)

3. Who could you imagine sharing this research with (in a letter, for example) and why? (Your answers to this question can help you sharpen your purpose, or consider another focus or purpose for your research.)

Our answers to these questions work together, feeding off one another, to help us arrive at a research project. For some writers, a topic and purpose doesn't really gel until they begin thinking about an audience. One student, Cary, wanted to research "something about the health-care profession." But she struggled to name a focus or purpose until she considered audience. She imagined writing this research as a letter to the children she planned on having someday so that they could see that she was making professional decisions with them in mind, even as an 18-year-old, first-year student. That "something" about the health-care profession was really her need to understand the risks and benefits of choosing nursing as a career. She read (or reread, more specifically) her goals and intentions as a researcher, and her project fell into place from then on.

Once we identify our purposes as researchers, possible contexts for our research emerge, and we can often arrive at rich and productive research projects that we find worth our time—and that inspire us to assume more active roles as researchers. Furthermore, we find a reason to reconsider what we think research is about.

First, we can see through Cary's example that research is not just an academic task. We research, on some level, every time we integrate new understandings with old, every time we seek to learn something from others. Sometimes this integration is prompted by something we experience: our parents kept telling us about the dangers of driving too fast on icy roads, but it wasn't until we slid off into a ditch the morning we were late for school that we consider the truth in their warnings. So we accept that icy roads are dangerous, but that's all we know. We then enhance that knowledge when we relate what we learn in science class—traction is difficult on icy roads—to our parents' warnings and our experiences. In this sense, we've been researching—at the most basic and fundamental level—most of our lives as we have worked to make sense of people and the world around us by asking questions, reading, and watching TV.

Second, not only is the researcher active, but the research itself is also active. It's a part of what Bruce Ballenger (and others) call "an ongoing conversation" (Ballenger 1999). This analogy is familiar to those of us working at colleges and universities. Your professors are expected to publish papers so that they will remain current on what's being said, learned, and challenged in their fields. Oddly enough, though, I hadn't heard of this analogy until research became a likely part of my job. Nevertheless, thinking of research as an ongoing conversation seems applicable to research of all kinds. If the analogy is a good one, why aren't undergraduate students (as well as high school and middle school students) taught to view their work this way? Research teaches us what people have been saying about a subject, the different perspectives they bring to a subject, and, at times, what remains to be said. When we read our sources or conduct an interview, we are entering into a conversation about a subject with a history, a base of common knowledge, and a desire to address the questions and issues that motivate the discussion. Good researchers do not merely eavesdrop on that conversation; they contribute something to it.

The impact of context on creating a worthwhile research project doesn't end with tailoring topics and audiences or with thinking about research as an active and familiar process. Context is crucial in helping us clarify our purposes for writing and make decisions about sources. Consider the following scenarios:

A. In an English Composition course, you decide to research diabetes because you're concerned about your grandmother's declining health.

B. In a nursing course, your professor assigns you to research diabetes as a part of a case study on a diabetic patient.

Each of these situations will impact your purpose as a researcher and the kind of research you will conduct. For your English Composition class, you will probably be most interested in learning the symptoms of diabetes so that you can convince your grandmother to see the doctor. In the nursing class, you find that your research should focus on the treatments for diabetes, more specifically the side effects of those treatments because, as a future nurse, you are concerned with patient care.

Furthermore, these situations will help you decide what kinds of sources you should examine. In the English Composition class, you may have more freedom to draw from popular sources such as the article you find in *Healthy Woman* about the warning signs of diabetes for women in their fifties. However, this source will probably be unacceptable for your nursing class. The nursing instructor will think medical and nursing journals more appropriate. As we advance in our course work, our research is often expected to be more specialized.

Use the following questions to help you begin your research process and to help you determine the expectations of your research and your options as a writer:

1. What is my purpose for reading about this topic and sharing my research with a particular audience?

2, What does my audience and purpose suggest about what I need to learn and share through research?

3. What is the "common knowledge" associated with this topic? Is there a place for this common knowledge in my research? Why?

4. How specialized should my sources be in light of my purpose and audience (as well as the requirements of the assignment)? What are useful and appropriate sources?

These questions help us to read our context and determine the expectations for our research—for example, the sources we can draw from, the form and tone of our essay, the role of personal narrative in our essay—and name our goals as research writers. Our purpose will likely sharpen or modify as we continue our research, but imagine how much more productive—how much less overwhelming—our first trip to the library will be if we can run a search on "diabetes, women, symptoms" rather than just "diabetes."

The Search

Beginning the Search

We begin our research into a topic before we ever set foot in the library, visit the women's shelter, surf the Internet, interview the diabetic, or write to the Environmental Protection Agency for information. Our work starts when we begin searching our own minds for what we know about a subject and what remains to be known, given our purposes and audiences as researchers. We carry sources around with us: conversations with our parents about "flower power"; an MTV special on 1960s rock and roll bands; reruns of *The Wonder Years.* We've gathered information one way or another our entire lives. We're the place to begin searching, and this beginning place automatically encourages us to take on a more active role. Take some time to list the sources of your knowledge about the topic you are researching. While all of the sources you list may not be appropriate for your essay, list them anyway because they may trigger new ways of looking at your topic.

Collecting Sources

I almost titled this part of the discussion "Finding Sources," the term we commonly use. However, we can "find" four-leaf clovers, but I hope we don't associate (only) luck with conducting research. I can "find" my dog's stuffed elephant once I stumble over it, but I don't trust that that I'll stumble on the right journal article when I go to the library. Yes, we might very well feel lucky or unlucky depending on the day, or might trip over the perfect book on the way to the copy machine. But good research asks us to leave less to chance.

I prefer to think of "collecting" sources. This term implies more control on the part of the writer, and seems more accurate. When we "collect" Nolan Ryan baseball cards, we aren't just satisfied with what we "find." We're more discriminating. We're not as interested in the common cards as we are with his rookie card. We're not looking for cards we already own. We're looking for the card that will add something to, or complete, our collection.

We should bring this same discriminating mindset to the research process. Not every article we find on boarding horses, for example, will suit our purposes as researchers when we're searching, specifically, for ways to maintain good nutrition for the horses we board. We can't leave the library with the first three articles we find. If we do, we usually face big problems when we start writing.

Evaluating Sources

Researchers need strategies for evaluating the sources they find so that they can collect the best sources for their project, those sources that will contribute something to their specific discussions on a topic and will be appropriate for context. These strategies involve another, more traditional form of reading. The following questions can help you identify suitable sources:

1. *Is the publication credible for your purposes?* Certain publications are known for a particularly liberal or conservative bias, for example. Some publications are written for a general audience (glossy magazines with pictures, by and large) and some for a specialized audience of knowledgeable peers (the seldom glossy, rarely illustrated journals with plain covers, containing articles with colons in the titles). You can make early decisions at the computer terminal or in the reference section by paying attention to the publication in which possible sources are located. Noting the type of publication is especially important when running an Internet search. If you are unfamiliar with the publication, scan the entire journal (even a couple of back issues) so that you can identify its bias and can begin thinking about how you will work with or against that bias in your own writing. If all else fails, ask around.

2. *Is the writer credible for your purpose?* If you are researching the need for stable family structures to an audience of single mothers, it can work against you to use Dan Quayle's definition of family, especially if you don't address the controversy surrounding his definition. Likewise, Richard Simmons might not be the nutritional expert you want for a nursing class project, unless your purpose is to survey popular advice on nutrition.

3. *Is the discussion appropriate for, or applicable to, your project?* Scan the
    content of the source, primarily for the main point or purpose of the
    discussion. The article you find may be about Daisy Buchanan's charac-
    ter in *The Great Gatsby,* but if it concentrates on her as a representative of
    the upper class, it might not pertain much to your analysis of "pink
    clouds" as a window into her inner life.

Realize that while scanning might serve your purposes early on, you'll eventually need to read and reread sources, especially those you end up using.

Recording the Search

For any source that you are seriously considering, use the following suggestions to help you organize and save time during the rest of the research
process:

1. Record all bibliographic information that you'll need. If you don't end up
    using the source, you haven't wasted much time. More importantly, if you
    decide to include the source at the last minute, you'll be able to without
    another trip to the library.

2. Make copies of the serious contenders.

3. Use a highlighter and annotations during initial and subsequent readings
    of a source in order to guide you when you return to it—but be selective
    when highlighting. If you highlight everything, you are probably not read-
    ing closely enough and may be in danger of plagiarizing your source.

    Annotation strategies:

    a. Star the main point of your source, and restate it in the margin.

    b. Underline all subpoints or arguments made in support of the main
        point. (Distinguish subpoints and arguments from examples.)

    c. Record in the margins questions that you have about what's being said.

    d. Box key terms.

    e. Star conclusions, if reached.

    f. Write your questions/observations in the margins so that you can
        record your train of thought while reading the source.

4. If a source has "made the cut" after your evaluation process, write a
    summary paragraph for that source and a paragraph in which you explain
    what this source can offer your discussion. The more effort you put into
    the summary at this point, the more prepared you'll be to introduce your
    source in your essay later on.

    Suggestions for writing the summary:

    a. It is customary to refer to the writer and the title of the source in the
        first sentence.

b. Identify the main point of the article—not just the subject of the article, but also (and more importantly) the purpose of the article.

c. Record how the writer achieves the main point.

d. State conclusions, if reached.

Revising Purpose

An initial search can be full of frustrating and pleasant surprises. Be prepared for the frustrating ones (the perfect book that someone else checked out) and leave yourself open to the pleasant ones. Depending on the sources we find, it may be necessary to modify our research projects. Perhaps we set out to research the environmental problems associated with overflowing landfills, but research led us to some articles about what some communities are doing to address this problem and we wonder if our own college campus could implement some of these measures. Now we may be more interested in researching a proposal for a recycling plan to be submitted to our student government association. In short, the sources we "read" (whether they are magazine articles, interviews, documentaries, etc.) can prompt us to respond in ways we may not have anticipated. They can take our thinking in new directions, help us arrive at more focused discussions. As you read your sources, pay attention to how they are pushing you to reconsider what can be done with your topic.

More Than Quoting: Reading for a Purpose

Our past experiences may have taught us that research is about quoting experts on a subject in order to support the assertions we want to make. We get the impression that we need a quote from Georgia Newman to support our claim that child-care costs are skyrocketing (even though that comes as little surprise to us as single parents). Consequently, we often see research as a matter of finding those sources that agree with us, then quoting them a "respectable" number of times, often determined by how much our writing "looks" like research.

There is a role for the expert source in research. Earlier in this piece, I made reference to Bruce Ballenger's *Beyond Note Cards* (1999). It is important, in my mind, to demonstrate a familiarity with Ballenger's work since he has published two books on the research essay. Expert sources lend credibility to our discussions. Furthermore, as we advance in course work, our teachers may expect us to be familiar with the key sources and scholars in that field.

We reduce the purpose of research if we see it only as a process of reporting and quoting sources. With this view, the research we conduct merely covers "old ground" or echoes the positions we held before we even started the research process. Ideally, research should be a discovering and deepening process, and as we enter college, teachers increasingly expect research to enhance thought, not just to restate original positions. We begin by reading more closely.

Introducing Sources

Typically, the first time we use a source, we should mention the author (by first and last name) and, if appropriate the title (from that point on we can just refer to the source by the author's last name). If the source is especially comprehensive (a government study on television viewing habits or a book on education reform), if a source is particularly credible but known only to people in that field, or if a source plays a primary role in our research, we should introduce our readers to the general scope and perspective of that source. That is, we should include summary paragraphs or sentences about the source. For example: "In 'No Wonder Johnny Can't Read,' Debra Keevan examines the educational standards of high schools in seven large American cities and concludes that standards, especially in reading and writing, have dropped dramatically in the last decade." Then we can begin using specific parts of Keevan's discussion for our purposes.

If it is important to establish the credibility of a source (especially to an audience who may not be familiar with that source), we should do so as part of our introduction of that source. Some sources require us to do very little: we only have to mention Roger Ebert if we are researching trends in independent film making, and his credibility is understood. However, many very credible sources do not have such name recognition. We'd need to point out that Debra Keevan is a 35-year veteran teacher, recently appointed by the President to a Department of Education Task Force.

Beyond "S/He Says": Taking Our Cue from Verbs

One of the features that distinguishes experienced research writers from less experienced research writers is the way that they represent and integrate quoted or paraphrased passages. Inexperienced writers have a tendency to rely on "s/he says" when referring to the content of a source. This tendency is often viewed as an indication that we are not as familiar with our sources as we should be. But there might be other reasons. Our early educational experiences emphasize reporting and quoting sources, which make us practiced in the kind of neutral stand with our sources that "s/he says" implies. Furthermore, this emphasis on reporting and quoting, on reading with little or no judgment of the content, has prevented us from developing our authority as readers.

As we pay closer attention to what our sources are saying in particular, and accomplishing in general, it becomes necessary to find a language that will help us accurately refer to a source. Our sources are likely doing something far more specific that merely "saying." Writers claim, argue, and challenge. Just as we are trying to accomplish a purpose when we write, so are our sources. Perhaps, too, expanding the language we have to talk about sources will also prompt us to read more closely. Finally, the language we use will often direct us in determining how else we need to work with a source once we've quoted or paraphrased a passage. Below is a list of some of the most common verbs used when integrating quoted or paraphrased material. It is not a complete list by far. The point is to choose verbs that say something meaningful about what we find in our sources and/or how we are using sources to advance our discussion:

States, Maintains, Claims,

Asserts:	Your reader expects you to specifically and accurately represent what is being asserted, etc.
Explains:	Your reader expects you to provide the explanation offered.
Suggests/Implies:	Your reader expects you to explain how you see your source suggesting or implying a particular meaning.
Reasons:	Your reader expects you to detail that reasoning.
Complicates:	Your reader expects you to explain how your source complicates the discussion.
Questions:	Your reader expects you to explain what your source is questioning and the basis for that questioning.
Argues:	Your reader expects you to summarize the argument(s).

What other verbs can you think of and how would they direct your work?

Once we move beyond "s/he says," we position ourselves to do more with sources than report from them. We can begin to talk confidently with our sources because we are better aware of what they are "saying." We can take exception with a conclusion they reach more easily if we realize that they are reaching a conclusion. We can add to their discussions if we notice that the reasons they provide for something are incomplete, and so on. When we begin talking confidently with our sources, using them to accomplish our purposes as writers, then we distinguish ourselves from inexperienced research writers. (See also Hint Sheet 5.)

Conclusion

Largely because of the research essay, I ended up with a C+ in my second semester Freshman Composition course. I was an English major at the time, and some people are surprised that I remained one. But I did because I'd had many more writing experiences before that spring semester that were positive, enlightening, and invigorating. I knew, on some level, to separate my writing abilities from my performance on that assignment, and on another level, I knew that I hadn't done the job of a writer to begin with; I merely lived through an assignment. It remains an experience that influences my work as a teacher today.

So, here's what I believe. The power to transform a writing experience (even about the economic repercussions of the Alaskan pipeline) lies not just with our teachers, but also, and more importantly, with us as writers. And that power rests in our authority as readers—to read an assignment, a topic, a context, and our sources, actively, specifically, and with our goals informing our every step.

Come to think about it, I never understood the big deal about the Alaskan pipeline anyway—the debates, the controversy, the high expectations. Who was involved? How did native Alaskans think differently than this girl who grew up in Texas? Were some of these economic repercussions tied to (more interesting to me) environmental repercussions? Whose lives were affected? (People are always more interesting to me than corporations.) There's a beginning.

Suggested Readings

Ballenger, Bruce. 1999. *Beyond Note Cards: Rethinking the Freshman Research Paper.* Portsmouth, NH: Heinemann.

———. 1998. *The Curious Researcher,* 2nd edition. NY: Allyn & Bacon.

Sharing Ideas

1. After exploring your beliefs about reading, move on to exploring your beliefs about writing in the same manner. For you, how connected are reading and writing processes? What does who you are as a reader predict about who you are as a writer?

2. As invited, write a class letter to Karen Schiff and Art Young in Chapter 12. You may want to move beyond their initial invitation and connect your reading of another chapter in this collection to your reading of their chapter. Direct their attention to things you've learned about reading literature, for instance, using the discussions in Chapters 7, 8, and 10 or any others.

3. How do you feel as you reread your own work? Under what conditions are you the best reader of your writing?

4. Try some of the suggestions Devan Cook offers in Chapter 13 and then write a note to her or to yourself or to your teacher in the form of a "read-

ing for revising" narrative. How does your relationship to your writing change if/when you read it rhetorically with revision in mind?

5. Like Gay Lynn Crossley in Chapter 14, tell/write out your own research paper narrative. What was your equivalent to the research paper on Alaska that she describes?

6. After reading Chapter 14, write a letter back to the research paper writer you were in high school, telling yourself what you could have done to make the research paper project more meaningful to you as a writer.

7. In a group, consider how the availability of information on the World Wide Web has changed and may continue to change your relationship to research. For this project, you may want to read ahead to Chapters 15 and 16, which may complicate your discussion in useful ways.

Part V

Reading Futures

I read for pleasure and to find out things, learn about things and worlds, people I don't know and am curious about. . . . I make notes of books I would like to read if I had the time. . . . If I love something I am reading all will stop until I finish the book no matter how long.

—Beth

When I was assigned readings, I would treat them as pleasure reading. Now I read books that a few years ago I would have abhorred—it finds its way into my writing: history, philosophy, theology, mythology—it doesn't matter. I usually read several books, both fiction and nonfiction, at a time so I'm always in the mood for something I have on the reading table—it keeps me from getting bored with one subject. I keep a dictionary beside me now when I read and write down definitions of words I don't know. I'm primarily a lubracubucularian (a person who reads in bed).

—Ron

Chapter 15

Reading and the Art of Berry Picking

Myka Vielstimmig*

On the Nature of Reading

```
<<How much formatting do you think
we need in this draft to Wendy?>>
                    <<well I'd like the most format-
                    ting we can manage. For me, the
                    formatting   is   the   text,   you
                    know?>>
```

The northern Athabascans have a verb stem that would be spelled *sas* or *zas*. There probably isn't a perfect English translation for it—*glean* comes close—but the same word is used in at least three different settings. In one, it conveys what a dog does to gnaw and worry the last pinches of meat from a bone. And then it is the word for how a berry picker's fingers tug and riffle the branches for the last ripe blueberry on the bush. Finally, the very same verb is used for what an audience does when they listen to the words of a storyteller.

I like that. How long ago—a thousand years?—the proto-Athabascans were saying "to listen" isn't just to hear or receive, but it is also to glean, gnaw, demand and pursue. In the alternative writing that we like to do, we encourage, if not enforce, the same kind of readerly persistence, participation, and production. Put simply, we ask readers to work.

It's also fair to say that readers have always worked—and they've had fun while

*Vielstimmig is German for "many-voiced." Myka Vielstimmig is the electronic writing partnership of Kathleen Blake Yancey, of Clemson University, and Michael Spooner, of Utah State University (in alphabetical order by institution). They write together separately via E-mail.

they were at it. Scholars used to think that reading was a sort of passive activity where the reader just soaked up what the author had to say. These days, we understand reading differently: we understand

[T]he "meaning" of the text is evoked as a transaction between the text itself, the reader's personal knowledge, the rhetorical situation, and the shared verbal meanings . . . The overarching guide in this process is the reader's attempt to impose a coherent and unified meaning on the text (Brent 1992, 71).

that readers "do." They make meaning as they read, and to do that, they work with the text. As an example of that, we might think about how someone reads a web page, clicking all the way—deciding which turn to take, which story to listen to, which self they will bring to the reading process. Readers of print texts do the same thing, only without a mouse. Contemplating an authorial point, their minds wander; encountering an evocative image, they link to related memories; immersed in a surprising turn of phrase, they participate in making the meaning of that phrase. Readers aren't passive; they're active—in ways we don't entirely understand yet.

This is perhaps even more true for non-literary (efferent) reading than for literary (aesthetic) reading. When you read a chapter like this one, you're not primarily in it for the pleasure; you're looking for information. In a sense, you're reading to update your system of beliefs or understandings—you're reading to learn. And learning is an inventive, interactive process: you have to participate, or learning doesn't happen.

Well, yes, but. It's true that some folks—notably Louise Rosenblatt (1938)—divide texts into those we read for information, which she calls *efferent,* and those we read for pleasure, which she calls *aesthetic,* as you say above. But it's also true that some texts permit both kinds of reading at once. In the hands of a good writer, a text on science that informs can be quite eloquent and thus pleasurable. It's poetic as well as rhetorical. And to flip the coin, a poem can teach: we can learn from it, even get information, say, about how language was used at a given point in time, or about the culture in which the poem was written.

We're not far apart on this, but just to clarify, I don't think Rosenblatt divides *texts* into efferent and aesthetic; she divides *readings.* Her example of the instructions on a fire extinguisher argues that the same text can be read for information or for poetry—which is the point you're making. Stanley Fish offers the example of a list of names on the board that his students read as a poem. Science writing can be elegant, yes, and a poem can be didactic.

I guess I think that this divide between informative reading and aesthetic reading makes a neat divide, sure, but it's a divide that often collapses in practice. Which means that already, even with the most conventional texts, we are already reading in multiple ways.

Out of rudeness comes rapid same question, out of an eye comes research, out of selection comes painful cattle (Stein 1926, 11).

I couldn't agree more: we're always reading in multiple ways. Still, that is not to say that differences are invisible. To our readers here, I meant just that when reading more efferently, they may be more conscious of the work that readers do—the rhetoric of reading, shall we say—because reading to learn is asking to be informed/persuaded/changed.

And as you can see, we use the very way we write to make reader participation obvious and central to both writing and reading. We think this kind of textual "conversation"—between a writer and a specific other like a teacher or friend; between a writer and several others, like you, the readers of this text; and between a writer and himself or herself—always takes place, *within* a text. We just like to make that conversation more obvious.

By interrupting each other, you mean? ;)

Of course, not everyone likes this. They say that we are making more work for the reader. Sometimes they say that we are obscuring the points we should make more clear. We disagree with these perceptions. We think we make both the writing and the reading more interesting.

More challenging, too, I'd say. But then too the reader is awarded more freedom this way, not less, since she or he is asked to play more than one role in reading the text. The reader can align with one voice, then another, then neither. When texts are written and read this way, more options are available.

You could say, in fact, that in a text like ours, the very possibility of options is highlighted.

Explaining Alt. Writing: Combining Forms/Genres

A landscape leavened by the ultimate equality of all texts offers no fulcrum for advocacy or change. (Hesse 1999, 41)

Suppose we put a poem right here. This is not a book of poems; this is a book of academic essays. What is the effect of putting a poem in the middle of this essay?

In a Station of the Metro

The apparition of these faces in the crowd;
Petals on a wet, black, bough.

Students are taught that this famous poem by Ezra Pound is important for how intensely visual it is, how compressed, and how it super-
poses one idea onto another. Pound is credited for the phrase "juxta-
position without predication," which is a
good way to describe his technique in the
poem here. He offers no predication—no
grammatical connection—between his
images. He doesn't say "these faces *look
like* petals" or "these faces *remind me of*
petals."

Nor is he using the familiar poetic
structures of metaphor, simile,
metonymy; he simply puts the one
image next to (or on top of) the
other, like layering one idea onto
another. He juxtaposes them:
faces, petals. By doing it this way,
he suggests a correspondence
between them, but he lets the
reader determine exactly what that
correspondence might be.

It's a visual technique, writing this
way. You could say he's writing like a
painter, because a painting doesn't predicate or explain. It's the juxta-
position itself—putting one image next to another *without* formally
connecting them—that is the reader's clue to the poet's meaning.

Ordinarily, you find a poem in an essay only when the poem is
there for the reader to study—when the essay wants to explain something about the poem to a reader. So then
the poem is used to illustrate a point that the
writer of the essay wants to make.

But suppose a writer puts a poem
in an essay and it's not for that
purpose, then what would the
purpose be, and what is the reader
to make of the poem? It's there not
to be explained, so it must be there
to contribute to the essay in some
other way.

It could be that the poem makes a similar point, but does so in a compressed way.
It could be that the image within a poem, or
a metaphor, locates the work of the essay in
a visual or aesthetic context that enriches or enlarges the essay. It
could be that the poem is like petals and the essay is like faces; they
connect in a way the reader establishes.

If readers read essays differently than they read poems, it could
be that the writer wants the reader to do just
that—to read differently, to think differently, to read visually, and to feel—all
within a single text.

Not to put too fine a point on it: for
readers to be aware of how they
read, and of the power that is reading.

   In recent academic work in
the field of composition studies,
written by folks like us—a publisher

and a professor—there are several examples of combining the different genres of poem and essay like this (see Amato 1999; Bishop 1995). In other recent work, you'll find the essay combined with autobiography (Bloom 1998; Villanueva 1993). Pacanowsky (1988) even wrote a short story on an academic topic and published it in an academic journal devoted to nonfiction—just to prove it could work. Crossing genre boundaries and combining genres in a single work is still not common, but it seems to be more and more acceptable to academic readers. Still, to readers new to combinatory writing—or what we could call alt.writing—the idea of what's expected, what's conventional in an essay, is disrupted, and the reader has to look for an unconventional way to understand the work.

Fortunately, many writers who combine genres in one work offer interpretive help to the reader. "This passion-play poem I kept hidden (and keep hidden still)" writes Janet Eldred (1999, 390). In referring to the poem, she gives it context and helps the reader interpret what the poem contributes to the essay. Villanueva (1993) creates a multi-genre work in which essay sections reflect explicitly on autobiography sections and (third-person) narrative sections.

Eldred and Villanueva want to be informative; you could say they want to persuade the reader, so they guide the reader in making connections that are useful to their informative purposes.

However, suppose we put a poem (or narrative or autobiography) into an essay and we don't say anything about it; suppose we just drop it in and move onward.

In a Station of the Metro

The apparition of these faces in the crowd;
Petals on a wet, black, bough.

What About Dialogue in the Essay?
What's with These Back and Forth Voices?

As texts have begun to change, some teachers and writers have argued that writers need to be especially careful in their writing. It's easy, these writers argue, for readers to become confused or misled by texts that work outside conventional boundaries. Since we aren't

Myka Vielstimmig is, of course, not simply a combined persona . . .
It is a position that openly demands that its readers make connec-

```
tions not being made for them, that they treat this text as hyper-
text, and that they know how to read hypertext. (George and Shoos
1999, 124)
```

supposed to read an argument the way we read a poem, they say, we as authors have a duty to help readers understand how the text we compose is to be read.

But our view of reading is a little more complicated than this one. We think that both reader and writer have equivalent, if somewhat different, textual responsibilities. We think of text as a place for writers and readers to create meaning together. Accordingly, writers take the first turn in making meaning. Readers take the second turn, a turn that the writer can influence but cannot determine. Even when reading conventional texts, readers rely on more than what the writers have created. For one thing, the reading of a text will be influenced by a reader's background and experience with the topics that the text is discussing. For another, the reading is influenced by a reader's own experiences as a reader.

Some days—like reading George and Shoos—I'm not so sure there's any difference at all between reader and writer. I mean, their reading of Myka is so inventive, it's like a total rewrite.

Obviously, a textbook discussing nuclear physics is easier to understand if the reader knows something about science. Less obvious perhaps, but just as important, the reader who understands the various ways such a text might be read will both learn and enjoy the reading of that text more. A reading of any text depends on more than what you know; it also depends on how you understand and can use your own reading strategies. We all have those strategies, of course; we just don't always think much about them.

Yes, this is where the rubber hits the (reading) road. Who is responsible, and for what? I can't speak for all authors, but I can speak to my own experience. Sometimes when I write, I do write in exactly the way you are suggesting: to be clearly and monologically explicit. The intent is to be clear, to explain sufficiently, to leave no doubt. There are occasions when that is a good

Yet another piece of the picture is the context from which the writer worked and the context in which the reader works. My interpretation of my sister's E-mail will be different if she's stabbed me in the back recently, regardless of what she's writing about this time. How a reader views the writer—reliable, unreliable, a stranger, a friend, an enemy—is part of the context or rhetorical situation. It becomes part of how one reads.

But let me make some trouble here. Don't you think what critics of alt.writing have in mind combines genre and the ethical side of the rhetorical situation? Their concern is with the writer's responsibility— an ethical matter—in view of what a reader might normally expect in, say, the genre of an academic article. If we think writing can change a reader's belief, then isn't it fair to expect the writer not to play games with the reader's head?

For example, we've been much in agreement so far in this

way to talk to readers—say, when a public figure is explaining why we should or should not go to war. But there are other occasions permitting another approach, not better, but different—in intent and values. Say, a text like this one, whose intents are many and not altogether congruent: to think about and to explain, yes—also to reflect upon, to provoke, to theorize, and to synthesize, as well as to question. The values such a text aspires to are different than those of the monological text: complexity, alternative views, energy, visuality, collage. In sum, it's not textual right or wrong, but textual propriety. Given a rhetorical situation, what works?

text, but suppose we disagreed. Suppose we end this chapter in disagreement—what meaning can a reader make of that, given that this is a chapter written by people they believe to be authorities? Don't they have a right to expect a coherent, unified statement from us? Or is that just tough luck in the postmodern world?

Then you're saying it *is* just tough luck for the reader. What the writer wants to accomplish—the writer's intents and values—determine what goes on the page. But this is the kind of dominance over the reader that some critics attack. You can say it's textual propriety, but I could reply that propriety lies in using manners that the audience expects.

Well, a couple of things here. In the first place, I'm not talking about a writer dominating a reader; I'm talking about writers and readers working together to create meaning. In the second place, all writers work from their own values, so this is so for all writers, not just alt.writers. In other words, a writer—or a team like us, say—will begin the exchange with his or her values, of course, but they also work hard to link to the values of their readers. In the third place, if all you get in a reading is what you expect, why bother to read at all? (Perhaps this is why the World Wide Web is so attractive to young readers especially. Who yet knows exactly what to expect there?)

The trouble is that when you dump a few conflicting voices together on a page, they all look to be of the same value. And if they look equivalent, then your reader doesn't have a good reason to choose one over another. Haven't you lost the power of persuasion, of change, of learning when you don't advocate for one or another of them? Isn't collage writing just another way of throwing up your hands?

But you assume a couple of things that I'm not sure are so. Are all the voices equivalent? I don't think so, and lots of readers of alt.writing don't either; in fact several of them have come back to us to claim agreement with one voice or another.

We should be concerned that the complexity, alternative views, energy, visuality, and collage that suit our intents and values may just alienate our reader. In our own terms here in this chapter, we might not provoke a reader to go berry picking with us; we might just be provoking.

So regardless of what theory might say, reader experience is that readers align themselves with voices that don't all seem equivalent. Second, collage isn't dumping voices onto a page, thank you very much. That is, I'll accept the collage description, but given the hours and hours we're spending designing this textual collage, *dumping* is beginning to sound pretty good.

Besides, I think authorial messing with a reader's head is much more likely in a very conventionalized kind of text, one that appeals to readers on the strength of its plausibility—say—the kind of thing you might read from the Ku Klux Klan.

(Or from critical theory? Heh heh.)

Precisely because it *looks* like a "normal" text—in its conventionality and faux reasonableness—readers are more inclined to take it at face value and not to question it, whereas the kinds of texts that we write, as the critics suggest, demand attention. I think demanding attention is ok, especially when it's obvious that . . .

. . . that we're doing this.

It puts readers on notice that effort is required, and that the text is unusual, so the appropriate signals in fact are sent. And of course, when we write this way, we run a risk, too: that the very readers we are trying to make meaning with will refuse. As one friend of mine put it, "What makes you and Michael think that as a reader, I should put up with this?"

Email from the editor of this book:
    i was interested to find the voices switched (i thought) somewhere in the middle. main speaker in the beginning is michael and the right side bolder type is kathi. and [later it's] vice versa (michael's "heh heh" always gives him away).
    but maybe you both rewrite both sections too?

Dear Reader,
  Don't buy this?
  Me neither.
—**Myka V.**

Now she's gettin it.

Okay, I can agree that the approach we take draws attention to itself, and this makes it hard to say we're sneaking anything past the reader. And yes, there's a risk here to the writer that the reader will simply refuse to play.

In a way, this reminds me of the art world's response to cubism. It drew attention to the constructedness of art; a viewer could no longer pretend that the canvas was three-dimensional. Duchamp, Picasso and company wanted to play in two dimensions, and they wanted viewers to appreciate how this revealed selectivity, idiosyncrasy, and, in a sense, technology (i.e., the role of technique) in the artist's medium, where

viewers were used to the idea that art held up a mirror to reality. Many
of their viewers, in fact, didn't feel they should put up with this; they
called Duchamp's *Nude Descending a Staircase* an "explosion in a
shingle factory."
Many of our readers, like those viewers of cubism, are used to

So both writer and reader are at risk here; on the other hand,
anytime you agree to make meaning with another human being,
you're at risk: of learning something new, of finding that what you
believed isn't quite accurate, of seeing that you may have to change.
Indeed, these are the points of making meaning together. Which does
return us to the issue of authorial responsibility. Our task is to make
the effort we are asking of readers worthwhile. Ideally, in such texts,
readers will make (their own) meaning, in multiple ways: that's the
fun part. As authors, we set a textual stage; as readers, they make their
own play upon it.

And let me invoke two more contexts here: (1). The world of the
media, (2). Conventional texts. Increasingly, we see genre lines
crossed, as you say. On TV, information and entertainment have
birthed a new hybrid genre, infotainment. The other night, I saw an
ad for a TV show on a video of a movie once shown in a theater. In
bookstores, we find texts like *The Agenda* (Woodward 1994), an
account of Clinton's early presidency that
pretends to historical accuracy at the same
time it offers imagined conversations and
thought processes. Woodward, the author,
himself identifies the book as a hybrid
form.

You mean a journalist is making up
his facts? Gasp! I am not at all
sanguine about the writer's hidden
role in all this.

Exactly. But it's not totally a flip issue. We also find texts that
mix genres in another way. In the novel *I Was Amelia Earhart*
(Mendelsohn 1997) for instance, the author tells the story of the
flyer's crash, her affair with her navigator, and the end of her life,
even though we don't know, factually, for a start, that she crashed
even. Besides, it's fiction: why should we
be captured by facts?

So you end up with imagined
events in an imaginative genre;
doesn't this make the mixed-genre
point disappear?

The point is that she wasn't merely
imagined, and neither was her navigator.
And at some still other point, some poor
student is going to miss a history question because she understood the
imagination of the novel as the truth of biography. Or perhaps truth
isn't at issue here at all, since imagination often gets us to a closer

truth than does fact. Still, it's helpful to
know which is which—fact or fiction.
Genre is supposed to help us do that.

Or used to do that. We have to
read differently now, you're saying.

On yet a third hand, historically, what
you read has never been precisely what
you've gotten. In the eighteenth century, an Irishman named Jonathan
Swift suggested that the problem of Irish poverty and hunger could
be cured by eating the very children who were starving. Now, you
could agree with that proposal, or you could disagree with it. Or you
could understand that he wasn't really making such a proposal at all,

Last year, a girl was raped by two
[men] . . . while they sang the
lyrics to our song "Polly." I have
a hard time carrying on, knowing
that there are plankton like that
in our audience. (Kurt Cobain, qtd
in Vowell 1998, 12)

There are just too many (I guess
you could call them) Unassim-
ilated Others out there. You
can't predict what every one of
them might do. (Michael's
daughter Nancy at 16, 1999,
personal communication, heh)

but rather suggesting the depth of despair to which conditions had
fallen. My point is that readers have always had to parse the text they
were reading—even 200 years ago, even before the World Wide Web,
even before alt.writing.

Making Sense of Reading

The task of the critic is to perform analysis on an
agenda of someone else's construction. . . . Design sets
aside past agendas, and treats them and their products
as resources in setting an agenda of future aims (Kress
1999, 87).

Design and critique. Ideas like these two from Kress offer a ready
frame for understanding some of what Myka does on the page. For
one thing, unlike conventional book chapters, we like to manipulate
type design in our writing. That's why we put different voices in different typefaces, change the margins often, and in some chapters we
even include visual art.

The computer
makes it easy these
days, but the idea of
doing this kind of thing is
an ancient one.
According to Kress, it
has simply been out of
our collective mind for
200 or 300 years, and it's
coming back now

From: Michael Spooner
          Kathleen Yancey
To: Joe Harris, editor CCC
Date: Wed, 30 Aug 1995
Subject: last revision

We decided that we don't want to
go as far as labeling each

because the computer makes messing about with type and pictures so easy.

And it turns out that the move to the visual accompanied the move to the printing press, in the late fifteenth century. The press itself had created new readers who needed clarity; one way of achieving that came from the visual. With both print explaining and the visual illustrating, readers found learning easier. But as Kress suggests, the visual is back   now—in part because of new visual media—television and the movies, for instance, not to mention the World Wide Web.

So this is the obvious visual part of what we could call "writing by design." Of course, there's a deeper end to critique and design. It's not that we just like an unorthodox page; it's a matter of *designing meaning* by managing more than one literacy (verbal and visual, for example) in the same space.

"speech" with our initials. Part of this is that we just don't like the effect; and part of it is our writing process—in many cases, the two different voices were composed jointly ("here: you say this...").

We've made a formatting change that will help the reader keep the two voices separate. Where there is a lot of back and forth between the voices, we use two columns; on the other hand, where one voice holds forth for a long spiel, we widen that column to take up most of the page. The obiter dicta continue to barge in from all sides.

The two-column technique not only helps the reader keep things separate, but enhances the sense of conversation—even of interruption. We think readers will see it as integral to the subject of the article.

Another issue that drives Myka is the sneaking suspicion that critique is not especially effective as a mode of change. The conventional book chapter, like the conventional school essay, is an argument, a "critique" in the general sense of the word. Many writing teachers are invested in critique—especially social critique—as their way of teaching writing, because they think teaching students to have critical minds (minds like critics) is the way to bring about positive change in society. That's good, and even true, mostly.

However, ironically, if you depend on the idea of critique this way, you are depending on society *not* to change, because when you lose the status quo, you lose the object of your critique. Then you have to build a new critique of the new status quo.

This didn't matter much when we thought of the world as a place where change was slow. The way we see the world today, however, is much more fluid than before. Some of this is just our way of seeing—our postmodern world view—but some of it is the result of actual rapid social and cultural change. So, in certain ways, we're losing the status quo every day, and this means that a focus on critique will keep some teachers more occupied (and frustrated) than they like.

It does, at times, seem like we are marking our way by dropping bread crumbs in an intertextual forest, only to look behind us and see that they have disappeared. (George and Shoos 1999, 126)

But any way you cut it, when you're doing critique, you're in a response mode; you are not initiating much change or anything but critique. That's why Kress says the task of the critic is to deal with an agenda created by someone before them.

On the other hand (and here we finally get to the fun part), if you take the idea of design as the way to teach or write or think, your task is not only to think critically but to think artfully.

Design is the essential textual principle for periods characterized by intense and far-reaching change. (Kress 1999, 87)

You have to select from elements you find around you and to shape something new with them. Or you place them against a new background so that you can see something new in them.

And Myka does this part, too; it's not just about typographics We gather thoughts from many different writers; these are our *found objects,* as they say in art theory.

He teaches *making,* I prefer *choosing.* . . . I want an aesthetic judgment, of course, but I want to judge a student's art as art, not as "critical practice." (italics added; Sirc 1999, 203)

And we're not so much interested in doing a critique of these ideas as we are in placing them in contact—juxtaposing them.
  We place them against each other—and against the background we paint with Myka's own voices—so that the idea collage we create by doing this shows something new about each of the writers we select. And something new is created in the uniqueness of the collage itself.

Faces, petals.

Humans attempt to make meaning in many different ways: and that's what reading is, making meaning. We attempt to comprehend what is written. We attempt to make sense of what is being said in light of our own experiences and reading practices. We hope that what is being said connects with us intellectually as well as emotionally, spiritually, poetically. Of course, we also react to what is said; to a certain extent, all reading is both a reaction based in critique—this is like me or not—and to a certain extent all reading is design—this is the meaning that I make with an author.

> Which brings us around again to the Athabascans. Just like listening to a good storyteller, making meaning with an author is a process for an active, nimble, persistent mind. In all reading, but especially when you read alt.writing, you have to gnaw the bone of the text. It's like picking berries in the woods; they're ripe and delicious and evasive. And you want to get every single one.

Works Cited

Amato, Joe. 1999. "Family Values: Literacy, Technology, and Uncle Sam." In: *Passions, Pedagogies, and 21st Century Technologies,* 369–86. Edited by Gail E. Hawisher and Cynthia L. Selfe. Logan, UT: Utah State University Press.

Bishop, Wendy. 1995. "If Winston Weathers Would Just Write to Me on Email." *CCC* 46.1 (February):97–103.

Bloom, Lynn Z. 1998. *Composition Studies as a Creative Art.* Logan, UT: Utah State University Press.

Brent, Douglas. 1992. *Reading as Rhetorical Invention.* Urbana, IL: National Council of Teachers of English.

Eldred, Janet Carey. 1999. "Technology's Strange Familiar Voices." In: *Passions, Pedagogies, and 21st Century Technologies,* 387–98. Edited by Gail E. Hawisher and Cynthia L. Selfe. Logan, UT: Utah State University Press.

George, Diana, and Diane Shoos. 1999. "Dropping Bread Crumbs in the Intertextual Forest." In: *Passions, Pedagogies, and 21st Century Technologies,* 115–26. Edited by Gail E. Hawisher and Cynthia L. Selfe. Logan, UT: Utah State University Press.

Hesse, Doug. 1999. "Saving a Place for Essayistic Literacy." In: *Passions, Pedagogies, and 21st Century Technologies,* 34–48. Edited by Gail E. Hawisher and Cynthia L. Selfe. Logan, UT: Utah State University Press.

Kress, Gunther. 1999. "'English' at the Crossroads: Rethinking the Curricula of Communication in the Context of the Turn to the Visual." In: *Passions, Pedagogies, and 21st Century Technologies,* 66–88. Edited by Gail E. Hawisher and Cynthia L. Selfe. Logan, UT: Utah State University Press.

Mendelsohn, Jane. 1997. *I Was Amelia Earhart: A Novel.* New York, NY: Vintage.

Pacanowsky, Michael. 1998. "Slouching towards Chicago." *Quarterly Journal of Speech.* 78.4 (Fall): 453–467.

Pound, Ezra. 1926. "In a Station of the Metro." *Personae*. New York, NY: New Directions.

Rosenblatt, Louise. 1938. *Literature as Exploration*. New York, NY: Appleton-Century.

Sirc, Geoffrey. 1999. "'What is Composition?': After Duchamp (Notes Toward a Teleintertext)." In: *Passions, Pedagogies, and 21st Century Technologies*, 178–204. Edited by Gail E. Hawisher and Cynthia L. Selfe. Logan, UT: Utah State University Press.

Stein, Gertrude. 1926. *Tender Buttons*. Los Angeles, CA: Sun & Moon Press.

Villanueva, Victor. 1993. *Bootstraps: from an American Academic of Color*. Urbana, IL: National Council of Teachers of English.

Vowell, Sarah. 1998. *Radio On: A Listener's Diary*. New York, NY: St. Martin's Press.

Woodward, Bob. 1994. *The Agenda. Inside the Clinton White House*. New York, NY: Wheeler.

16

Spiders, Flies, and Other Creatures of Reading's Brave New World

Hans Ostrom, Sarah Sloane,
Wade Williams, and Teresa Giffen

Sarah: Does it matter whether we're reading a story on the vertical plane of a computer screen or within the pages of a foxed, dog-eared eighteenth-century text that smells vaguely like leaf mold? Many readers and writers today sound terrified about what the computer will do to familiar acts of looking ahead of and looking back at the printed page, dog-earing the pages, scribbling in the margins. They clamor about the end of books (Coover 1992) or the decline of literacy (and by association, western civilization) (Birkerts 1994); they worry that the gaps in a postmodern metafiction are canyons into which all good sense, literary history, and cultural meanings and values have tumbled irrevocably. The abyss is the present, and it is dark and diminished: That is the way this argument primarily goes. I am not persuaded. What do we do when we read? We sweep our eyes across the page, stacking symbols together into familiar packets of words, phrases, and lines, and we animate that prose until it lights up and forms pictures and sounds in the mind. That's what we're doing today and that's what we'll be doing tomorrow, whether on a screen or on paper. A primary human activity is remembering, and reading always helps us remember. In the long run, it isn't going to matter at all where that reading (and remembering) takes place.

In the work of science fiction *Galatea 2.2* (1995), Richard Powers talks about his process of writing being like riding a train, leaning dangerously out from the locomotive to see what lines might be coming next. He wonders aloud what would happen "[i]f the line were memory rather than invention . . . " (55). I am thinking that if the line were memory rather than invention, Richard Powers would be reading rather than writing. The narrator of *Galatea 2.2* reads an article on "hippocampal association" and makes the following stunning connection:

> Every sentence, every word I'd ever stored had changed the physical structure of my brain. Even reading this article deformed the cell map of the mind the piece described, the map that took the piece in. At bottom, at synapse level, I was far more fluid than I'd ever suspected. (56)

I take as a commonplace that all texts act on their readers. But I realized recently that I no longer have a firm sense of what a story is, much less of what it does to its readers—a growing disorientation that no doubt stems from the time I spend reading the sprawling, paratactic, multivocalic, multiverse of postmodern texts on the World Wide Web, what Michael Joyce refers to as "narrative confetti" and what I prefer to call "digital fiction" (Sloane 2000). When we read, our minds change in response to that reading both biologically and metaphysically.

Consider what you do when you read a story by a favorite author, for example. Typically, you hear her voice inside yourself, interior to your head, as we commonly imagine the experience. Whose voice do you imagine as you read these words, however? Who do you hear when you read other authors who are strangers, too? How do you imagine me? Paying attention to the interior life of what happens when we read is one part of understanding this strange process of guided imaginings. Another important part of understanding reading fully, however, is to pay attention to the scenes of reading; that's where computers come into play. Look, for example, at some of the hypertext fictions recently posted on the web. (See the list at the end of this essay for some starters.) Whether we call it *ergodic literature* as Espen Aarseth does, *mystory* as Gregory Ulmer does, or *digital fictions,* we see on the screen a new pliability, loose borderedness, and paratactic sway to story. I propose that once we figure out the interior logic of these digital fictions, we can figure out what new ways these stories are acting on us. How do they change us, and how do they change the way we see the world? How much does that change have to do with the box through which they're presented (the delivery system), and how much has to do with new genres or forms evolving organically from weird contemporary culture?

Hans: Not surprisingly, Sarah's questions interest me. A lot. I wish I had answers that seemed half as interesting. From my vantage point, hypertext fictions change reading and writing radically, chiefly by fusing the two and changing them to *riting* and *wreading.* Hypertext is a site of multiple, simultaneous performances of invention, response, keyboarding, reading, imagining ("imaging"), interpreting, and . . . well—you know how to continue the list as well as I. Hypertext is light, in several senses of the word. It is liquid; its form, like that of a river, is a mirage, a momentary mask worn by energy. Hypertextuality is absolutely revolutionary. Is it also lethal? That is, has it killed "the book" (Birkerts 1994; Coover 1993)?

The other day I asked students in my upper-level fiction-writing class just that question, focusing on the victim, not the perpetrator: Is the book dead? Yes, most of them responded—at least dying, if not already dead. Their evidence—they had brought in brief written responses, by the way—was the deluge of visual and aural media—the Internet (including Internet radio), movies, cable TV, satellite TV, VCRs, and videocams. Some were saddened, even angered, by the apparent demise of the book; these are English majors, after all. Others said we should celebrate the appearance of new forms of writing and reading, such as hypertext fiction. A couple believed the health of the book to be robust. "Look at amazon.com," they said. "It's the Internet, but it's a conduit for books." To which, in a cynical mood, I responded, "That's just a phase." Ultimately, companies like amazon.com will be "shipping" virtual "books" over the Internet because it's much more efficient to sell people bits of light than to sell them packaged paper and ink.

Following are some excerpts, interwoven with my responses, from what one student, Teresa Giffen, wrote.

Teresa: In the interests of disclosure, a secret: I once supported an entire paper on ancient Greek rhetoric with evidence I gathered by applying the find function—ctrl+f—and a search string—word+words+song+speech—to an e-text of the Odyssey. I got an A.

Hans: What if I had read these sentences of Teresa's in 1980, let's say? I would not have known what she was "talking" about until I hit "I got an A." I very much like the other ironies, one of which is that the Great Books have become the Great E-Texts. To quote Casey Stengel, the Homer (as it were) of baseball, "Who'da thunk it?!" Teresa goes on:

Teresa: On the other hand, books have very few shortcomings. They are extremely portable (save for the *Oxford English Dictionary*, obviously). You can enjoy one in the bathtub, in a traffic jam, in a park, or while eating a snack. They are sometimes pricey, but libraries have largely alleviated this burden . . . But as book lovers, let's get down to the proverbial heart of the matter: books delight our senses. On a shelf, they invite our fingers to run across their spines. Their covers, contrary to the adage that I need not mention, can snare our attention and excite us. And a fresh book, to be quite honest, smells heavenly.

Hans: Here I like Teresa's practical analysis. Even when giants like Bill Gates stride the Earth, the book, physically, seems like a good idea.

And books, physically, have enormous appeal. This is something to keep in mind should you have to deal with a bibliophile, or "book addict," in your life. That is, to a large extent, it doesn't matter to the book addict what's printed on those pages; it's the feel of the book, any book—its smell, its graphics, the first words you see. Addict: "Hi. My name's Hans. I'm a book addict." Support Group: "Hi, Hans! (see Raabe 1991).

Unfortunately for this part of Teresa's (and my) bibliophiliac argument, there are probably more cyberphiles than book addicts out there, and the number must continue to explode every day. A recent headline (floating above a picture of a smiling woman sitting in front of a computer monitor) in *USA Today* proclaimed, "I LIVED FOR A MONTH ON THE INTERNET!" With regard to the issue of "post-literacy" (the condition of the book being literally or figuratively dead and of something else, such as hypertext, being very much alive), Teresa chooses the position of ambivalence:

Teresa: Although technology enables new forms of fiction, notably the hypertext fiction, these forms remain not inferior to, but simply different from, the traditional ones. The task of judging the superiority of the traditional over the innovative, or the innovative over the traditional, or the "out with the old, in with the new" compulsion, are not, contrary to Western thought, necessary lines of thinking. Ambivalence is not undesirable: after all, ambivalence tempers our whims and extremes. Perhaps these forms of media can coexist and, moreover, serve one another."

Hans: That is, Teresa seems to choose ambivalence over a false dichotomy and sweetens the ambivalence slightly with optimism. Questions like "Is the book dead?" are useful insofar as they start quick brushfires of thinking, speculation, debate, and—in the case of respondents such as Teresa— wit. My own view is that the book is no more dead than it was 100 years ago, but that it was less alive then than we might imagine. With regard to issues like this, I often think of poet Randall Jarrell's observation about a habit of thinking called Golden Ageism—or nostalgia. In the Golden Age, Jarrell cautions us, everyone was probably walking around complaining about how yellow everything looked. One hundred years ago and now, most people who read did so then do so now for light amusement, currency (news), and/or employment; with this in mind, the impact of hypertext on the reading and writing of novels shrinks as an issue.

Put another way, of all the people harvested by the Internet, what percentage of them read or write hypertext *fiction*? Less than 1 percent would be my guess. Are readers and writers of hypertext narratives as eccentric and irrelevant as bibliophiles?

I do have questions about reading that, for the moment, I consider deeper and more problematic. For instance, my colleague Wade Williams, who will join this essay soon, reminded me that most word-processing programs and even the "shell" (my word, not his) of hypertext are fairly conservative insofar as they mimic conventions of printed matter. What will happen, he asks, when the mimicry itself disappears and we absolutely enter an era of reading that weirdly fuses the medieval and the postmodern, when "reading" will mean chiefly interpreting not so much words of any kind (html or xml) but icons (pictures, images, image clusters) that are not just transmitted by but generated by electronic media? Let's say that one day, soon (now?), this electronic iconography dominates reading; but let's also say that, when it counts, printed matter, linear text, and conventional rhetorics and genres still rule society, in the form of laws, decrees, treaties, and contracts.

I would guess, for example, that Microsoft's business contracts are in the form of acid-free paper and indelible ink. While we happy consumers are swimming along the Internet in html or xml, the fundamentals of our lives will still be controlled by people who write and interpret good old-fashioned laws, legal briefs, appeals, contracts, sentencing guidelines, tax codes, lending policies, and treaties. Another way to phrase the problem: Even as we celebrate new textualities and delight in the questions and possibilities they produce, might we also ask to what extent, if any, word processing, cyberspace, hypertext, the Internet, and so forth have changed the fundamental situation of . . .

- Women worldwide (repression, rape, health, education)
- Workers worldwide (sweatshops, distribution of wealth, health care, job security, psychic health)
- The environment (are computers merely extremely effective tools to helps us describe—but not fundamentally change—the impact of human society on Earth?)
- Economies (fundamentally, how different is Bill Gates, as an economic creature, from Rockefeller or Carnegie?).

All of which is to ask, and I am not asking it rhetorically, does it matter whether our reading and writing (riting and wreading) are changing, or have changed, "radically"?

Sarah: Wow. Hans and Teresa raise so many interesting points and questions that I feel like a spider approaching their web of ideas, à la Wendy Doniger. Doniger has written a great book called *The Implied Spider* (1999) in which she riffs on the narrative theorist Wolfgang Iser's idea of "the implied reader." She says that all the great myths and legends together imply a reader who is a spider, who weaves connections between creation myths of Bali or the Bible, for example. She also says that "the contexts themselves are embedded in the texts if we know how to look for them . . . " (Doniger 1999, 45). And she suggests we learn how to look for them, to weave them together, to treat readings as more like conversations. Wendy Doniger traces the metaphor of the spider itself as it has been used over time, from a mystical Hebrew text, the *Zohar,* in which God is likened to a silkworm that "wraps itself within and makes itself a palace" (Doniger 1999, 62), to the sixth century *Upanishads,* Walt Whitman's poems, and the philosopher Kierkegard's use of the spider as a metaphor for leaping into the unknown. And I feel a bit like Kierkegard's spider myself right now, alight on an unwieldy web, the silk threads taut, fraught, and spinning out before my very eyes.

I can see the remarks made by Hans and Teresa ask me to become a particular kind of spider. They ask that I respond as a spider attentive to forms and possibilities; they ask that I remain alive to the ecologies of writing, to explore how the millennial winds blow through familiar forms and voices on the Internet or on the page. I can do that. They're also asking me to become a spider who can glide across the webs that always exist above the printed words, the invisible traces of conversations echoing before and after what is said. Right. Now. I imagine the conversations that have always existed around the texts we study in school as a sort of Oulipian poetry collection: a book of poems that is invisible to the human eye and that only dogs can hear.

But I have to say I infinitely prefer the web to the argument, the collaborative structures of narrative to the agonistic rhetorics of debate teams. So, I guess I am more spider than fly, and I definitely am more interested in rambling stories than clipped, curt, box-shaped arguments on the page. And the delivery system, the computer that computes these various genres, doesn't trouble or distract me much at all. I think the novelty of computer-based stories and rhetorics opens a window into the way all delivery systems affect what is said; but I don't think the computer is any more pernicious or sinister than the pencil is; and the companies that create software and hardware aren't to be suspected of evil hegemonies or homogenizing acts any more so than are New York publishing houses, the owners of radio stations, or any of the many other collaborative commercial endeavors that depend on getting out products to make a fast buck. Computer-based texts are not a new devil; they're an old devil in a new blue dress.

The web that Hans and others are spinning here, I think, is one that is woven with a healthy paranoia about the directions the Internet is taking us, about the hidden ideologies and epistemologies underlying the networks of hardware and software that connect us. It is a concern, if paranoia is too strong a word, that recommends a skeptical approach to claims of new cyberliteracies, or postsymbolic discourse or virtual wreading and riting.

An interesting set of essays published recently (Selfe and Hawisher 1999) explores the misplaced missionary zeal that underlies the claim that international computer networks are neutral purveyors of information, that there are no implicit claims or economic systems or assumptions about position and power underlying the simple exchange of E-mail messages from Aberdeen, Scotland, to Aberdeen, Washington State, for example. Sometimes harsh critics of the "wahoo!" rhetoric about global literacies and global economies fostered by computers, Selfe and Hawisher help us see that although the World Wide Web may exaggerate or distort existing hegemonic practices, it does not *create* them—nor does it provide an antidote to them. Ethnocentric ideas, national biases, capitalist assumptions, and racist and sexist "gazes" still thrive on the Internet. (One need only look at the web pages about any South Pacific island to see the continued workings of "the tourist gaze.") Ultimately, the essays in that collection caution us, the rhetorics of liberation and transformation that inform so many of our discussions about digital technology may not only be false, but irresponsible.

My guess is that once the novelty of the computer fades, we'll see that this particular delivery system of text represents a difference in degree, but not in kind. That is, many of our choices of how to compose, with whom we compose, and what we say are themselves always embedded in culture and context and chunks of past ways of thinking and feeling. That's life. But ultimately I have another question: How are the computer-based stories that Hans and colleagues are wary of any different from various other artistic movements of this century, including French dadaists, the Italian futurists, the American metafictionalists, or so many other paper-based literary experiments? What's the difference between Stuart Moulthrop's *hegirascope,* for example, and some Oulipian stories (Matthews)? My point is that the delivery system of story is often of little relevance, and the fact that we can play around with form, with delivery, with constraints like the one Teresa imposed on herself, is an aesthetic game not tied to computers alone. I can imagine a round of Scrabble that might be as inventive, collaborative, and creative as anything on the World Wide Web today, especially if it were played by cheaters.

Finally, I think the past 10 years' conversations about whether the book is dead is about as interesting as the past 50 years' drivel about whether the novel is dead. It doesn't matter. It's either here or not, and time will tell. There are really only two routes (and variations thereof) that the book as information delivery system can take: it can continue to coexist with the literary forms (hypertext fictions, MUDs, web soap operas, *Postmodern Culture* essays) that the Internet supports, or it can be erased by the Internet. In any case, I am confident that stories and cultures will survive the changes. All writing involves reading; all reading involves writing. Computers ultimately bring little new to the essential practices and products.

Hans: Yes, but! Yes, I appreciate Sarah's bracing bit of fatalism: A brave new world (Huxley 1932) is either here or it isn't. But the same sort of fatalism could apply to other pressing questions of the moment. One could also say that violence, racism, and ecological disintegration will either continue to plague the planet, or not; it doesn't matter; time will tell. I hasten to add that the analogy I want to make is between two fatalistic responses, not between our topic of reading and these massive ills. Whether we want to make such fatalistic moves is debatable, and I invite our readers to debate: Do we have any control over this technology? If not, why not? If so, what kind of control, and how should we use the control? To play off of Wendy Doniger and Sarah, are we spiders or flies?

Also, if one can reasonably show that the "delivery system" of "story" fundamentally changes "story," then asking questions about the delivery system is hardly irrelevant; indeed, it is crucial. Is there any doubt that in the past 500 years or so, the "delivery system" of "the book" defined "story," hugely influenced who wrote and read, shaped—for good, for ill, for in between—whole societies (Raymond Williams 1961)? True, if we only ask a question like "Is the book dead?" and leave the arena, then we are drivelers; but I take the question to be only introductory, a step into an arena in which we ask how delivery systems and means of production change "story," reading, and writing; change education; redefine notions of "intellectual property"; change or reinforce existing structures of culture (literature, rhetoric, law, politics, economics, and so on). And yes, I too can imagine a highly creative game of Scrabble, but in fact Scrabble is not the "delivery system" at the heart of our brave new world. Computers are.

Sarah: Right back at you. It seems to me that there are many ways of reading our culture's preoccupation with computers, but fatalism isn't a particularly good one. I wouldn't recommend it, either. Fatalism presupposes that "events are fixed in advance for all time in such a manner that human beings are powerless to change them" (Webster's) and ultimately that's a poor attitude with which to approach any problems—from the important ones that Hans notes above, to the simpler ones such as how stories appear on the page or screen. We can change things, and we do. I think since we're composing at the threshold of a new century, some of the millennialist rhetoric current in the news has inflected our own thinking about technology today. I'm saying instead of being fatalistic, we should be realistic, flexible, and open when we observe a switch in delivery system such as we are seeing today. I'm saying we need to pay attention to the important features of the reading and writing cycles—such as who gets to speak, what stories get said, and who gets to read them—and less attention to the hyperbolic screeds of the millennialists who in the seams between the centuries see the good old world dying and a bad new world order starting.

For goodness' sake, technologies have conveyed stories since our ancestors painted hunting scenes on the smudged walls of a cave. The word *technology* itself simply means art or craft or skill; etymologically the Greek *techne* is linked to the Latin *texere,* to weave. All the computer is doing is offering us a new loom for our stories. And we should resist the attempt to transmogrify the computer into some wholly unrecognizable force that is going to blow up reading and writing as we know it, in the form of some narrative Armageddon that will destroy stories forever. I don't believe it. My guess is that once the novelty of the computer fades, we'll see that this particular delivery system of text represents a difference in degree, but not in kind.

Finally, I guess I'm ultimately urging us toward a spiderly appreciation for the magnificent structures writers spin out of air, whatever medium or delivery system brings those stories home. And in your readings, I'd say, don't cling too much to the past but enjoy the playful pastiches, the visual and audible cultures of the story on-line today. It's okay that they're different from what you're used to.

Hans: Makes sense to me. I would add, as I prepare to depart the text and welcome Wade to it, only a few things. I'd say, yes, don't cling too much to the past, but also don't automatically reject the past or mindlessly accept what's new. Teresa's view, expressed earlier, is appealing in part because it looks critically at both "the book" and "hypertext." To modify Sarah's entreaty slightly, it may or may not be okay that the story on-line is different from what you're used to. Judge for yourself: how, why, and to what extent is a particular story on-line different? How effective is the "loom" analogy Sarah draws, or other analogies we (and you) have used when discussing computers and reading and writing? And judge yourself—your criteria of judgment. But, as implied in my reference to Golden Ageism earlier, I certainly agree with Sarah that "end-time" rhetoric isn't appropriate to discussing cyberspace, although it is interesting to observe that, in the United States at least, the chief cause of apocalyptic thinking these days (the Y2K problem) seems to spring not so much from a reactionary reflex as from a recognition of how ubiquitous computers have become.

To some degree, the potential impact of "narratives on line" on our culture pales in comparison to other potential effects. I am thinking mainly of the effect of computers on privacy and on social relationships. Concerning the latter, Jon Katz (1999) has written an interesting piece in *Rolling Stone* that includes a profile of one Jesse, whom Katz labels a *geek* (and thanks go to Jeffrey Early for drawing my attention to this piece). Katz writes:

> Jesse has a thriving social life, but not in the sense that most people traditionally use the term. It exists almost totally in his head, on screens,

online, on the Web sites, conferencing systems, chat and messaging programs, games. Jesse stays in touch with some friends nearly every single day but knows little about their offline lives, their families, their states of mind. His friendships are characterized by a stream of gifts— games, music, software. It would never occur to him to tell a friend that he was happy or sad. (50)

Leaving aside the epithet *geek* (which doesn't get us very far), and assuming Katz's profile of Jesse is accurate, we might ask how representative Jesse is, might ask ourselves what we think of his "social life," the way he "reads" himself, his identity, the sense in which he exists chiefly on-line. No doubt you know more people like Jesse than I do, and maybe there are even some similarities between you and Jesse. Indeed, you are part of a new kind of "first generation" in the United States, in the world—the generation that has not known a world without computers, a generation that, because it has "grown up with" computers, seems uniquely positioned to answer the questions we have raised here, to question some of the answers we have given, and most especially to think of different, maybe better, questions.

Wade: Like the question of whether the book is dead or not, like the medium of hypertext itself, on-line dialogs resist closure. But the conventions of print and academic writing impose their own boundaries, and I've been given the task of wrapping up this discussion. Unfortunately, I'm left with more questions than answers: What are we to make of all this? Are the transformations fostered by the new technology of hypertext ones of degrees or kind? Is the medium, as Marshal McLuhan argues, the message? And, how can we know? First, we need to define the subject a little. Are we talking specifically about stories, fiction, literature? Or are we talking about acts of writing and reading themselves?

If we are talking just about, to use Sarah's phrase, digital fictions, then I am certainly sympathetic to her position. Narrative is the ur-genre. It has survived many delivery systems, many technologies of the word: the alphabet, papyrus, the pen, paper, the printing press, and, probably, hypertext. But I would agree with Walter Ong and others that stories have been transformed by technologies. Orality imposes an economy on invention, arrangement, style, memory, and delivery (the five traditional canons of rhetoric) different from that of handwriting and, later, print literacy. Stories, which are so fundamental to the sustenance of culture, will survive. Why not, as Sarah states, appreciate these "magnificent structures"—whether Dickens' *Great Expectations* or Joyce's *Afternoon*—as they exist, as they are enabled by the possibilities of a particular technology, rather than decrying the first change in narrative form as the downfall of civilization. Yes, certain avant-garde literatures predate the World Wide Web, as do literary theorists such as Roland Barthes who seem to anticipate the Web so presciently. In many ways, however, the possibilities of hypertext enhance the experience of reading and writing; it foregrounds (or it can more readily foreground) the intertextual, multilinear and polyvocal properties of fiction that are always already present—even in the printed text. Let's celebrate the play of imagination.

But I want to temper that enthusiasm with a healthy dose, not of paranoia, but of skepticism, à la Hans and Teresa. And here, I think, we need to look at the whole package: how will new technologies of the word affect reading and writing? The question is ambitious, and the evidence is still unclear. We can turn to hypertext theorists such as Jay David Bolter, George Landow, and Stuart Moulthrop for predictions, forecasts, and speculations, but the fact remains—we're living through these transformations, we're insiders trying to look inside. We can't really know where all these shifts are going to lead: the evidence is still too ambiguous. We can, however, turn to history for some possible answers. Since the Scientific Revolution, technologies have always been introduced under the auspices of progress. We see this with the telescope, the compass, the cotton gin, the combustion engine, the air conditioner, the birth control pill, the splitting of the atom, and so on. Each is couched in a rhetoric of progress, efficiency, and control. And there's no doubt that many of these technologies have enabled changes that have made our lives . . . I almost wrote *better*. Perhaps *easier*? No, I'm uncomfortable with that word as well. But I'm not giving up my car, and I'm still writing on a computer. I'm no Luddite, and neither, I suspect, are many people who claim the title, but I do try to be a little skeptical. And it's hard when we're bombarded daily with messages about how much easier life would be with products X, Y, or Z.

My point is that there is very little discussion of the social effects of these technologies. We discuss cloning, but the ethical line is being moved by degrees, unseen, until one day we'll look back and wonder how we got there. Can we apply the same line of reasoning to current technologies of the word? To E-mail, word processing, hypertext, and the like? Will we look back and wonder how we got there? I can already do that with E-mail. Every morning I get to my office and immediately check E-mail; it has changed how I organize my day, how I get information, how I communicate with those around me. I ask myself, how did I ever live without E-mail? The same question can be asked of word processing and the Internet. Or, try this experiment: make a list of every technology of the word that has been introduced since the 1970s: e.g., telephone answering machines, VCRs, CD players, cell phones, modems, fax machines, personal computers, laptop computers, E-mail, the Internet, voice mail, camcorders, and on and on. Next, ask yourself, could I live without this or that, or any of these?

Many—perhaps most—acts of writing and reading done on the

computer or in cyberspace are still governed by the conventions and expectations of print literacy. We speak of the paperless office, but many of us still write on-line as a means to producing hard, printed, tangible text. Many of my students inform me that they still need to revise on hard copy. We are, it seems, somewhere in between the old world of print literacy and new world of electronic literacy. Word-processing programs conceptualize electronic text as an extension of traditional print culture. For example, Microsoft Word uses features and functions such as desktop, cut and paste, file, document, pages: all familiar and comfortable traces of print literacy. Of course, it doesn't have to be that way. The familiar page on-screen is, in the end, virtual—ultimately, a string of ones and zeros somewhere deep in the recesses of my computer. But, such print-oriented features still (comfortably) shape how I produce and interpret electronic text.

So, in the end, if the printed text ends at all, it will do so with a whimper and not a bang. I suspect we'll continue to approach our reading and writing with the conventions of the book. Of course, different communities on the World Wide Web will organize themselves and their forms of discourse differently; some more conservative and some more innovative. We already see this. But the high-use communities, particularly the information sites such as news, are still governed by the conventions of the book. Is there any technology on the horizon that will threaten the hegemony of the book? The most significant is probably voice recognition and activation technology. And here, I confess, I only have questions: what will happen if (and when) the physical acts of writing and reading are rendered unnecessary? In 10 years will anyone use keyboards (or pen and paper) anymore? Is this brave new world of reading and writing a difference in degree or kind?

Related Questions

Think about what you do when you read. What are you seeing right now, for instance? Where does that vision come from? Whose voice do you hear, what voice do you almost hear, echoing in the very back of your head? You might think, too, about who you become when you read. Is this essay (so far) demanding that you become a certain kind of person? Does it matter if a teacher assigns the reading you do? How does this sentence change things for you: Are you sometimes tempted to forego this whole enterprise of analyzing word-coupled-to-word, the tired task of using familiar symbols to build a lighthouse in your brain? How does your own history change according to the memory palaces you enter via the printed word? Do you care? What would make you care?

Some Digital Stories

The Garden of Forking Masques by Katherine Wren
http://members.tripod.com/~liveKate/

Gregory Ulmer Hypertext Fiction
http://207.82.252.253/cgi-
in/linkrd?hm___action=http%3a%2f%2fwww%2eva%2ecom%2eau%2f
parallel%2fx2%2fjournal%2fgregory_ulmer%2findex%2ehtml

Beehive
http://www.temporalimage.com/beehive/bee_core/in2x.html

Fences: A Womyn's Web
http://english.ttu.edu/kairos/2.2/features/reflections/emily.htm

Works Cited

Aarseth, Espen. 1997. *Cybertext: Perspectives on Ergodic Literature*. Baltimore: Johns Hopkins University Press.

Basbanes, Nicholas. 1999. *A Gentle Madness*. New York: Owl Books.

Birkerts, Sven. 1994. *The Gutenberg Elegies: The Fate of Reading in an Electronic Age*. Boston: Faber & Faber.

Calvino, Italo. 1979. *If on a Winter's Night a Traveler.* Translated by William Weaver. New York: Harcourt, Brace, Jovanovich.

Coover, Robert. 1992. "The End of Books." *The New York Times Book Review,* June 21, pp. 1, 23–25.

Coover, Robert. 1993. "Hyperfiction: Novels for the Computer." *The New York Times Book Review,* August 29, pp. 1, 8–12.

Doniger, Wendy. 1999. *The Implied Spider: Politics & Theology in Myth*. New York: Columbia University Press.

Front Page, *USA Today,* April 15, 1999.

Huxley, Aldous. 1932. *Brave New World*. Garden City, NJ: Garden City Publishers.

Joyce, Michael. 1990. *Afternoon, a Story* [computer software]. Cambridge, MA: Eastgate Software.

Katz, Jon. 1999. "Geeks." *Rolling Stone,* April 29, pp. 48–57.

Mathews, Harry, and Alastair Brotchie, eds. 1998. *Oulipo Compendium*. London: Atlas Press.

Motte, Warren. 1986. *Oulipo: A Primer of Potential Literature*. Lincoln: University of Nebraska Press.

Powers, Richard. 1995. *Galatea 2.2.*

Raabe, Tom. 1991. *Biblioholism: The Literary Addiction*. Golden, CO: Fulcrum Publishing.

Selfe, Cindy, and Gail Hawisher, eds. 1999. *Global Literacy Practices and the WWW.* London: Routledge.

Sloane, Sarah. 2000. *Digital Fictions: Storytelling in a Material World.* Norwood, NJ: Ablex Press.

———. 1999. "Postmodernist Looks at the Body Electric: Email, Female, and Hijra." In: *Feminist Cyberscapes: Mapping Gendered Academic Spaces.* Edited by Kris Blair and Pamela Takayoshi. Norwood, NJ: Ablex Press.

Ulmer, Gregory. 1989. "Derrida at Little Bighorn." In: *Teletheory: Grammatology in the Age of Video,* pp. 212–243. New York: Routledge.

Williams, Raymond. 1961. *The Long Revolution.* London: Chatto & Windus.

Sharing Ideas

1. What was your readers' response to Chapter 15, by Myka Vielstimmig, to the argument for and practice of alt.style?

2. Use Chapter 7 by Darrell Fike to read Chapter 15 by Myka Vielstimmig. What does each reading lens—mimetic, pragmatic, objective—add to your reading of this multivocal text?

3. Where else in your reading life have you found alt.texts? What demands do these make on you as a reader? How willing are you to make such changes in your reading style?

4. Look at other chapters in this collection. To what degree do they too partake of alt.style? To what degree are the essays of your classmates composed in alt.style? Are you encouraged/allowed to write in this manner? Why or why not?

5. As a group or class, compose a multivoiced response to the authors of Chapter 15.

6. Choose four or five provocative statements from Chapter 16 and play the doubting and believing game with each statement. For me, one such statement is this: "Once the novelty of the computer fades, we'll see that this particular delivery system of text represents a difference in degree, but not in kind."

7. Join the doomsayers, the enthusiasts, the skeptics, the pragmatists of reading and writing in the 21st century. What do you think first-year college writing classrooms will be like in the year 2025, 2050, and 2075. On what do you base your predictions?

Part VI

Hint Sheets
for Students (A–K) and for Teachers (1–5)

The reading process for factual texts is like pulling out a tooth, is like sucking on a lemon, is like sitting through a boring class; the reading process for imaginative texts is like smelling a rose, is like seeing a sunset, is like tasting chocolate, takes me to the world inside the book, allows me to think, imagine, and feel. Reading the writing of my peers is like looking into people's characters/minds—you get to see how they think, feel, organize thoughts. It is sometimes like looking at a big yard full of yard-work to do—it can be overwhelming but after the work is completed you can see the difference. You have gathered new ideas/techniques from other writers.

—Anonymous in-class freewriting response

Hint Sheet A
The Process Cover Sheet

Wendy Bishop

The process cover sheet ranges in length from a paragraph to several pages, sometimes functioning as a mini–"how-I-write" essay. Sometimes I request a letter from author to prospective reader, sometimes a short essay of self-analysis. At a minimum, the text should cover the actual, physical conditions of the writing of the paper under discussion, as well as the major decision points the author took in the drafting and revision process. Equally, this is a location where the writer can give himself or herself credit for the thinking and writing activities that aren't supposed to appear in a final, carefully proofread draft—the wrestling-with-ideas-in-writing that naturally must take place in order for a piece of writing to grow and develop.

The following samples are portions of the process cover sheets submitted with the five narratives in this book. As writers submitted each draft, they also submitted revised narratives of their drafting journeys.

While reading these, make notes on the different issues and subjects the authors covered. Also, you should note instances where they didn't seem to tell you what you needed to know or places where you'd like to hear them explore their processes even further. Analyzing their cover sheets should help you draft a better cover sheet of your own.

Narrative 1: Kirk Parrott

This paper was an easy one to write since I had the story fresh in my mind. Not too long ago I'd been arguing with my mom about all the ways they used to torture me and whether or not I'd do that to my son. This was one of the images that was conjured up during this discussion, so when this assignment came around I immediately realized that this is what I should write about. That got the problem of deciding on the subject out of the way, which made me much more confident about my writing, because that's what usually deters me first.

Once I began typing it was easy to develop the story. This was probably where I spent the most amount of time, as I usually do. If I can get started then I don't have any problem. Its when I start the paper, stop and wait until later, and then start working on it again that I get confused as to what I was trying to say. It's just like trying to verbally tell a story, stopping until later, then trying to pick up where you left off. I just can't seem to get back into the same voice or style to finish the story. That's what made the revising of this story so incredibly difficult. I'd add in some new sections and they'd just appear to stick out, or not flow with the rest of the story.

Overall, I probably spent about 4 hours writing the paper without stopping for any breaks. During that time I'd write the original draft and read over it several times, making corrections wherever I saw necessary. My revising didn't last nearly as long as the actual writing of the paper. I did spend a good amount of time revising without actually getting anywhere since I'd add something and later decide it just didn't sound right. I'd really appreciate any ideas you could give me on how to improve my essay. Please give me ideas as to how to work those improvements into my paper.

Revision of this paper was a breeze. The people I worked with during the revision of this paper gave me good criticism on my paper rather than cheesy answers. The alternative for the parts that didn't work really helped the most. For someone just to tell me a part of my story doesn't work won't help me. I obviously thought it sounded all right or I wouldn't have left it in there. If they give me an idea as to how to make it better then it helps a lot more.

Narrative 2: Lysa Moorefield

For my beginning rough drafts of this paper, I did not even hit the subject of reading—I concentrated more on my English class from my freshman year in college. I explained some of the papers that we had to write in class, and that was basically my main focus. I made a five-page written paper out of this, and after one revision in class I knew I was going to have to change the whole basis of my paper. After revising and thinking, I changed to fall semester, and concentrated on both History and English.

Since my first written draft was only three pages, I had a little bit of confidence that I could rearrange my five page written document into something that had to deal with reading.

I could not really remember a lot about reading when I was younger, except that I hated it, so I decided to write on myself looking back at my fall semester in college. Specifically, American Civilization and English 1101.

I feel that I explained myself pretty well in the way I felt about reading and how it has changed through the years. In my paper, the one main objective that I wanted to accomplish was to make the reader interested in my story, and also make them relate to it in some way. In my conference with you, Wendy, I took everything you told me and used it in my final project. All and any comments that were on the side margins were put to use in the end.

I did most of this paper in the Academic Center, and even typed my final paper there. Rewrites and proofreading were mostly done at home, but there was a lot of time put into this paper. It is nice to write about experiences that have changed myself as a reader and a writer because those are things that I would not normally discuss.

Narrative 3: Chris Olson

Beginning with my first draft, I quickly became troubled with the way it was coming out of my brain onto the paper. I knew what I wanted to write about, but it just did not seem to want to come out. In my first draft I completed three pages, which were read in class by my peers. Surprisingly, they liked them, so it was possible that I was being too hard on myself. Although my classmates liked the first draft of the paper, I did not. In my opinion, I was not expressing the emotion and feeling that I felt so strongly about in the paper. It was not a clear reflection of what state I was in during the early years of learning to read.

I knew what I wanted to accomplish in the second draft. Reading has been so emotional for me, so I wanted to capture that in the paper. I find it harder sometimes to write about things I feel very emotional about because I see it in my head very clearly, which makes me leave out detail.

In planning the second draft of my paper, so I would not leave out detail as I did in the first draft; I took a piece of paper and made a list of all the topics I wanted to cover. Then next to each topic I wrote what was troubling or emotional about each one. This helped when I began to put the paper together. When I was lost in emotion I could look back on the reference sheet.

In revising the second copy, I looked at the reference you made on the copy. In two places I added more description or a scene to elaborate the setting. I also went through the paper and fixed the spelling and grammar errors.

Narrative 4: Dawn Maria Lieber

I wrote this narrative using the prompts given to us in class. I wrote about the things I read in different rooms of my house. I compose all of my work on the computer so I just started thinking and typing about my encounters with reading all different types of media as a child. I started by drawing a sketch of the rooms in my house. This was fun for me so I continued and I did the majority of the work in that one sitting. I save my Saturdays for my long papers. I did minor revisions and changes throughout the 2 weeks that followed.

I usually wake up on Saturday and turn on the computer. Once it is on, I need little inspiration once I find a general idea to write on. I live in a loud dorm, so I constantly have people running in and out of my room. I throw out some ideas to them and see how they react. I got a good response to all the stories I told so I chose those to be included in the paper. If I see an interest in a certain part of the story, I go back to the computer and expand. I also find myself explaining the story more in detail when I verbally communicate, so I go back and add all the details that I forget to write in the first draft.

I had a lot of fun thinking about the different experiences I have had as a child. It was almost hard for me to choose which ones to use. After listing these different readings I threw them together and tied it with a paragraph for the introduction and a sentence for a conclusion. This was my framework. Within that framework, I touched up each story. I added little lies that I thought worked well and enhanced the paper. It turned out they worked well because the little inventions I added were more conceivable than the parts of the story that were true. Even though I liked the stories, I did not like the way I had arranged my paper.

My editing group liked the paper a lot more than I did. I listened to their advice and took much of it into consideration, but for reasons I cannot explain, their ideas did not help in the direction that I looked to take this paper. Nobody in the group gave me any type of criticism or response to work from. They were too polite and it seemed as though they were refraining from a critique.

Two weeks later, I sat for another revision and I switched my introduction and conclusion. It worked well. Immediately I was more content with the paper and the way it flowed.

I did not feel like there were structural problems that I wanted to change for my portfolio copy. After putting this paper aside for a couple of weeks, I realized how much fun it was to write and how much I enjoy this paper.

The very final revision done by my classmates was very positive. They felt as though it was an extremely funny paper and there was nothing for me to change.

Narrative 5: Rob Adams

My inspiration for this essay was the phone conversation mentioned within. The freewriting exercises we did in class also helped. They really got me thinking about reading as a child. The memory is a strange thing—there are things in there I've lived but don't know about yet.

The first half of my rough draft came very easily. I was interrupted by a phone call, went to sleep and tried to finish the next day. This was a big mistake. My thoughts weren't flowing anymore and I found myself writing in a different voice than the night before. That aside, I came out with about five pages worth of material.

Our in-class editing workshop was a big help. They pointed out a few places that needed work that I had never noticed. They all acknowledged that my stop/restart point was noticeable. However, they couldn't really help me with it. I knew that was my biggest problem. Overall, their reactions were positive and nobody seemed bored. I felt no need for any radical changes.

The professional draft came out a little better. The feedback from my writing group members was almost all positive. They all commended me on my cover-up of the problematic stop/restart point. The only changes I made to this version were correcting a few typos and minor tweaks in wording here and there.

My goal with this essay was to appeal to a very general audience. I think anyone over age 10 could read this. In high school, I tended to use a lot of big words to impress my teachers, but I don't think that will work in college. I'm looking forward to essay 4 so I can take this topic in a new direction.

Hint Sheet B
Summary of Inventions for Beginning a Literacy Narrative

Wendy Bishop

To continue to explore how reading connects to your writing life, try any or all of the following explorations:

1. *Reading Home.* Think of a house, apartment, trailer, or living space from your earliest years, years when you were learning to read and write—for most of us, this is preschool through elementary school. From memory, draw a floor plan of that living space. Then, number each room in the living space, including, if it applies, outdoor areas. For each number, in a list at the bottom of the page, remember a literacy story—stories of learning to read or write in the broadest sense, from reading "forbidden magazines" in the bathroom, to parents reading to you in the bedroom, to hiding out outside with a book, to trying to type a story for Mother's Day, to reading family fights, to reading how your older sister got dressed for a date, and so on. Write enough notes for each numbered location to remind you of this story later. Finally, choose the most memorable reading memory and cluster or freewrite a bit of this experience on a separate sheet of paper.

2. *Timeline and/or life map.* Draw a horizontal or vertical line that moves from age 1 to your present age or school level. Mark off important events in your reading and writing life. Or, draw a curving line from left to right down the paper, drawing stick-figure representations of events concerned with reading and writing, and continuing from the upper left-hand corner of the paper to the bottom right-hand corner in a life map. Choose one of these events—the one your forgot about and only "found" by completing this exercise—and write about it in a freewrite on a separate sheet of paper.

3. *Describe your reading process.* How do you read and what do you read? Where do you read? What keeps you from reading, helps you read? How does reading connect to your writing? As a writer, when are you reading? Do you have a different process of reading for writing than reading for reading?

4. *List your all-time favorite books, preschool to the present.* Come back to and add to this list over the course of several days. You might do this by listing your ages of reading—preschool, kindergarten, grades 1–3, grades 4–6, and so on. Freewrite about your favorite preschool/kindergarten book: What do you remember liking about it? What were the conditions under which you read it or it was read to you? What do you remember about the plot and illustrations? Go to a bookstore or library and reread the book. Then freewrite about this reading experience a little further.

5. *What do you know about readers and nonreaders?* List four friends or family members who read and four more who do not read. What are their reading habits and reading choices? What in their past or present makes them the readers they are today? Does their attitude toward reading connect to anything you know about their attitudes toward writing? Choose a favorite book of yours, read in the past year, and offer it to each of these eight people to read—what would their responses be, and how would you try to convince each to undertake this reading?

6. *Is it possible to be a writer who doesn't read or a reader who doesn't write?* Explore the ramifications of either situation by thinking first about the connections you can draw between your own reading and writing processes and then that of others.

7. *Imagine you have a younger brother or sister who is just starting college this fall.* He or she has neglected his or her reading and writing but suddenly wants to get serious. What are your ten best tips for becoming a better college writer? A better college reader? Write these in an engaging way with enough detail to be really helpful to this person whose success you really care about (ignore the number of times he or she has avoided your good advice in the past!).

8. *In a week or ten days, reread all these writings about reading for writing* and draw some conclusions about what issues, themes, learning you find that you didn't see as you did the initial draft.

Hint Sheet C
Discussion Questions and Activities for "From Books and Articles to Websites and Newsgroups"

Dan Melzer

Discussion Questions

- What are some similarities and differences between reading texts and "reading" websites, films, advertisements, and so on?
- What "alternative" forms of reading have you done in your classes?
- What approaches do you take to reading websites? Films? Plays? etc.

Activities

- Provide definitions of *reading*. Share these definitions and then apply them to alternative reading material such as websites and films.
- Undertake an alternative kind of reading—a movie, website, or advertisement. Discuss the way you *read* this material compared with the way you read print text.
- Observe and *read* people at the mall or on campus. Discuss the ways we read people like we read print texts.

Being an Active Reader

Discussion Questions

- What techniques do you use when you're reading?
- How do you know what to underline?
- What does it mean when you highlight "everything"?
- Is faster reading better reading?

Activities

- By sharing copies of a common text or looking at a text your teacher puts on an overhead projector, practice active reading together as a class. Suggest (and evaluate) a variety of reading strategies.
- Bring in a difficult reading from another class and practice annotating each others' texts.
- Use a reading journal to summarize your reading for your writing class or for all your classes.
- Practice summarizing short texts together. What do you learn about the art of summary?

Reading Is a Process

Discussion Questions

- What is your reading process? Do you "preread" or reread?
- Compare your writing process to your reading process. How are they similar? How are they different?
- Compare your reading process for different classes. What process do you go through in each class? Is your reading process different for each class?

Activities

- In class, reread an essay you were already assigned to read outside of class. Discuss the advantages of this kind of rereading.
- As a class, discuss your reading processes. Compare the processes you go through in different classes.
- Practice reading aloud in class, either with professionals' or with peers' essays.
- Share your metaphors for reading by responding to the prompt, "For me, reading is like . . ." What do you learn about yourself and other readers in the class?

The Reading/Writing Connection

Discussion Questions

- Do your professors connect reading and writing? If they do, how do they make the connection?
- Is the reading you do in most classes "fact finding," or do you read for comprehension?

- Does reading improve writing? If you think it does, in what ways?
- Are there classes for which you don't read what's assigned?

Activities

- Discuss the reading and writing you've done in college. Do your professors connect reading and writing? What connection have they made? Do they ever connect the reading and writing done for different classes? With what results?
- Discuss quotes from writers talking about their reading habits, and the way their reading connects to their writing. Your teacher may provide these, or you can find them by doing some research for there are many books available that interview professional writers about their composing practices.
- In a small group, have a "true confessions" session about reading. Talk about all the times you didn't do the assigned reading for classes, and how that affected your writing. Summarize your confession session to share with the whole class.

Hint Sheet D
Ways to Respond to a Literary Text

Wendy Bishop

1. Choose a resonant phrase or crucial word and begin clustering in response (example: "I look at his face . . ." or "Call me Ishmael"). Draft a prose riff or poem beginning off cluster ideas.

2. Write a letter to a character, narrator, speaker, or author—ask questions, give responses.

3. Write a reversal—change gender, actions, scene, or simply reverse language.

4. Write an extension—take the piece an hour, day, or week beyond its current ending.

5. Write a treatment—what contemporary movie stars would you have star in this text and why?

6. Explore the narrator or a character—use the following metaphoric prompts to add to your understanding of the narrator/character:
   - He/she is the kind of person who wears . . .
   - He/she is what color?
   - He/she is keeping what secret(s)?
   - He/she has this dream . . .
   - He/she would like to say but never says . . .
   - He/she is what kind of fruit? What kind of landscape? What kind of time of day?
   - What job should this person never have? What kind of a car does he/she drive?
   - This person is what kind of weather? and so on.

7. Drive words
   a. Write down your own personal drive words (words you like the sound or meaning of) in categories:
      - three words for plants (e.g., aloe, hibiscus, rhododendron)
      - three words for animals (e.g., Manx, Doberman, catfish)
      - three words you just like (e.g., cinnamon, phenomenologist, melaleuca)

- three words for food (e.g., chocolate, cellophane noodles, orange calabash)
- three words for parts of the body (e.g., index finger, collarbone, Achilles tendon)

b. Choose five drive words from the text you're studying—words that resonate or have odd significance, interesting locations, etc.

c. Choose two of your own drive words and two of the text drive words and freewrite on each for 1 minute (4 minutes total).

d. Begin an initial draft of a poem or prose paragraph.

As a group: Do the drive word exercise by sharing one personal and one poem drive word from each group member. First freewrite, then compose a text together.

8. Recast an issue or scene.
   - If the text talks about love and food, freewrite about love and food.
   - If a text talks about moral and ethical decisions/turning points, freewrite about those in your own life.
   - If the text has a lyrical description of X (summer, winter, the coast, etc.) freewrite about X in your own life.
   - Draft your own text in a situation contemporary to you (create a word meal for a current lover, describe a current living landscape for a distant friend, etc.)

9. Explore the text's rhetoric and style.
   - Write a parody (new subject, same linguistic style).
   - Change genre (turn a poem into a prose passage by filling in gaps and recreating sentence patterns; turn prose into a poem by lining out, cutting, repeating, altering the rhythm).
   - Write a reply to the text using the same style (or a reply for a character in the text).

10. Collage your text (any of the above exercises) with those of members of a group.

Intentionally

- Write drive word passages or poems using the same drive words and then read in a chorus (alternating or in a round).
- Cluster from the same core word and then share the resulting freewrites by reading a sentence at a time, around the group.
- Let several of the "created from text" characters speak together—put them into a scene or dialog together after you flesh them out with metaphoric prompts.
- Do a call and response—one person reads a passage and everyone writes a response (do this one time for each group member) then read the entire set in compositional order (or in a set alternation).

Randomly

- Cut and paste sentences together from individual writings or choose three or four phrases for the group to freewrite on and then share in a round reading.

Obviously, these "creative" moves are all variations of similar exploratory patterns:

1. Resonate to the text (read, reread, discuss, share, annotate, puzzle, highlight, etc.).
2. Respond to the text (perform, talk, freewrite, relate to own experience, etc.).
3. Enter the text (manipulate genre, voice, syntax, theme, etc.).
4. Transform the text (turn into own text, extend text, layer the text, hide the text, etc.).
5. Share an evolutionary text (with traces of the original obvious perhaps only to those who shared the journey).

This is not about competitive art-making, it's about understanding and experiencing.

Hint Sheet E
Small Group Exercises for Reading and Responding to Literary Texts

Wendy Bishop

Directions

- Choose three of these exercises to complete together; one group member types up copies for all group members (for this, choose from 1, 2, 5, 8, 9, or 13).

- Choose seven more exercises to complete in your own reading/writing journal over the next several weeks.

1. Using your literary text, create an outline script for a movie and cast the movie. Who would play characters and why? What would have to be changed to appeal to contemporary audiences, if anything?

2. Write the author of your literary text a substantial letter, and ask about issues that intrigue or baffle you.

3. You're the editor of a publishing company that has received this manuscript. What revision advice would you give the author to make this text more popular/accessible/a best seller (a) for your contemporaries and (b) for your parents?

4. Think of five very different people that you know. How would each respond to this text? If they're resistant to it, how would you argue to convince them to "try it"?

5. Choose a character from a story, novel, or poem. Speculate about what happens to them an hour, day, week, or year later (or choose two—1 week *and* 1 year).

6. Your younger sibling or a good friend is going to read your literary text next term in first-year writing. What advice do you have for him or her about getting into, understanding, and enjoying this text?

7. Would you like to read more by this author? Why or why not? In this genre of story, novel, poems? Why or why not?

8. Speculate on why you think your teacher chose to assign this literary text for this class. Would you suggest that it be used again? Why or why not?

9. Speculate on what this author might write next (or what you'd like to see him or her write about)—consider genre, topic, style, and so on.

10. If this author came to campus to read his or her work, would you attend? Why or why not? Would you invite anyone to go with you? What do you think the author would look like, sound like? What part of your text do you think he or she would choose to read and why? What part—story, poem, section—would you like to hear read aloud and why?

11. How are your (a) culture, (b) values, and (c) life-style similar to and/or different from the character or themes of your text? How does each influence your reading of this text?

12. Tell about one unexpected connection you made to your own life, based on your reading. Freewrite in order to explore that connection a bit more.

13. Lucky 13. What from this author's writing style—techniques, voice, subjects, way with words, sentences, paragraphs—could you steal to spice up your own writing? Be detailed, quote some of the writing, and explain why it's particularly useful to you.

Hint Sheet F
Collaborative Project—Reading Ordinary Lives: Personal and Cultural Ideologies

Kim Haimes-Korn

This assignment provides a condensed explanation of the writing and collaborative activities described in Chapter 8. You can either complete the activities as you read the chapter or initiate this assignment after reading and class discussion.

Collaborative Project—Reading Ordinary Lives: Personal and Cultural Ideologies

Americans in particular should study their popular arts the better to understand themselves. The media inform their environment, make suggestions about ways to view themselves, provide role models from infancy through old age, give information and news as it happens, provide education, influence their opinions, and open up opportunities for creative expression. Culture emanates from society, voices its hopes and aspirations, quells its fears and insecurities, and draws on the mythic consciousness of an entire civilization or race. It is an integral part of life and a permanent record of what we believe and are. While future historians will find the accumulated popular culture invaluable, the mirror is there for us to look into immediately. (from *Handbook of Popular Culture,* M. Thomas Inge, ed. 1989)

For this assignment we will focus on how to create our own knowledge—through a collaborative learning project—as well as examine the ways collaborative learning can contribute to our knowledge about ourselves. For this project, you will work in groups to research an ideology that influences thought and behavior in our culture. This project draws on the classical notions of the "commonplaces" and upon Crowley's (1994) more modern term, *ideology,* which she defines:

Ideologies are bodies of beliefs, doctrines, familiar ways of thinking that are characteristic of a group or a culture. They can be economic, ethical, political, philosophical, or religious. (76)

Group members will work together to choose an ideology that is somehow reflected in images, words, things, and behaviors of our culture. Your purpose in writing about this ideology is to discover more about how this idea or group of ideas has worked its way into the culture and how it manifests itself in our attitudes, beliefs, values, behavior, and language. You will examine our culture in light of the "language, myths, rituals, life-styles, establishments which are all symbolic forms for the expression of the attitudes and values of society" (Inge 1989, xxv). The project asks you to go beyond general assumptions and explore multiple layers of your ideology through rhetorical analysis. For example, if you choose to look at dominant beliefs about success, you would work to define how you see those ideas and then go on to examine how these beliefs, ideas, and images find their way into our thoughts, language, behavior, and images.

This collaborative project might require some group meetings outside of class. It is each member's personal responsibility to make the group work. You should take your participation seriously because you will rely on one another to complete this project; therefore, you are expected to act as a contributing and responsible member of your group. It will be up to you to make this a productive learning experience.

As a group you will be required to submit the following assignments that make up the parts of this project. There are many steps (activities explained in Chapter 8) along the way, but the following represents an overview of the project as a whole:

1. Construct a definition and explore the origins of your subject:
    *   Create and administer a questionnaire to give you an idea of how other people feel about your subject.
    *   Identify, collect and discuss the artifacts of your culture and the ways they reflect beliefs about your ideology.

2. Write a collaborative paper in which you discuss your findings. This paper should pull together your individual work and analysis of your questionnaires and artifacts. The voice and content should represent both the individual and the group (quote from individual exploratory writings).

3. Present your findings to others. This presentation should be more than a mere listing of your findings. Instead, this presentation should somehow represent your findings and artifacts in a creative manner that will be interesting, informative, and perhaps even entertaining, to a live audience. Find a way to make your presentations *interactive* so they involve members of the class in activities and discussions (consider supplementing with video, powerpoint, audio, drama, websites, visual images, etc).

4. Write a series of individual exploratory writings along the way that will contribute to your group knowledge of your subject (submit as a portfolio at the end of the project). The individual responses:

- Exploratory 1. List of Ideologies: Magazine and Artifact Analysis
- Exploratory 2. Individual Elaboration of Group Ideology
- Exploratory 3. Design/Administration of Questionnaires
- Exploratory 4. Analysis/Interpretation of Questionnaires
- Exploratory 5. Reflective Narrative: Personal Interpretation of Cultural Ideology
- Exploratory 6. Process of Group Work and Evaluation

5. Write a "Process of Group Work and Evaluation" in which you analyze and evaluate your work and group members on this project. As part of this writing you will be asked to evaluate, by the way of a letter grade, all members of your group (including yourself) after you have completed the project (see full assignment in Hint Sheet G).

Hint Sheet G
Group Process and
Evaluation Assignment

Kim Haimes-Korn

The assignment asks you to critically reflect on your collaborative work as you analyze your group work and participation. These guidelines can be used with the activities described in Hint Sheet F or in conjunction with any other collaborative work throughout the class.

Group Process Paper and Evaluation

The following guidelines will help you organize this writing, which is an examination of the processes you went through in relation to your collaborative work in groups. The questions posed should help you to examine this subject fully, but do not feel restricted by these questions. In this writing, explore the specific working dynamics of your group, your individual role in the group, and the particular group project itself. Following this description you should complete an individual evaluation for each member of your group (including yourself).

The Group: For this portion examine your group's processes. Be as specific as possible and discuss your individual contribution and how your group worked as a whole. How did you contribute to your group and what role did you find yourself in within the group? What specific roles did others take on in the group? What were the points of success? realization? failure to communicate? negotiation? compromise? How did you feel along the way? Did those feelings change as time progressed? How did you collaborate and negotiate the final text or presentation? What did you learn about working with others? What did you learn about collaborative writing and learning?

The Project: How did the project work for you? What about the project made it work—or not work? How did it contribute to your overall ideas about learning, knowledge, reading, and language? Do you have any suggestions which might make the project more successful in the future?

Evaluation: Evaluate, by way of a letter grade, each individual member's performance (including your own) in the group. Include each person's name and a short explanation of the roles they played (according to you) and why you assigned the grade you did. Be as complete and fair as possible in these explanations, because your response should reflect the reasons behind your evaluation.

It is important that you treat the evaluation portion of this assignment with the utmost respect. Engage in honest, specific reflection about your learning and participation in the project.

Hint Sheet H
Class Reading Survey
Wendy Bishop

	Strongly Agree SA	Agree A	Un-certain U	Disagree D	Strongly Disagree SD
1. It's the writer's fault if I can't understand the text.	☐	☐	☐	☐	☐
2. Reading is a solitary activity.	☐	☐	☐	☐	☐
3. One is born a good reader.	☐	☐	☐	☐	☐
4. Reading is irrelevant to my everyday life.	☐	☐	☐	☐	☐
5. Good reading is fast reading.	☐	☐	☐	☐	☐
6. It's only reading when you're reading printed texts.	☐	☐	☐	☐	☐
7. Reading sucks.	☐	☐	☐	☐	☐
8. English majors love to read.	☐	☐	☐	☐	☐
9. Reading is a social activity.	☐	☐	☐	☐	☐
10. Reading is difficult and unnatural.	☐	☐	☐	☐	☐
11. If I write as I read, it helps me think better.	☐	☐	☐	☐	☐
12. Women are better readers than men.	☐	☐	☐	☐	☐
13. It's not reading unless it's done for school.	☐	☐	☐	☐	☐
14. Reading is to gain information.	☐	☐	☐	☐	☐
15. I never read unless it's assigned.	☐	☐	☐	☐	☐
16. Reading is for correct meaning/comprehension.	☐	☐	☐	☐	☐
17. Reading is not a solitary activity.	☐	☐	☐	☐	☐
18. When I read, I "revise" or "rewrite" what I'm reading.	☐	☐	☐	☐	☐
19. Reading is exploration.	☐	☐	☐	☐	☐
20. If I talk about my reading, I understand it better.	☐	☐	☐	☐	☐
21. I like to read.	☐	☐	☐	☐	☐
22. Reading culture(s) is like reading print.	☐	☐	☐	☐	☐
23. Reading is a waste of time.	☐	☐	☐	☐	☐
24. There is no such thing as a nonreader.	☐	☐	☐	☐	☐
25. Reading is escape.	☐	☐	☐	☐	☐

A. I am: ☐ Male ☐ Female

B. I consider myself (primarily): ☐ African American ☐ American Indian ☐ Asian/Pacific Islander ☐ Hispanic ☐ White

C. I am a ☐ Freshman ☐ Sophomore ☐ Junior ☐ Senior & Major: _____

D. I was raised in a (circle one): 1 2 3 4 5 household
working class middle class upper class

E. Overall, I consider myself: ☐ an eager reader ☐ a reluctant reader

F. I'm most often (choose one): ☐ someone who reads mainly for school or work ☐ someone who reads mainly for pleasure ☐ someone who reads both for school/work and for pleasure

Hint Sheet I
First-Year Writing Students' Descriptions of Reading

Wendy Bishop

Suggestion: Before your read the descriptions of others, complete the exercise they completed yourself.

1. Write several metaphors for reading. For me, reading is like . . .

2. Vary this by differentiating between reading factual reports (e.g., text-books), creative writing (e.g., literature—poetry, fiction, drama—or genre writing like mysteries, etc.), or literary writing, and the reading of your own writing or peers' writing in writing classes.
   - For me, reading novels is like . . .
   - For me, completing assigned school writing is like . . .

   Or more simply—
   - For me, factual reading is like . . .
   - For me, imaginative reading is like . . .
   - For me, reading my own writing, is like . . .

3. After you complete these freewrites, compare yours to those shared below. Are there commonalties? Major differences? Alone, as a journal entry or with a group, try to characterize the patterns of readings noted here:

   Factual reading is like having my nails pulled out of my feet slowly. My mind is already made up and I cannot really imagine what is going to happen because it already has.

   Imaginary writing, if good, can be awesome. You can really get into it and not want to put the writing down. If you do put it down, you will be thinking of it all day.

   My own text is very hard to read because I know what I want to say so when I read my writing I am basically just skimming the work and not proof-reading it properly. It is very hard to read my own work because no matter what I get, I think it sucks.

   Student reading is also tough because one can be a Shakespearean while others can be a Bo Jackson.

When I am reading factual style works, I am like a child. I try to retain all that I am exposed to. For me, the process of reading factual text is like reading a list. I try to arrange all of the needed information into an order that makes sense to me. On the other hand, if I am reading imaginative or creative works, my eyes gloss over the words with no thought as to why the author chose the words or style or topic of discussion. I read imaginative work for pleasure and I do not receive any pleasure from working a text. For me, the process of reading creative works is like viewing the sunset. The first time can be beautiful but it loses something every time. Reading student writing is like passing a gall stone. It is painful and I make every attempt to avoid being put in that situation.

For me, the process of reading factual texts is like listening to the news.

For me, the process of reading imaginative texts is like letting your mind run free and thinking about what that text means to me. It is probably different for everyone. It is similar to watching a play. One person might see something that another person may not.

For me, the process of reading student texts is like learning a new word.

To read factual text can be boring or fun. It just matters what the fact has to do with.

Imaginative writing I think has the most potential to be a better writing. It can be wild and much more exciting.

Student writing is like reading something that generally has more meaning to you. You relate better to the writing.

My reading process for factual writing is like reading a test. It is strict and filled with facts, causing the reader to be uptight or tense.

My reading process for imaginative writing is like going to a movie or a fair. It is entertaining and relaxed and comfortable.

For me, the process of student writing is like having a baby. It's a painful experience. I struggle to get it done but once it's done I am relieved.

For me, the process of reading factual texts is like going to the dentist for a root canal at 8:00 on a Saturday morning.

For me, the process of reading imaginative texts is like going to the dentist for a root canal at 9:00 on a Saturday morning.

For me, the process of reading student writing is like standing between a rock and a hard place—will I honestly cause tension between classmates?

For me, the process of reading my own texts is like a Sherlock Holmes mystery, scrutinizing every little detail and finding out what went wrong.

For me, the process of reading factual texts is a struggle. I find my mind drifting off to another place. I feel as if it's being forced upon me and that I have no choice but to read it.

The process of reading imaginative text is much easier. It's not something you have to think about, it's something you enjoy. I can't really see it as a process, because it just flows much easier.

I read student writing as something I could have written myself. So, at first, I am very easy on it. I pick out only the good points. But then I get more critical with it and think of ways it could be different. Yet, as a whole, I like reading students' works because it is something I can closely relate to.

For me, factual material is like putting a stew together—if you read or skip over something, everything is messed up or will fall apart.

For me, reading imaginative material is like a bird gliding over the oceans. It's fun. And free.

For me, reading my own writing is like cleaning my room. I have to make sure nothing is wrong and everything is in the right place.

For me, the process of reading factual texts is like watching the president give a speech.

For me, the process of reading imaginative text is like sailing on the sea.

Reading student writing is like watching a show for the first time; you're not sure whether or not you're going to like it.

Reading your own writing is like watching the same movie over and over again. You really don't want to see it anymore.

The reading of factual text is like pouring boiled water on my leg.

The process of reading imaginative texts is like walking under a waterfall and just dreaming. Reading imaginative writing is an escape from the everyday problems I wake up to. Putting myself in the book.

For me, the process of reading student writing is like going to work without getting paid. I have to help them out.

Reading is like a fast-moving train that you always want to get on.

For me, the process of reading student writing text is like a teeter-totter board. Sometimes it is really interesting while other times it makes you want to jump off and do something.

Reading student writing is like going to hear an unknown band. Sometimes it is a pleasant surprise and sometimes you want your money back.

Reading factual writing is like studying for a test I'll never take.

Reading imaginative writing is like an escape, an experience, a journey, a thrill ride, a letdown.

Reading imaginative writing is like a wonderful vacation that makes returning to the real world a disappointment.

Reading is like another dimension where even though you're not a character, you're a part of the book.

Reading student writing is like searching for an identity among all the extras.

Hint Sheet J
First-Year Writing Students' Advice for Improving Your Reading Process
Wendy Bishop

40 Ways to Improve Your Reading—Advice from Four Reading Groups in One Writing Classroom

Suggestion: Make a composite list of the best advice from these advice givers.

- Decide which advice you (and your group) finds valuable and why.
- Are there exceptions or warnings you'd add to any piece of advice here? How much does reading context matter to reading advice?
- Finally, add any advice that you think has been overlooked.

Aim for your own list of top ten advice statements, perhaps with brief explanations for each.

Group A

1. Eat something before you read; otherwise hunger preoccupies your thoughts.
2. Make the noise be constant—total silence or total music to avoid distractions (like the TV).
3. Keep a pen and paper near to write down important things (when you write you remember things).
4. Take a short nap before you dive into reading; otherwise you'll fall asleep and retain nothing.
5. Read a certain amount of pages at a time. Make goals, then when you finish that goal, take a break, then start over.
6. Keep a dictionary near; look up things you don't understand!

7. Be comfortable when reading (not too comfortable because you don't want to fall asleep).

8. When reading peer work, really pick it apart (it helps the writer).

9. Clean your room before reading, this way you won't get distracted or want to do other things.

10. Don't be overly critical; go into reading with an OPEN MIND!

Group B

1. Read a text outloud to help with comprehension. When a text is read outloud, it allows the reader to catch mistakes or pick up on things previously missed.

2. If you fall asleep reading the book, wake up and go right back to the book.

3. Highlighting or notetaking helps with remembering important passages.

4. Read with a snack or drink to keep you from interrupting to go to the fridge.

5. Make a schedule for reading and stick to it to keep from procrastination.

6. Carry the book with you since you'll never know when you'll have some free time.

7. Read and reread the text to help with memory.

8. Find a comfortable environment in which to read and to aid with comprehension.

9. Take the reading slow and don't rush so you fully comprehend the material.

10. Take breaks from the reading when you feel your mind beginning to wander.

Group C

1. Read in a comfortable setting (eat, drink, lounge).

2. Fall asleep reading, sleep, wake up, and read again—it's okay.

3. If highlighting is distracting, outline and read more than once.

4. Read about things that you're interested in (when you need to find a paper topic, choose materials that interest you). There are a lot of choices out there; don't feel limited. Research!

5. Take notes. You can review your notes to refresh your memory on what you read.

6. Research the author—it helps to better understand the author's purpose behind writing the materials that you are reading.

7. Ask others for their input about the book you are reading. The more info you have about the book, the better able you are to plunge into the work and understand it.

8. Read aloud. To hear your own voice can sometimes help to commit the words to memory.

9. Stand while you read. It's a change from the usual way of lounging and reading. Trying new things breaks the monotony.

10. Set a reading schedule (pages per day) for longer works. Planning helps in accomplishing a goal.

Group D

1. When reading something that is not interesting, sit up. Be in a comfortable position but not one in which you can easily fall asleep.

2. Take notes, underline or highlight to keep attention. This helps you focus on whatever you are reading and helps with studying it later.

3. It's better to read in intervals of 20 to 30 minutes than try to do it all at once and not understand anything. When reading for a long time, you lose focus and don't understand what you read.

4. If you get tired, take a nap or move around, then get back to it. Example: wash your face.

5. When reading a novel for class, don't focus on trying to learn something. Read it for "pleasure" and the meaning usually comes later.

6. Don't procrastinate and save reading until the last minute. Spread out the assignment. This makes it a lot easier and more pleasant and you will get more out of it.

7. When reading a textbook, look at pictures, headings, extra comments, to get a full idea of what you will be reading before actually doing it. This helps give you an image of what you are reading.

8. Make sure lighting is to your satisfaction because poor light strains your eyes and could make you fall asleep no matter what position you are in.

9. Have snacks on hand for a quick break; avoid taking too long a break to make a snack.

10. Skim, then read profoundly, then take notes/summarize every few pages. After you're finished with the book, put all the notes together to get a full meaning of the book.

Hint Sheet K
Ideas for Revision Based on Rhetorical Reading

Devan Cook

Use these suggestions to make connections between dramatic, purposeful, rhetorical reading and revision.

Speakers

1. Take another look at your sources to let their voices blend or converse with yours as you revise.
2. Then, after you've written a new draft, read it aloud to see whether what you've written has the voice you want.
3. Read aloud to someone else so the two of you can decide about the piece's tone—does the persona sound harsh, sarcastic, abrupt, lazy? Is that what you want to convey?
4. Then talk over what you've written with your listener. Ask them what they think about any new ideas you had when you read. Ask them what they think about what you're saying.

Subjects

1. Reread your sources to see if you've changed focus or direction since you read before writing your first drafts; you're different now.
2. Reread sources to double check your facts.
3. Read off the subject to get new ideas.

Purposes

1. Role-play by reading your draft aloud again. Does what you've written support your purposes for writing?
2. Read to discover how other writers achieve their purposes: read examples you admire of the genre or style you're writing in.

3. Read to learn text conventions, the signs writers use to show readers what to expect.

Audiences

Read to learn special conventions that may apply—what's different about the ways botany papers and English papers are written, for example? Remember:

When we read, we write.

When we read, we change.

It's usually worthwhile to read, write, read, rewrite—one more time.

Hint Sheet 1
Teaching "Interpreting Poetry: A Song of Reading"

Darrell Fike

Suggestion for Discussion

It might be helpful to discuss the idea of interpretation by asking some basic questions about the complicated factors that surround any act of interpretation. In particular, the following questions focus on the implications of initial context, literal versus figurative uses of language, the question of intention, a reader's life and literacy experiences, and the idea of misreading.

The questions below use bird song as an example. You could use song lyrics, part of a famous speech, or a bit of "overheard" conversation as alternate examples.

Using bird song as an example:

Context

Should we assume even that interpretation is possible, since the exact moment and original situation in which the call was made has passed?

Literal/Figurative

Should we assume the songs are literal, or might they be arias of irony or metaphorical motifs?

Intention

Might a bird sing without the intention of expressing anything but singing?

Reader's Experience

Do our past experiences with bird song influence our interpretation of what we hear now?

Misreading

Should we consider that what we hear may not be exactly what is sung?

Suggestion for Writing Activity

Develop a writing assignment based on each of the interpretive strategies. Or use previous writing assignments and have students revise or reread them based on class discussion of each of the strategies.

Some Possibilities

Mimetic   Write a description of something. How hard/easy is it to depict the object or person exactly? Would two people depict the object the same way? Can you think of ways to use particular examples or details of the object to convey a sense of the universal aspects of the object to a reader?

Pragmatic   Choose an emotion. Now write a poem or descriptive passage using images and language that will cause the reader to feel that emotion. How does writing to achieve this effect shape your writing process?

Expressive   Write a poem that expresses your powerful feelings about someone or something. How hard or easy is it to do this? Do you have to be "inspired" to write this kind of poetry? How can you write about feelings in away that someone else will be able to feel what you feel?

Objective   Write a poem or choose a favorite you have already written. Examine the poem for its structure. How can you make the parts fit together better? Does doing so add to or take away from the poem's appeal to you? Now let someone else read both versions. Which seems to work better for the reader?

Suggestion for Reading Activity

Choose a poem and have your students apply all four strategies to their readings. Ask them how their understanding/experience of the poem changes as they use each strategy. Does one strategy work "better" than the others? If so, why? Does it depend on the kind of poem that is read or on individual reader's preferences?

Hint Sheet 2
Investigating Why We Read (or Not)

Jennifer Ahern

1. On the board, develop a class list of favorite books. Discuss what makes these books their favorites. Are they books from their childhood? Books they read in high school English classes? Now, develop a separate class list of five to ten books "every college student should read." Is there a difference in the types of books students select? Can the class collaborate and reach a set list of five or ten? Use this list-making exercise to discuss school reading versus pleasure reading, reading that is "good" for you, reading lists and how they're selected, and what makes a good book.

2. Ask students to describe their oral literacy backgrounds. Were they read to as children? Was storytelling valued in their community or culture? Make a class list of nonprint texts every college student should read, discuss how that reading differs (or not) from print text reading, and explore the place of oral literacies within classroom and home community contexts.

3. Ask students to discuss the process they use to choose a book, magazine, or article to read. Is it based on others' recommendations (like Oprah's book club or a roommate's suggestion)? Or, do they read based on what they should for their major, degree, class, intellectual development, or what's good for them? Do they talk or write about the reading that they're doing?

4. Brainstorm with students about reading and writing connections in their school reading. What kinds of activities did/do they do? What kind of writing do they think supports reading (rather than serves it)? Have they ever had positive reading and writing experiences? Perhaps get students to practice this kind of activity by having them do any one of the following:
   - Rewrite an ending to a novel, short story, or TV episode.
   - Create a dinner party scenario (dialog or not) with all the key players of their favorite novel or TV show (complete with menu, seating chart explanation, conversation starters . . .); guests may be dead or alive.
   - Write a letter to an author, the editor of a magazine, or to a former teacher (what they wish they could have read, what they really wanted to say about the book . . .).

5. Brainstorm with students' items to add to either list in the article. What suggestions do they have for surviving college reading or pleasure reading? Is it realistic to ask college readers to try to read for pleasure? Do they identify more with Kathy (college survival reader) or with Jessica (reads when she can; thinks reading makes us better people; but still reads what she'll be tested on).

6. Bring in books that have writing all over them: notes in the margin, notes on the last page, underlined passages. Discuss active reading, writing during the reading process, interacting with a text. (My students are amazed when I bring in textbooks and paperbacks that have my hand-written comments throughout—they are typically not allowed to write in books in high school or they are afraid to mess up the book.)

Hint Sheet 3
Teaching with "An Open Letter"
Ormond Loomis

1. Consider the range of your "reading," using an expanded definition of *read.* Make a list of all the items you've read in the past week, not including students' papers or the pieces you've given as class assignments. What type of items are most numerous? Which items do you enjoy most; which have the greatest emotional significance for you; which do you give the most intellectual significance? Ask your students to do the same exercise and compare their lists. To record the results for your class, you'll have to collect their lists and tally them, but I expect you'll be surprised with the results.

2. Require students to include MLA references to a variety of print and nonprint sources. Books and periodicals are routine for most students, but how does a writer cite a cereal box? The detail needed to document sources becomes more interesting and important to cite accurately when authors use several types of sources. When writing critically about the sinking of the *Titanic,* students might refer to the book by Richard A. Boning, the play by Christopher Durang, or the film by James Cameron. They share the same title, but they require different information to document them on the "Works Cited" page. Similarly when citing Cameron's work, students might refer to the standard video edition, the wide-screen video, a video edited to delete potentially offensive scenes, or the printed screenplay. Careful critics should be aware that such differences exist, and they need to document for readers the sources they use.

4. Develop with your students a list of authorities you mutually respect and establish the characteristics of each that would be important to explain to readers. For example, how do you and your students regard George Foreman, George Lucas, George Orwell, and George Will? What do you base your impressions on? Which of the authorities would be best to cite to persuade for audiences you may want to address? Next ask students to write three or four variations on sentences they could use to introduce one of the authorities as a source in an essay. You might see sentences like these:

   "According to George Foreman, former prizefighter and author, . . ."

"George Foreman describes his fight with Mohammed Ali in *By George.*"

"In *By George,* author George Foreman, who once held the world heavyweight boxing title, . . ."

4. Ask your students to "read" your appearance and write notes on what they assume about you from the way you dress, move, and speak. Then invite them to discuss their assumptions and explain the basis for them. Do your students share common stereotypes about you because you're a writing teacher, because you teach at a university, because you have a background in English, or because of other attributes? This activity works best during the first or second class meeting. You may, or may not, want to respond to your students' assumptions by commenting on how close their assumptions are to your perceptions about yourself. You can vary the activity by having students work in pairs or small groups to "read" each other.

5. Ask your students to watch an episode of a popular TV show such as *The Simpsons.* It can be one that you show in class or one that you assign on a particular channel, date, and time. Then have students write about the social issues the episode raises. You may want them to brainstorm in class about the variety of topics they felt the program touched and the position the show took on issues. Encourage your students to cite specific sequences of action, quote characters precisely, discuss characters' apparent motivations, and distinguish the screenwriters' views from their characters'. You can combine this activity with a research essay assignment by having students find what media critics have written about the show and writing their own assessment of the show.

Hint Sheet 4
An Examination of Teaching
<u>Sankofa</u>

Camille Cain, Akua Duku Anokye, and Jamie Barlowe

As an experiment, we asked a teaching assistant who was taking a socio-linguistics course with Duku to run an experiment in her class. Camille Cain is a young African-American woman who is, herself, still learning how to navigate the academic waters. She was teaching a Composition I class of nine Euro-American and two African-American students primarily coming from the rural areas of Ohio and suburban Toledo. The class met three times a week for 50 minutes each. Camille reports:

Day 1

On the first day I told the students that they were going to watch the opening 20 minutes of a film. After the film, I asked them to complete an in-class writing assignment evaluating and responding to the segment they viewed. The students wrote for the remaining minutes of the class period, approximately 25 to 30 minutes. I instructed them that they should at least have one page completed by the end of class time.

I observed a reluctance in the students to write a response, and some of them stopped writing before time because they said they had no more to say. During the viewing of the film I noticed students were not as attentive and concerned with watching the film during the voice-over of Oscar Brown, Jr. Some of their facial expressions reflected resistance. They didn't seem to take the issue very seriously, possibly because they didn't believe it was dealing with an issue that was relevant to present conditions. I also believe this had a significant effect on the writing they produced this first day of viewing *Sankofa*.

Initially, I didn't realize the task that I had asked my students to perform. However, as I reflected on the scenes in the film, looked at my students, and saw the frustration and confusion on their faces, I realized that this was not an easy in-class writing assignment. Especially, when they only had 20 minutes to write and maybe 5 to 10 minutes to think about what they saw in *Sankofa*. I think this shortage of time also constrained many of the students and influenced their limited evaluation of the 20-minute segment. It's difficult to take in such complex information and decode its meaning or symbolism. The portion of the text shown was extremely difficult to understand, decode, and recognize.

After class I had an interview with one of the students for her class project, and she talked about *Sankofa* and her feelings. She said, "I really don't mean to be so short about responding but I just don't like seeing movies like that. It's not that I don't care or I'm not interested, but I just don't know what to say because its not me and I feel like I'm still blamed for the past." She is a Euro-American student who said that slavery in school was not depicted the way it was in the film. Another student asked me before leaving, "What was that and what happened to her?"

Day 2

On day 2 the students were shown the same 20-minute segment of the film. However, this time, before viewing the excerpt, they were told some of the history and culture underlying the film, the important cultural symbolism, and other significant historical facts about African culture and slavery, as well as some information about cinematography. The students watched more intently and were more enthusiastic. At the end of the class period following the 20-minute segment, the students were told to write another response about the film using the background information. The response had to be typed, double-spaced, one to two pages long, and returned on the next class meeting, which was Friday. They asked me if they were going to see the rest of the film on Friday.

I observed them watching for the issues and symbolism I spoke about. They were interested in seeing what I told them or at least recognizing the information I provided. I think they were more receptive to the film because they could apply to the film something they knew or had been introduced to as new knowledge. I am sure this new knowledge had a significant effect on their responsiveness. Their frustration with the first day's viewing was replaced with curiosity. Some of the students just left the room shaking their heads and saying, "Wow, that was deep."

Day 3

On the last day of the experiment the students turned in their typed responses and completed viewing the film. They were anxious to see the rest of the film to answer some of the questions they had proposed in their first writing responses.

Analysis of the Writing

While reading their papers written on the first day, I noticed a defensive attitude in a few of the students' writing, whereas others tried to discuss the film and offer an analysis. One student wrote, "To be completely honest, I don't really understand the movie we just watched . . . I don't really like watching about slave times . . . So watching it doesn't make me comfortable." Some questioned why whites are still being blamed for the past errors of history. Another student felt that watching the film didn't make one bit of difference and he wanted to talk about the Cleveland Indians game from the night before. I believe the inability to accept the present as a result of the past and the inability for European Americans to admit and humble themselves to the atrocity of slavery creates this defensive attitude.

Another student discussed the initial scene with Mona and was able to recognize that it represented the Africans' passage into slavery. This is significant because many people are ignorant to the middle passage that was endured by the people who were to become slaves. Her recognition of this fact allowed her to decode the information she took from the 20-minute segment. The student told me after class that she can't imagine the suffering, dehumanizing, and powerless feelings of a people who were once kings and queens. She is an African-American student. Another student who had seen the film in high school noted the difference between *Sankofa* and other Hollywood depictions of slavery. He concluded that this film better represents history because it refuses to "sugar coat" the experience. He also noted the composition of the film, in which Mona/Shola travels back in time. He understands this movie as a sign of the pain and suffering of slaves and that people in our modern times should not neglect our history but reflect upon it.

I found that many of the students were quite interested in seeing what happened next and where the film was taking them. They expressed interest and sympathized with the conditions of slavery, while questioning the events of the first 20 minutes of the film. One of the students noted the difference in attitudes of slaves born on the plantation versus those who had experienced the passage into slavery. She discussed the resistance to rebellion against the slave owners by the plantation-born versus the "stolen" slaves.

The second responses were more in-depth and detailed and written in conjunction with the historical background given on the second day of the experiment. These were written with more positive energy and less defensiveness. The students seemed to appreciate diversity more and had developed a sense of self-awareness. Here are a few of the responses from the students:

> I believe this movie goes back into those years to make people fully aware of the suffering and agony experienced by African Americans. There is much ignorance still in today's society which makes life harder for everyone . . . I feel that I have benefited greatly from watching this film [because] my past views have been dispelled and I am more open to the lessons history has to teach; I am really glad we got to do something like this in class. Not only was it a change, but it really opened my eyes to something new, and made me really change the way I think about slavery and African culture in general;

I didn't really ever take any of these situations (sexism and racism) that I have
mentioned into consideration when learning about slavery and for that I am
ashamed. I didn't really think it could be that bad, but now I realize that I was
very wrong because I was ignorant myself.

One of the students discussed the cinematography. He talked about the lighting in particular scenes that "cast shadows" and made the scene more realistic. He had to remind himself that it was a movie. Another student wrote,
"Before we started watching the movie, I really wasn't looking forward to
watching *Sankofa* because I didn't think it had anything to do with me. My
feelings all changed after seeing *Sankofa*." Finally, the student who was defensive in the first response was still defensive in the second but more empathetic
about some of the issues presented in the text.

I also looked at the rhetoric used by the students in developing their
essays. In the first paper I noticed that the students wrote with minimal
sentence variety and inadequate and inconsistent facility in the use of
language. The writing in the second paper was more organized but still
included some paragraphs with unrelated topics and organizational problems.
The level of interpretation in the second paper increased tremendously, and the
rhetorical strategy of compare and contrast was clearly demonstrated in the
writing. This indicated to me that the students were not only analyzing the text
in the context of the past but also in the context of the present.

The second paper displayed self-awareness, an appreciation for diversity,
and a more in-depth view of current society and the history that produced it.
In the first response their self-awareness and appreciation for diversity was
numbed and exchanged for self-justification and confusion. Instead of sympa-
thizing or trying to evaluate the text in its context, the students took it as a
personal attack. This could be attributed to the lack of knowledge and background information that was not provided on the first day but given on the
second.

When comparing the writings I found that many of the students wrote
with their emotions more in the second paper than the first. There were feelings of empathy, apology, self-awareness, understanding, and anger. They
showed a new knowledge about the subject that they were discussing. They
wrote with more confidence even though their organization and development
was somewhat inconsistent.

I found that the information provided before the text was shown invited a
more positive response. Thus, I think the use of introductions that provide
background information and cultural presupposition, in this instance the heavy
reliance on oral tradition, gives the student more of an opportunity to interact
with the text, to read it accurately and respond to it in substantive ways.

Conclusion

Jamie and I have been teaching for many years. We felt, if we wanted to see whether this paradigm would work, we should expose the pedagogy to a new teacher. Camille became a willing member of the team after her first semester as a teacher. Her observations, comments, and insights were the result of her wrestling with the theory and application of this project. Our conclusion is that if a teacher is willing to suspend her own biases in order to research other cultural ways of knowing, she can expose her students to such a paradigm with good success. As teachers, we have devoted ourselves to enlightenment. We think that this process is ongoing and replicable.

Camille's experience lays the framework for reflecting on this method for decoding texts. Our next step is to widen the field of film to other visual literatures in order to determine if the process will be successful. Camille had been in classes with both Jamie and Duku. As a result, she was very familiar with our teaching styles and able to emulate some of our methods. We will continue our experiment to see how successful it will be with teachers who have not been exposed to our personal teaching styles, philosophies, or methodologies.

Hint Sheet 5
After Reading "Making Peace with the Research Paper"

Gay Lynn Crossley

I've had the most success teaching the research paper—and the kind of active and meaningful research I encourage in Chapter 14—by working with a student's idea. While brainstorming for her research topic, she asked if she could write her research in the form of a letter to her brother. She wanted to research the drastic measures some high school boys were taking to "make weight" for wrestling competition, in particular the risks of those measures and alternatives to them. She came from a wrestling family: her father coached; she'd worked as a student trainer; and soon her brother would be joining his high school wrestling team. She wanted her research to dissuade him from starvation diets and rubber suits, and she wanted to inform him of healthier alternatives. Her researched letter was purposeful, engaging, and demonstrated a real use of sources. Her work stood out.

Since then, I've required students to write research letters rather than research essays, and lately have used the research letter as part 1 of a two-part assignment. Students now revise their research letter for a college-level class, appropriate for the kind of research they've conducted. In this two-part version, I do not require students to formally document their research letters. Give credit to borrowed material and accurately quote direct material, yes, but no parenthetical documentation or "Works Cited" page. Separating the formal documentation from the research letter allows us to talk meaningfully about plagiarism issues and academic integrity—the concepts behind them rather than the rules about them. Furthermore, the letter draft allows them to focus on integrating their sources and working purposefully with them, and to save the details of documentation for the next draft. Of course, students also gain valuable experience when they have to make a range of decisions about revising their informal letters into more formal research essays.

The advantages of the research letter, whether alone or as a draft of a research essay, are clear: students tend to choose more focused and personally relevant topics; students tend to identify more meaningful purposes for writing because they have a real audience in mind; and students tend to spend more time with their sources and use them productively because they really are trying to say something to their audience about their topic. Plus, it opens a door for us as teachers when we advise students about their projects. One student told me that he wanted to write a letter to President Clinton about the environment. I asked him if he was familiar with Al Gore, and if so, what he thought his letter to President Clinton would really accomplish. This student pretty quickly revised his project into a letter to the college about inexpensive ways to enhance its environmental campaign.

Sample Research Letter Assignment

At this point in the semester, we apply what we've learned about writing—about substantiation, purpose, voice, and structure—to researched writing. Rather than write a research essay, though, each of you will write a "research letter." In this letter, you will share meaningful information on a personally relevant topic, information you've found through research, with one or two people you know.

We must first choose the topic that we want to search again and begin identifying our reasons (our purposes) for searching into that topic and for wanting to discuss it with someone in particular. Look at the list of topics you generated at the beginning of class today, and consider your specific reasons for wanting to research this topic. Then, consider who you might want to discuss this topic with, in light of your reasons for wanting to think about this topic.

The potential purposes you arrive at through this invention strategy will help you (a) to narrow your topic so that you can treat it adequately in the space you have; (b) to determine possible sources for your research; and (c) to identify possible audiences for your letter. You may end up modifying or sharpening your purpose as you go, but an initial "reason for researching" will help you to make some early decisions in the research process.

You are required to integrate three sources into your research letter. I require only three so that you can work more fully with the sources you do include in your essay. I expect you to read/study your sources closely—to analyze the arguments they make, the evidence they offer, the assumptions behind their arguments, and their conclusions and perspectives. This kind of analysis will not only help you to understand the claims these writers make, but also help you to determine how to get your sources "talking to one another." Over the next week we will talk more specifically about what's involved in analyzing a source.

In your research letter, I'd like you to focus on integrating borrowed material into your own prose. That is, I'd like you to concentrate on creating the necessary transitions and introductions that will let your reader know why you are making use of a particular source at that point in your essay (in other words, your purpose for using that source).

We'll talk more specifically about integrating borrowed material. To help you focus on integrating your research, I will not be expecting you to formally document your research in your research essay. You should, yes, indicate that you are borrowing from another's work—another's words, ideas, and so on—by referring to the article and author before you quote or paraphrase material from that source. However, you need not worry at this point about a "Works Cited" page or parenthetical documentation.

We will be talking much more about the research process in the next couple of weeks, but for now, let me share with you what I'll be looking for in your research letters:

1. Established and fulfilled sense of purpose
2. A high level of interaction between you and your sources (avoid simply reporting)
3. Integration of three sources (at least two of which must be print sources)
4. Productively constructed voice (in light of the purpose of your letter and your audience)
5. Research letters 6 to 8 pages in length

Sample Research Revision Assignment

For this essay, you will revise your research letter into a more formal research essay appropriate for an academic context. The research essay letter assignment gave you the opportunity to focus on making research count in your discussion, on using your research to further clarify or complicate your own thoughts on the subject at hand, and on integrating that research productively. It is my belief that the letter format encourages you to suspend your concerns for the more formal features of academic research (the very features that often distract us from doing anything more with our sources than report from them). Once you have your research letter, then we can shift our attention to reshaping that research for an academic audience, using in the process an appropriate system of documentation.

To prompt your revision of the research letter, think of a course in which you can imagine researching the topic you chose for your letter. Consider also how well your purpose for researching that topic in the research letter would fit that kind of course. You may need to narrow your focus or modify your purpose, but imagine how you would revise your discussion if your reader were an instructor in another course. Next week, we will discuss in conference these very possibilities—how you might imagine your research letter into a research essay, and the kinds of changes that revision will involve.

Expect to revise in substantial ways. You will need to do far more, probably, than add some documentation and a "Works Cited" page. More than likely, your focus will need to be tightened and your purpose modified, and, depending on how productive your research is and how much you modify your focus and purpose, you may need to gather additional sources. If these changes occur, then there will need to be other revisions: chances are the structure of your discussion will be revised. Furthermore, since you are revising a letter to someone you know personally (probably not an academic) into an academic research essay, very likely the voice in your writing will change to some extent. My point here is that revisions in purpose and focus imply revisions in structure, and that changes in rhetorical context will necessitate revisions in style and voice.

Contributors' Notes

Jennifer Ahern—(Florida State University, teaching writing and literature)—I have stacks of books and magazines all over the house, Stephen King novels, murder mysteries, *National Geographic, UTNE Reader, Style,* clothing catalogs, so I can read in five- and ten-minute snatches of time. I enjoy reading E-mails from friends, watching TV (I'm a junkie), especially "The X-Files," "Law and Order," and Atlanta Braves games. I'm currently taking black-and-white snapshots of my family and friends—caught in the act of reading.

Akua Duku Anokye—(University of Toledo, Associate Professor/Director of Composition)—I read everything I can lay my hands and eyes on. When I was a kid, and as a matter of fact even now, when I am riding down the street, I read the billboards and license plates. At the table I read cereal boxes, anything with words. I love African folktales, fairy tales, legends, Greek and Roman mythology. There is always some new Zora Neale Hurston material to read. I love the way she captures my story. It feels like she was listening to my grandmama speak. I like to read when I am troubled and need an escape. Sometimes when I can't fall asleep, I read and forget to sleep. There's always a pile of magazines and books nearby. If I am not on the move, I have some kind of reading material in my hand—menus, recipes, directions—you name it, I read it.
Jamie Barlowe—(University of Toledo, Associate Professor of English/Chair of Women's and Gender Studies)—I have always loved reading as a means of escape, inspiration, education, and transportation to places and times I could not physically go. And I always took reading for granted as my right and pleasure, that is, until I began to study slave narratives. Then I learned that reading was a privilege denied to slaves to shut them up in "mental darkness," as Frederick Douglass put it. Teaching himself to read and write by various means, Douglass learned that slavery was a condition imposed on him. Reading, he said, "enabled me to utter my thoughts" (*Narrative*). Other slave narratives relate similar stories of slaves gaining power through reading and writing, despite the punishments they had to endure for becoming literate. I have never taken reading for granted again. **Camille Cain**—I am a second-year graduate student who enjoys reading short story fiction. I enjoy reading outside because my imagination takes off like a DC-9. I can't explain why outside has this effect, but it does.

Lisa Albrecht—(University of Minnesota, Alumni Distinguished Professor of Teaching)—I'm always picking up something to read. I stick mostly to the alternative press and read lots of newspapers, magazines, and periodicals by women, people of color, working people, and gay and lesbian folks. I've taught basic writing in General College at the University of Minnesota for fifteen years. I also teach undergraduate and graduate courses in Women's Studies. I'm Chair of the Minneapolis Commission on Civil Rights; in that capacity I've had to read a great deal of legal writing that's really tough to digest. I'm currently working with activists and educators to start an adult education center in the inner city in Minneapolis. I love reading books about teaching and popular education. Give me a women's mystery and it's like eating chocolate! Run into me and you'll find at least five different magazines in my backpack.

Wendy Bishop—(Florida State University, Professor)—I like to read E-mail from friends. I like to read aloud (or be read to) and to share what I'm reading (poetry, magazines, newspaper articles), especially standing at the kitchen counter when friends or family are hanging out. One of these summers I'd like to spend weeks browsing through the "I should read this" books I've collected for the past ten years that are overflowing my bookshelves. Pleasure reading for me means disappearing into women detective novels while hidden away in a quiet room eating a snack. When friends ask how I get my writing done, I explain that I don't read (watch) TV all that much.

Devan Cook—(Boise State University, Assistant Professor)—Several years ago, I learned (read) that Cybill Shepherd reads for an hour a day to maintain her "mental health." I identify with Cybill—we're both from Tennessee, and once both of us were blonde. She's taller and funnier than I am; I've accepted that. I've always read to maintain equilibrium: stay upright, on my feet. But now it was as if Cybill gave me permission—almost a prescription—for pleasure reading. I prefer what my daughter calls "beach reads": adventure, intrigue, mysteries, homicides. If Cybill were still moonlighting, she would solve them all.

Every day since, I've wriggled into my favorite chair for an hour and ignored everyone and everything except the current book. Around me, the world shakes itself off, straightens, regains its composure. If I lose track of time or return to read later for relaxation or reward, so much the better. I wonder what Cybill's reading?

Gay Lynn Crossley—(Marian College, Assistant Professor)—I think I had two sets of encyclopedias before my parents ever brought me home from the hospital: a children's set and the official set of *Encyclopedia Britannica*. That's pretty much the way it went from there. Our house was filled with books. My earliest memories are of my father reading *Tom Sawyer* to me, back when beautifully illustrated, hard-backed books were more common, and of me asking him to pause while I took in the picture of Tom and Becky going into the cave. By the time I was in fourth grade, I had made the discovery that books held power. The knowledge to become anything I wanted to be could be found in books. So when I wanted to become an astronomer, I turned to books on the solar system. When I wanted to become an architect, I checked out books from the public library on house design.

Once when I was angry with my parents, as ten-year-olds can be, I went directly to the library for books on witchcraft so that I could study how to cast a spell on them. And it's the books I remember most vividly, not the telescope or the drafting board my parents got me, or the fact that none of my spells worked. It's the books. Their power over me continues today. They decorate my home. They fill up empty space under beds, in drawers, and on tables. And I pretend that I possess them as they possess me. Currently, on my bedside table, sits a book on chaos theory, a collection of short stories by Edith Wharton (one of my favorites), and a book on diet and nutrition for multiple sclerosis patients. Some things don't change from childhood. I'm still the girl who believes that if I can read about it, it's mine.

Darrell Fike—(Valdosta State University, Assistant Professor)—This morning I read the back of the shampoo bottle as I stood in the shower. I wondered what the world would be like if there was some global catastrophe and the writing on the shampoo bottle was the only writing left. Would "lather, rinse, repeat" become the motto of our nation? Would "super shine and extra body" become a greeting of respect, and "propylene" and "glycol " become the most common children's name? Would teachers spend hours discussing the hidden meanings of the ingredient list?

This is the kind of reading I enjoy—looking for the poetry and the wonder in writing of all kinds. As a college teacher, I read student essays and textbooks all the time, so it is fun for me to take the same analytical skills I use in my work and use them in fun and interesting ways that help make reading an adventure.

Kim Haimes-Korn—(Southern Polytechnic State University, Assistant Professor and Writing Program Director)—When I was a child I used to share a room with my sister. At a point when my parents thought I was old enough they converted our old den into a new bedroom for me. When the room was finished it looked mostly like a young girl's room except for one remnant of the old den—a bookshelf in the closet filled with my parents' books. Although I was told that these books would not interest a kid, I secretly read them on my own. Every night, with a flashlight, I would hungrily read book after book. My parents were later very surprised to hear that I had read *Atlas Shrugged, Rosemary's Baby,* or the latest in pop psychology.

I remember these days with fondness and I still think of myself as a voracious reader. I read quite a bit and continue to experience the secret joy of falling into a story. I like to read journal articles about teaching, magazines, student writing, the newspaper, and I always keep a novel at my bedside to read before falling asleep. I like to read with my son, Garrett, and share the stories I loved as a kid. I also like to drive and listen to audio versions of stories that I might not have time to read in print. Most of all, I like a good story—something that will push my imagination and help me know people a little bit better as I experience thoughts beyond my own.

Ormond Loomis—enjoys reading at home in the evening, among the shelves in libraries, in waiting rooms, and on airplanes and trains. A composition teacher at Florida State University, he would rather read anything than writing that's assigned as part of his job. His favorite printed works include essays by Steven Jay Gould, stories by A. S. Byatt, and articles in *Newsweek.* He often reads books and magazines from back cover to front, perhaps because he's left-handed.

Dan Melzer—(Florida State University, teaching writing and literature)—In the spirit of my essay, I like to read a lot of things: short stories and novels, movies, websites, E-mail. My most common reading condition is on the bed with a cat on either side of me and the door shut so I can't hear my girlfriend watching "Allie McBeal" in the living room. I always look forward to reading a good story, and I keep a supply of short story books within reach at all times. Not only do I enjoy these stories, but nothing improves my writing more than reading. The best piece of advice I can give to writers is to read, read, read.

Hans Ostrom as a boy read *Full Cry,* a magazine about hound dogs and their owners, to which his father subscribed. Currently he is reading and collecting the mystery novels of Rex Stout. **Sarah Sloane** reads digital fictions, alien abduction stories, theories of

Scottish rhetoric, and L=A=N=G=U=A=G=E poetry. She has also been known to read the directions on the back of seed packets, to read web-based soap operas, and to frequent cyber-cafes. **Wade Williams** reads nature writing and eighteenth century literature and appreciates narratives involving Bart Simpson. **Teresa Giffen** has read the fiction of Italo Calvino and books about rhetoric, partly because Professors Sloane, Williams, and Ostrom (University of Puget Sound) assigned them. Having completed her B.A., she is once more in control of her own reading agenda.

Karen Schiff—(Clemson University, Assistant Professor, Interdisciplinary Humanities and Literature)—After sifting through E-mail and dealing with the administrivia of university life, I sometimes get a chance to wolf down *The New Yorker,* or nurse a Sunday newspaper for the entire week. These days, though, I'm just as likely to fall asleep over Buddhist psychology. This summer I tried reading Italian train schedules . . . and sometimes it worked. Once, though, it resulted in an unnecessarily long train ride . . . No matter what country I'm in, I scrutinize the words on fruit stickers, since I find paper doodads like that strangely fascinating. Novels generally wait until summer vacation (even those by David Malouf, who's Australian, and great!). But every now and then I thumb through poetry books, more or less at random, searching for a crystalline combination of words that will make my heart/mind leap. **Art Young**—(Clemson University, Professor)—I read a newspaper most every day. I get a morning paper delivered, and I like to begin my day with a cup of coffee and the paper. When I get so busy that I can't read the paper until evening, and maybe not even then, I get frustrated, and my day begins on a sour note. I often read the paper inside out (that is, the inside sections first, particularly sports and comics) and back to front (start with the last page of each section). I'm intrigued by how I am drawn to the sports section to read about a game I saw in person or on TV the night before—after all, I already know what happened. Maybe I want to relive the experience, especially if it was a victorious one, or maybe I want to see if the reporter's perceptions of the game match my own. I enjoy reading literature of all kinds, but I'm surprised at how little time I have for such reading, since I am an English teacher. I spend many hours a day reading E-mail, memos, reports, students' writing, my colleagues' writing, professional articles, magazines (especially *Newsweek* and *The New Yorker*), letters, bills, etc. On the other hand, recently I've been looking around for and reading poetry about love, and when I find one that moves me, I share it with a special someone. I am an incurable romantic.

Susan Taylor—(Brevard Community College, teaching writing)—I like to read absolutely everything—from a cereal box to an Edith Wharton novel (my copy of *The House of Mirth* is falling apart)—and always at the same time if possible. Most of the time I read student essays because they are my favorite type of texts. Although I love TV, QVC in particular, what students have to say about textuality is what keeps me reading and thinking.

Deborah Coxwell Teague—(Florida State University, Director of First-Year Writing)—For as long as I can remember, reading has been one of the best parts of my life. I grew up the eldest daughter of an ultra-conservative Southern Baptist minister, and the list of things I wasn't allowed to do was longer than I ever want to recall, but one thing I could do as much as I wanted was read—and I read a lot—mostly novels. Lots about my life has changed since those restrictive days, but one part that's stayed the same is the enjoyment I get from reading. Right now, I'm anxiously waiting for

Thomas Harris' *Hannibal* to arrive in the mail. I loved *Silence of the Lambs* and *The Red Dragon,* and I'm looking forward to losing myself in Harris' new thriller. Books I've enjoyed reading recently have been Ursula Hegi's *Stones from the River,* Toni Morrison's *Paradise,* Judy Blume's *Summer Sisters,* Frances Mayes' *Under the Tuscan Sun,* and Charles Frazier's *Cold Mountain*—five very different types of writing, but each a pleasure in its own way. A few weeks ago I discovered a new writer—new to me anyway—a poet—Mary Oliver. I've fallen in love with her imagery and ideas and can't get enough of her writing.

Myka Vielstimmig—If Myka Vielstimmig is a co-writer, does that automatically mean that Myka is a co-reader, too? There's some confusion on this point. The Myka one of us knows reads widely—art and architecture, theory and practice, poetry and novels, comics and cereal boxes. The reading this Myka likes best is on-line, where (as it happens) you can find all of these, sometimes even together (except for cereal boxes). But the other one of us isn't sure that everything we both read goes into Myka-the-writer. As far as this one of us knows, Myka should be completely in the dark, for example, about *Soap Opera Digest,* the ingredients in bratwurst, and *Soldier of Fortune* magazine (and cereal boxes). (FYI: Myka Vielstimmig aka Michael Spooner, Director, Utah State University Press, and Kathleen Yancey, Pierce Professor, English, Clemson University.)